THINKING ABOUT LANDSCAPE ARCHITECTURE

What is landscape architecture? Is it gardening, or science, or art? In this book, Bruce Sharky gives a complete overview of the discipline to provide those who are new to the subject with the foundations for future study and practice. The many varieties of landscape architecture practice are discussed with an emphasis on the significant contributions that landscape architects have made across the world in daily practice.

Written by a leading scholar and practitioner, this book outlines the subject and explores how, from a basis in garden design, it "leapt over the garden wall" to encapsulate areas such as urban and park design, community and regional planning, habitat restoration, green infrastructure and sustainable design, and site engineering and implementation.

Coverage includes:

* the effects that natural and human factors have upon design, and how the discipline is uniquely placed to address these challenges
* examples of contemporary landscape architecture work—from storm-water management and walkable cities to well-known projects like the New York High Line and the London 2012 Olympic Park
* exploration of how art and design, science, horticulture, and construction come together in one subject.

Thinking about Landscape Architecture is perfect for those wanting to better understand this fascinating subject, and those starting out as landscape architecture students.

Bruce Sharky is a professor at the Robert Reich School of Architecture at Louisiana State University, Baton Rouge, Louisiana, USA, and a registered professional landscape architect.

His interests in landscape architecture are varied and have evolved over the years and through work in varied locations and countries. He has worked professionally in Los Angeles, San Francisco, and Winnipeg, as well as in state government. He has lectured and taught design courses in countries as varied as China, Chile, Japan, and Israel, and was a Fulbright Scholar in Mexico and Portugal. He had a private landscape practice in Anchorage, Alaska, for 15 years prior to taking on the position of director of the Robert Reich School of Landscape Architecture, Louisiana State University. In 1990, Professor Sharky was honored as a Fellow of the American Society of Landscape Architects for his years of service and contributions to the profession.

"The book establishes definitions of methodology, scope of work, outlook, and design concepts for students and professionals alike. It touches succinctly and clearly into the history and evolution of the profession and of the scale and typological landscapes that professionals are committed to today. It also defines the amplitude and limitations of a profession difficult to define. A book much needed at schools, as well as in private corporations and public institutions."

Mario Schjetnan, FASLA, Landscape Architect/Architect

THINKING ABOUT LANDSCAPE ARCHITECTURE

PRINCIPLES OF A DESIGN PROFESSION FOR THE 21ST CENTURY

BRUCE SHARKY

Routledge
Taylor & Francis Group

LONDON AND NEW YORK

First published 2016
by Routledge
2 Park Square, Milton Park, Abingdon, Oxon OX14 4RN

and by Routledge
711 Third Avenue, New York, NY 10017

Routledge is an imprint of the Taylor & Francis Group, an informa business

© 2016 Bruce Sharky

British Library Cataloguing-in-Publication Data
A catalogue record for this book is available from the British Library

Library of Congress Cataloging in Publication Data
Sharky, Bruce, author.
    Thinking about landscape architecture : principles of a design
    profession for the 21st century / Bruce Sharky. — First edition.
        pages cm
    Includes bibliographical references and index.
    1. Landscape design. 2. Landscape architecture. I. Title.
    SB472.45.S53 2016
    712—dc23   2015029624

ISBN: 978-1-138-84717-0 (hbk)
ISBN: 978-1-138-84718-7 (pbk)
ISBN: 978-1-315-72693-9 (ebk)

Typeset in Univers
by Keystroke, Station Road, Codsall, Wolverhampton

To my parents Louis and Beatrice who brought me into this world and my mother Sophie who prepared me to stay.

CONTENTS

CONTENTS

CONTENTS

FIGURES

PREFACE

The job of the artist is to go to the edge and report back.

Yo-yo Ma[1]

When thinking about landscape architecture, gardens are often what first comes to mind for most people. Garden design certainly engages the professional practice of many landscape architects. A garden is thought of as a place of beauty, simplicity, and pleasure. The Greeks referred to such a place as Arcadia, an idealized bucolic setting, a place to write poetry and consider philosophical questions. *Locus amoenus* is the Latin phrase with a similar meaning as a pleasant rural or garden setting offering one a place of comfort and to enjoy beauty. The idealized garden of the Greeks and Romans was seen as a safe place where one could enter to attain a sense of well-being. A garden setting had overtones of regenerative powers for healing as in caring for one's body and soul. We will learn in the following chapters that the ancient ideals of a garden were the genesis of contemporary landscape architecture. We will also explore what it means to be a landscape architect in the twenty-first century and the place in the world for this young and robust creative profession. We will also learn that the regenerative powers ancient cultures attributed to gardens now engage the creative work of today's landscape architects. This work involves the regeneration of damaged landscapes, responding to the impact of global issues such as sea-level rise, and rebuilding derelict urban neighborhoods and transforming them into more livable and walkable communities.

Thinking about Landscape Architecture is intended for several audiences. It was written for a general audience curious about the profession and the nature of what a landscape architect does. This audience might be considering hiring someone with capabilities appropriate for a potential project, considering that a landscape architect would be the appropriate profession to seek professional advice. This audience may have heard of the profession while researching possible design consultants. This audience would feel confident in knowing what to expect when hiring a landscape architect and be able to ask good questions before hiring after reading this book. A second audience consists of two groups of students. The first group has already enrolled in the major at a university and is taking an introductory course where a text such as *Thinking about Landscape Architecture* has been assigned by the faculty. As a text, it would provide these students with a well-rounded understanding of the broad-ranging facets of the profession they have embarked upon. The second group of students is one researching potential majors with landscape architecture being one of perhaps several possibilities. This group is seeking more in-depth information than might be available from a career counselor or popular publication so as to make an informed career decision.

Someone who has had a productive, fulfilling, and varied career in the profession wrote this book. I, the author, initially chose chemistry as my major upon entering the university as a freshman at the University of California at Los Angeles (UCLA). At the end of the second year I decided to change majors, having researched many possibilities that included landscape architecture. I proceeded with the paperwork transferring to the University of California at Berkeley where I would be able to study and earn a bachelor's degree in landscape architecture. After graduation followed by a year of travel by land in Latin America, and completing my apprenticeship years in the profession, I returned for advanced studies to earn an MLA degree with an emphasis on regional and coastal resource planning. My career has included working for private landscape architecture consultants in San Francisco, Los Angeles, and Winnipeg; a position as a park planner for a city park department; and as a researcher in the lieutenant governor's office at the state level. A brief stint working with an NGO in California involved lobbying activities associated with the passage of landmark coastal management planning legislation establishing the California Coastal Planning Commission. I also worked as a landscape architect for a consortium of oil companies, planning and implementing a landscape restoration program along an 860-mile-long oil pipeline corridor across the State of Alaska. My academic experience has included several North American universities including California State Polytechnic University-Pomona and my current tenure at Louisiana State University as well as shorter periods as a visiting scholar at international universities including Mexico, Portugal, Chile, Japan, Israel, and most recently in China. I established with a partner and long-time friend a successful landscape architecture consulting practice in Alaska, that included the design and overseeing construction of over 200 parks, numerous school campuses, office parks, government facilities, and urban design projects in nearly every corner of the state. I currently teach studio design as well as a sequence in the landscape technology stream at the graduate and undergraduate levels in the Robert Reich School of Landscape Architecture at Louisiana State University.

This breadth and depth of my experience in the profession have prepared me to write *Thinking about Landscape Architecture*. I believe the perspective that I bring should provide the reader with a sound and comprehensive understanding of the profession. While the experience described above is primarily North American, international teaching and travel augment my understanding of the profession, giving it an international grounding. While requirements for preparing and entering the profession may vary by country and continent, there is near uniformity in what landscape architects do, the services they perform, and the theoretical and practical basis of their work, regardless of the country. Stewardship, working in harmony with nature, and incorporating human needs are basic values that guide the professional practice of landscape architects worldwide.

Note

1 Barry Mazur, *Imagining Numbers* (Picador, New York, 2003), p. 6.

ACKNOWLEDGMENTS

Acknowledgments are in order here. In writing this book, while it is the words, thoughts, and ruminations of the author, I am indebted to a lifetime of influences, exchanges, and teachings of faculty, classmates, employers, professional associates, students over the years, and many others who have guided and inspired me.

I want to make a special acknowledgment to those at Taylor & Francis who made the publication a reality, including my editor, Sadé Lee. There are undoubtedly many others at Taylor & Francis to whom I owe a debt but whose efforts were conducted behind the lines.

I want to acknowledge the very capable graphic assistance of Jidapa Chayakul (MLA graduate research assistant) assigned to work with me from the Robert Reich School of Landscape Architecture at Louisiana State University. Jidapa prepared the line drawings of historical precedence for Chapter 4 and the illustrative maps and diagrams in Chapter 3.

I wish to acknowledge the very valuable support of the Louisiana State University administration and Board of Supervisors as well as my College of Art + Design: Dean Alkis Tsolakis and interim Director Van Cox of the Robert Reich School of Landscape Architecture for their support in the form of a sabbatical leave that enabled me to conduct valuable travels to photograph in many locations and the uninterrupted time to research and write.

Images and photographs from third-party sources are referenced in their respective figure captions. All other photographs are those of the author.

Early on, *Principles of Landscape Design* was the working title for this book project. The more I thought about the title and what motivated me to start this project in the first place, the more it had to do with providing students with an understanding of the potential of the profession beyond the mere basics. I considered what made landscape architecture special and unique among the design professions, believing that it was a profession for the twenty-first century.

The world we have inherited with its many challenges requires a special breed of designers—problem-solvers—who are uniquely prepared to make significant contributions to solving the environmental problems in the world we are facing nowadays. The aim of this book is much more than a source to inform people considering landscape architecture as a possible career choice. It is meant for people who wish to make a difference in their lives, in the lives of others, and for the sustainable preservation of the environment through design. It seems the current title better suggests the story that follows, beginning with the first chapter.

CHAPTER ONE

INTRODUCTION: WHAT IS A LANDSCAPE ARCHITECT?

Landscape architecture is one of those little-known professions with a substantial legacy of extant built works that have added value and beauty to cities and regions throughout the world. This legacy has included parks, gardens, college campuses, greenway systems, and all manner of designed places where people live, work, and recreate. The aim of this book is to present a window onto the world of landscape architects and the principles that inform their work in designing the outdoor places and environments we enjoy and pass through during our daily routine. The chapters are liberally sprinkled with photographs of significant projects designed by international and award-winning practitioners. The landscape architects of these works have incorporated ecological and design principles that are infused and informed by cultural and historical considerations to create built works following the highest design standards. Many visitors have admired and enjoyed this work without knowing whose hand was responsible for their creation. The reader will also come to realize that the knowledge, skills, and experience of landscape architects have prepared them as credible participants in seeking solutions for some of the significant environmental issues of the twenty-first century. These issues include diminishing water sources and water quality, global warming, loss of biodiversity, human health and quality of life issues in urban areas. Landscape architects have a growing voice, while working at the table with others in creating strategies to solve these and other issues affecting the quality and the very survival of life on this planet.

The target audience for this book is university students enrolled in the early landscape architecture design courses, students taking a university survey course from a menu of general study courses, and for those considering landscape architecture as a career choice who want to know more in order to make an informed decision. The students in Figure 1.1 are midway through their landscape architectural curriculum towards earning a Bachelor of Landscape Architecture degree. The group represents the diversity of students who are attracted to the profession, including international representation.

Landscape Architecture: A Design Profession for the Twenty-First Century

Landscape architects often work in close association with other professionals, including architects, civil engineers, various scientists, and others in the planning and design of a range of urban, rural, natural, and cultural settings. Landscape architecture is a relatively new profession, at least in name. The name was coined in the mid-nineteenth century and the young profession established its identify and growing influence, beginning with an early pioneer of the profession: Frederick Law Olmsted. Olmsted, along with Calvert Vaux, designed the American park icon: New York's Central Park and later the Emerald Necklace, a system of parks and greenways celebrated and enjoyed by the city of Boston, Massachusetts. These two projects are noteworthy in two vital respects. New York's Central Park was the first large-scale urban park in America with a design influenced by the estates and parks in England visited by Frederick Law Olmsted. While the design of Central Park was steeped in the naturalistic and Romantic tradition of Capability Brown and other early English landscape architects, the park was seen by Olmsted as a means of providing relief from the crowded tenements of New York by providing healthy passive, outdoor recreation spaces framed in a naturalistic setting. Olmsted also applied these natural and Romantic traditions he found in his travels to England to the design of the Emerald Necklace, another landmark urban park of nineteenth-century America. Olmsted's design for the Boston greenway park system also helped to reduce the recurrent flooding from winter storms. What we see on the surface are large expanses of lawn composed in a series of grand outdoor rooms, defined by planted forests of mostly native trees. The park was in essence the basis of the newly created storm-water infrastructure system designed to reduce periodic flooding in downtown Boston. So in the early years of the profession, a tradition was established where the landscape architects assumed an almost messianic point of view to deal with social as well as environmental issues, in addition to creating aesthetically appealing and functional green urban open spaces and parks. With Olmsted and the early landscape architecture pioneers, a professional tenet advocating stewardship for the environment and the goal of creating healthy livable communities was inaugurated. Later in the twentieth century, the profession firmly embraced and advocated the concept of land ethics and creating greater value by incorporating what has become known as sustainable and resilient design strategies: plans and designs that will be sustainable places where people live, work, and recreate now and into the future. And these created landscapes can include design strategies that will make the resulting landscape resilient to the negative impacts of storms and other naturally occurring phenomena.

The profession of landscape architecture is well positioned to participate in solving some of the fundamental problems facing communities, cities, and global regions. The academic preparation and professional practice career trajectories prepare practitioners to create design solutions that consider the environmental as well as the social, economic, practical, and aesthetic factors. Landscape architecture, like engineering, is an applied discipline that uses scientific-based knowledge to inform planning and design solutions. The practical application of scientific knowledge is the basis for landscape architects participating in identifying solutions to such global issues as global warming, increased scarcity of adequate safe water, loss of biodiversity, and problems related to sea levels rising. The involvement of landscape architects in these issues occurs in collaboration with other disciplines. What the reader will realize while reading through the following chapters is that landscape architects have a rightful and meaningful place at the table when dealing with global-scale environmental issues, just as they do at the local and regional levels. Among the design professions, landscape architects have assumed the role of good citizens of the environment.

Landscape architects are involved in various realms and on many scales. Employment opportunities can be found in many realms of practice. There is a diverse range of professional career options open to graduates, including private, public, and academic practice as well as the emerging areas of practice involving non-governmental organizations. Landscape architects are engaged in private practice, working with multiple design disciplines and with scientists in a wide range of land resource planning and management investigations.

Landscape architects were key designers and planners of the City Beautiful Movement,[1] a movement that contributed to making the rapidly expanding cities of the post-industrial era more humane and desirable places to live. One of the early legacies of Frederick Law Olmsted was his role in the establishment of the system of US National Parks, beginning with Yellowstone and Yosemite. Early landscape architecture pioneers had a significant impact on the park movement in the United States, including the design of urban park systems that have provided enjoyment and, to a considerable degree, healthy recreation opportunities for cities, beginning in the early twentieth century and the post-World War II period and up to the present day. The design work of landscape architects can be found in iconic examples of urban design, an area of importance to the profession that has been re-energized as older areas of central cities have found new ways to reinvent and make more livable, healthy central urban neighborhoods.

In addition to the work of landscape architects at the national, state, and city project scales of development, members of the profession have collaborated with natural scientists and land resource managers tasked with creating and maintaining our system of natural areas set aside to preserve and enhance large tracts of nature preserves, coastal areas, and river corridors. Landscape architects have played a central role in attempts to identify and preserve cultural heritage sites. They have worked as part of teams of planners, designers, and engineers, assisting in route selection and later landscape restoration and landscape installations associated with national and state transportation networks, oil pipeline corridors, and large mining extraction enterprises. And of course, landscape architects have been responsible for the design of private residential gardens and commercial properties. Other types of projects for landscape architects have been either as the principal designer or associated with teams who have designed golf courses, destination parks such as Disney World, eco-tourism resorts, ski resorts, and the list could continue. And, finally, landscape architects have participated in addressing the impact of natural disasters, such as hurricanes, by contributing to the rebuilding or developing strategies to increase the resilience and sustainability of communities affected by floods, fire, earthquakes, and other natural disasters. The profession appeals to individuals interested in creating more livable, environmentally responsible, safe, healthy places for people. These people must have a range of interests, skills, and passions steeped in the arts and the natural sciences.

The skill set developed by landscape architects is applied to the processes of problem solving and design. If you like to draw, write, and interact with people, you will most likely acquire a range of effective verbal communication, drawing, and computer skills. Interestingly, the profession has embraced the application of a growing range of computer representation software, including various technical drawing, animation, and photo-simulation programs. Hand drawing remains important and those skilled in the use of various media, including pencil, watercolor, and pen and ink, continue to be valued. Model making is another skill that is used to help clients better understand a proposed design. Model making can involve quick constructions out of clay or cardboard or more elaborate models using laser-cutting machines and 3-D printers. Landscape architects have found themselves at the cutting edge of computer applications to enhance their work and increase their efficiency in communicating design ideas and solutions.

Landscape Architecture: Science or Art?

> The old slow art of the eye and the hand, united in service to the imagination is in crisis . . . no other medium can as yet so directly combine vision and touch to express what it's like to have a particular mind, with its singular troubles and glories, in a particular body.[2]

Another worthwhile topic to consider as we set out to explore the profession is whether or not landscape architecture is an art or a science. The short answer—as you probably will guess—is both. Since it is in fact both, this is the underlying reason that people choose to become landscape architects. Landscape architecture is arguably not readily considered an art form, as is the work of a studio artist, for reasons we will briefly review. Landscape architecture is considered a profession, whereas artists see their work as a calling, not a profession. The word profession suggests someone who provides a service to others and indeed, landscape architects do perform a range of design and planning services for others as their prime endeavor. Artists, on the other hand, do not normally work to serve others except when a commission is involved. Still, landscape architects produce designs that follow their creative instincts and ambitions as an artist might in applying paint on canvas or creating sculpture from stone or metal. It is probably much more challenging for a landscape architect to produce a work of art than an artist, considering the former must incorporate such practical matters as user safety, zoning and regulatory criteria, and functional design standards (such as vehicle turning radii). The artistic expression is manifest in the choices the landscape architect makes in creating (designing) the physical forms and spaces inspired by their artistic sensibilities. The two garden walls shown in Figure 1.2 are very different aesthetically. The wall in Figure 1.2A provides a straightforward division between two spaces. The wall in Figure 1.2B not only provides the desired separation between two spaces, but also it can be accepted as a sculptural piece, visually attractive in addition to serving its functional intent.

Most landscape architects consider what they do and how they approach their work as having characteristics of both art and science. They see their discipline enabling them to be both creative and inventive as well as incorporating pragmatic and scientific interests to inform their work. While the words art and science appear on different pages in a dictionary, their application is anything but mutually exclusive. And the successful practitioners

Figure 1.2 Two very different wall designs: A: Parc André Citroën, Paris, designed by landscape architects Gilles Clément and Alain Provost, and the architects Patrick Berger, Jean-François Jodry, and Jean-Paul Viguier; B: Garden wall in Scottsdale, Arizona, by Steve Martino, landscape architect.

apply their artistic (creative) and scientific (pragmatic) skills, knowl-edge, and experience to what they do and the work they produce. Design is another component in the equation that can add clarity to the definition of what a landscape architect is. The result of their efforts is that something physical is to be made: they make things and make places. As we will see in a moment, the act of design is guided by the word *intent*. Design intent guides much of a landscape architect's creative work.

It is any one or a combination of the triumvirate (art, science, and design) that attracts people to study landscape architecture. Landscape architects are makers of things (landscapes) and the making requires the acquisition of a body of knowledge and spe-cific skills honed by experience that are applied, using one's creative imagination in creating places of beauty and utility. The American designer Charles Eames states: "Art resides in the quality of doing [making]. Process is not magic."[3] What Eames means by "process is not magic" is that art is a process that can be learned. One can learn and follow a series of steps or tasks toward discovery, finding truth, and gaining knowledge to organize what is learned to solve problems or create logical relations, such as functional relationships that result in producing a garden, a skateboard park, or a public plaza. The artistic component of the design is made by applying one's skills to produce something that can be appreciated by others as beauti-ful or that expresses important ideas or feelings. What is created is much more than functionally appropriate. What is created must also appeal to the senses. In the case of a designed landscape, a place is created where one can enter, move through or partake in some programmed set of activities. The created place feels comfortable to be in and perhaps one feels inspired walking through. In market-ing these are called value-added features. The made place or object offers far more than just utility or functionality. Elbert Hubbard further ties together art, the making of art, and the importance of process: "Art is not a thing—it is a way."[4] In other words, art is not simply a made object but also a creative process. Landscape architects apply the process of design that includes phases of research, discovery, synthesis, and eventually place-making, to create gardens, parks, recreation and sports facilities, college campuses, residential and mixed-use communities, arboreta, walking and bicycle trail systems, and urban spaces and streets.

When Frank Lloyd Wright says: "Art is a discovery and develop-ment of elementary principles of nature into beautiful forms suitable for human use,"[5] he is really talking about design. Design implies a function or utility, while art generally does not. When Wright talks about discovery and development of elementary principles, he is describing the process of gathering and analyzing data and applying the scientific method to arrive at some truth or set of facts.

Returning to the original question: is landscape architecture an art or a science? Why not both: art and science? The creative activities of landscape architects are informed by scientific knowledge and their own observations and experiences. They apply their knowledge to understand what they do. Through their creative ambition, landscape architects produce built works that are not only functional but are also beautiful (attractive to the eye and other senses). Their work can also improve the health of the environment and increase the desirability and economic value of the community where they practice their art and science. There is a potential for the practice of landscape architects to be a science in the way we think about ecology, horticulture, and geology as sciences. But, in fact, landscape architects, at least the present-day practitioners, might consider themselves applied scientists and not true research-based scientists. Landscape architects are not typically engaged in what one thinks of as scientific research. Rather, landscape architects draw from and are informed in their work by the body of knowledge scientists report as the result of their research. There are of course exceptions in the case of landscape architecture university faculty, who are engaged in research that is guided by scientific methods and protocols. Those individuals drawn to the science aspects of landscape architecture tend to pursue an academic career where time and resources facilitate pursuit of the scientific questions and their own curiosity about the world.[6]

Landscape Architects Must Balance Practical with Artistic Considerations

In practice, a landscape architect must find a balance between practical considerations with legal and economic and artistic expression. Ultimately the spaces they create through the process of design are said to resonate experientially, taken in by all of one's senses not just only visually. A space can be described as one comfortable to be in or a pleasant space to move through. Successful created landscape spaces are imbued with elements of comfort in addition to being practical and useable. Well-designed spaces for public use feel safe to be in and one feels welcomed psychologically if the design has considered the needs of all potential users, including those with physical disabilities. The landscape architect must contemplate a range of practical considerations when designing, such as the correct turning radii for vehicles or bicycles, or the correct dimension, such as a seat height or walkway width. Sightlines to enhance attractive distant views or baffle less attractive ones must also be considered. Design of landscape spaces considers orienting the layout of activities within a space either to be exposed to sun when desirable or to block the sun to prevent moderate to extreme hot air temperatures or glare. These and other practical considerations are part of the lexicon of landscape design.

Landscape architects also select materials for walks or gathering places as well as walls, fences, site furnishings, and other constructed elements. Material selection criteria might include durability and ease of maintenance and selecting complementary colors and textures. Perhaps the single most important design consideration landscape architects must devise is solutions for the modification of terrain. Landscape architects prepare site grading plans to guide the modification of existing landforms not only to accommodate intended uses but also to provide the proper handling of surface storm-water. Site grading most often provides the physical underpinning and visual structure of a designed landscape. Some grading decisions emphasize aesthetic design objectives and other decisions have to do with practical considerations, such as creating the correct slope and shape of the topography to accommodate an intended use or structure, such as a building, a parking lot, or an athletic field. Think of a golf course and the critical importance of terrain grading in creating a challenging as well as an aesthetic golfing experience. Other influences a landscape architect must consider during the design process are wind direction and force, solar orientation, growth of plant materials over time and seasonal changes throughout a year. Designed landscapes should be understood as places to be experienced, experienced by all the senses. A successful landscape design is one where the landscape architect has carefully orchestrated a range of considerations: physical, temporal, natural processes, and aesthetics. One needs to be a generalist, applying diverse knowledge with creativity to produce outstanding places and experiences.

Academic Preparation

The academic preparation for landscape architecture consists of curricula that contain a range of technical and design subjects as well as courses in the natural science and the arts.[7] Embracing both art and science can enhance one's creativity as well as result in producing innovative design solutions. Each (art and science) can inform the other. For example, doing research on natural plant succession can lead to an idea or concept for selecting and arranging plant materials in a planting plan. By developing a concrete understanding of the horticulture requirements for sustaining healthy plant growth, a landscape architect will have the necessary knowledge to design a roof or wall garden. Observing how plants are spaced and distributed in the natural landscape can inform spatial arrangements for site design or a planting plan. How art might inform science is a more slippery enterprise. A design concept may require research in several areas in order to figure out how best to realize and support a viable design idea. Extending your thought process to include both the sciences and the arts can trigger bold ideas or problem-solving strategies. One of the key skills to develop as a landscape architect is observing and learning from the places you pass by or through and visit in your everyday life. Developing keen observation skills and reflecting on what is observed and experienced adds to your knowledge base and understanding. This means you have more to draw from when presented with a new design project. Travel and reading are certainly important aspects of this idea of developing as a consummate observer. Experiencing new places, new environments, new landscapes all contributes to your process of learning. The sciences are often magnificently beautiful in themselves (think of the cosmos or the wonders of genetic code). The sciences can be the key to unlock new artistic possibilities and artistic expression in the practice of landscape architecture.

The Design Studio Environment

Academic preparation in landscape architecture places emphasis on studio courses. The method of instruction in a studio course presents students with design or planning projects—real or theoretical—to be solved, with the requirements of the projects described in a brief or project statement. Students may work independently in developing their solutions (design proposals) or in small groups with the teacher interacting with individual students by offering advice and giving substantive feedback (suggestions) during a student's progress. The work of the students is their own, developed through a process of self-discovery, eventually to arrive at a design solution to a large degree satisfying their understanding of what is required and their own creative sensibilities.

Career Opportunities

There are several career paths a landscape architecture graduate can take when practicing their chosen profession. These paths include:

- academic
- public practice or service
- private practice
- non-traditional practice.

There are many career paths landscape architects can take that not only include becoming designers of outdoor places but also involve participation with other professionals and scientists in developing management plans for natural resource areas, or developing plans and programs for repairing and restoring damaged environments, such as hillsides mined for gravel and coal, and improving animal habitat. Landscape architects have been involved in coastal restoration and restoration of other ecosystems that are threatened and damaged by natural disasters such as hurricanes. Landscape architects are employed by highway and other public infrastructure departments involved in the planning of route selection and later landscape restoration and enhancement. The list could easily continue but the reader should get the message: the work and skills of landscape architects go far beyond what is contained within garden walls. Urban design is yet another area that finds landscape architects vitally involved. Urban design includes the redesign of street corridors to enhance pedestrian use and safety, as well as establishing attractive and vibrant places for shoppers, workers, and visitors in sections of cities, and the design of plazas, establishing inviting and highly useable public spaces in new developments. The knowledge, skills, and problem-solving processes of a landscape architect are applicable in just about any facet of life, limited only by one's imagination and passion.

The workspace of the firm shown in Figure 1.3 is organized in an open office configuration, where professionals share a large open space not divided into individual, walled-in cubicles. The open office format is popular among design professionals and gives everyone a sense of knowing what is going on, the kinds of projects others are working on, and it also promotes group engagement. In situations where privacy is required to work or meet with clients or other professionals from other firms, private spaces or meeting rooms are provided.

Figure 1.3 The work environment of a landscape architecture firm.

Support professionals such as accounting and marketing may have their own spaces to work in, so as not to disturb or be disturbed. The workspaces are often designed with low partitions (note none are used in this example) so that a designer may work without direct eye contact with others when seated. Note in the foreground of Figure 1.3 larger tables that allow several people to work together on design projects when interaction is desired. The principals or partners may have individual offices in order that their telephone calls and conversations with others do not disturb the professional employees in the adjoining open work area. Also note the presence of computer monitors at each workstation. Each workstation has two monitors. The dual system facilitates the multi-tasking necessary for efficient computer-aided production. While difficult to see in Figure 1.3, the dress code in this office and generally in most offices in America is casual and comfortable.

Landscape architects are found on the professional staff of government agencies at the national, state, and local levels. Government entities such as national and state parks agencies as well as city park and recreation departments employ landscape architects, thus offering career opportunities that are challenging and productive throughout one's career. The preservation of a nation's historical and cultural heritage is an area of government that has grown significantly, requiring staff with professional expertise and training to manage these valuable facilities and landscapes. Landscape architects who are interested in history and culture have become integral professional staff in the planning, design, and management of landscape and cultural heritage sites. Governmental planning organizations, such as city planning departments, have long employed landscape architects. Just about any government agency will have landscape architects on its staff. Surprisingly government agencies such as national defense, housing, natural resources, transportation, and even departments of state will have landscape architects on their staff; primarily planning and designing facilities such as embassies or military installations. Working in these agencies most often engages teams composed of multiple disciplines. The work may include design of projects but more often it is overseeing the design of contracted consultants. The multi-disciplinary teams have primary responsibilities in planning, policy and regulation development as well as a review function, evaluating submittals of pre-construction documents to check for conformity with agency regulations and design and planning standards.

Another career track in landscape architecture is to become an educator. To do so in North American and most European universities requires a terminal degree, which is a master's in landscape architecture (MLA). In most other parts of the world, a doctoral degree has become the norm. An increasing number of candidates entering the teaching track have a bachelor's degree from just about any discipline in the humanities, sciences, engineering, business, and social sciences, and then enroll in landscape architecture graduate studies to earn a master's degree or even a Ph.D. The job description for a faculty position often requires candidates to have professional practice (in private or government) but this is less critical if candidates can demonstrate a history of research or scholarly accomplishments. A record of accomplishment can be demonstrated by published work in books or journals and awards. While teaching and research are the primary activities of faculty, they may engage in outside professional practice and some university programs endorse outside practice, particularly if faculty can demonstrate that their practice contributes in a meaningful way to their teaching and scholarly activities.

Non-traditional forms of practice have provided fulfilling and productive careers for landscape architecture graduates. The computer and design skills developed in school have led to employment in industry and non-governmental organizations. Landscape graduates have used their computer skills and interest to join municipal and state planning departments or industry, providing geo-spatial or graphic representation capabilities in support of various functions. Landscape graduates have found work in film production, particularly for documentaries or educational markets. The FedEx Corporation at their Memphis, Tennessee, headquarters hired a landscape architect several years ago, based on his design and especially his computer graphic skills. He was hired to produce web-based training manuals as well as assist in the production of marketing media. Another example of a non-traditional track is a student who was hired by the National Trust for Public Lands to assist in assessing potential strategic purchases of properties. Other individuals became public school teachers, ministers, and technical staff for various humanitarian agencies such as Catholic Services. The writing and editing skills of several other graduates have helped them to become editors of popular trade magazines. The knowledge and skills learned in school have enabled graduates shown in these examples to create professional careers limited only by their imagination and resourcefulness, together with a bit of persistence and patience.

Steps to Becoming a Professional Landscape Architect

Landscape architecture is recognized as a profession similar to architecture and engineering in most Western, European, and Asian countries. In recent years the profession has gained professional standing in several Latin American countries. The rate of acceptance has met with mixed success in others. Those in the profession see a bright future, particularly as problems of ever-increasing scarcity of resources, environmental degradation and pollution, and rapidly expanding urban growth make achieving more healthy, livable, and sustainable development a priority. Landscape architects, given their education and professional experience, are viewed as contributors to identifying and creating sustainable solutions in a world of expanding urban centers and scarcity of resources, and which is fraught with environmental problems.

Many countries have established a path to achieving professional status in the design professions, including landscape architecture.

The path begins with academic preparation followed by a period of apprenticeship in preparation of licensure or other form of establishing one's credentials to practice. Let's review the path or steps typical when becoming legally if not administratively a professional landscape architect.

Path to Becoming a Professional

In the United States, professional licensure is required before one can legally practice and charge clients fees as a landscape architect. There are two primary prerequisites before taking a national examination: academic preparation and an apprenticeship. In other countries there is generally no formal licensure requirement based on an examination. Generally, successful graduation from an accredited program plus a period of apprenticeship is sufficient.

There are approximately 80 accredited landscape architecture programs in the United States. The Landscape Architecture Accreditation Board (LAAB), together with procedures for carrying out the Board's responsibilities, have been established under the auspices of the US Department of Education to determine if a university's landscape architecture program has met specified minimum standards of academic preparation. Standards include specified course subjects and contents, faculty academic preparations and accomplishments, adequacy of the physical plant, and administrative support. Accreditation determination, if successful, identifies a university's program as accredited for a set period of time (typically six years). A university may offer accredited programs at the bachelor's or master's levels, or both. Course work includes landscape history and theory, landscape technology, plant materials and planting design, studio design, special topics seminars, and other university-required courses. Some professional landscape curricula also include horticulture, soils, and land surveying. The students in Figure 1.4 are seen working in the field and in their design studio where they may work on projects assigned on an individual or teamwork basis. Often the landscape planning projects are community-based projects and may be designed to include many project types from residential, neighborhood, community, and state levels, and in remote areas involving national parks, wetlands and river corridors and resource extraction sites. Students may also work in teams on a variety of project types at the regional scale, involving hundreds and even thousands of acres (100–500 hectares), and working with geographical information software to analyze and formulate planning and design strategies.

Figure 1.4 A: Landscape students gathering information during a field trip to design a project site; B: Faculty giving students a critique of their work in progress.

One of the requirements when a candidate applies for licensure is proof of having graduated from an accredited program and having been employed as an apprentice for the minimum length of time required by the licensing jurisdiction. Serving as an apprentice in the employment of a professional landscape architect or other recognized design professional is a prerequisite for being recognized, in addition to having an accredited degree in most countries outside of North America. In the United States, one must also successfully pass a nationally administered examination. In the United States, one obtains licensure at the state level, not the national level, whereas in European countries professional credentials are administered at the national level. Each state in America has established its own minimum number of apprenticeship years and the number varies from none (in the case of Mississippi) to three (the state of Washington, for example). The number of years of apprenticeship required by the majority of states is one year but it can also be longer in other states. A candidate is then required to take the national landscape architecture registration examination. Having graduated from an accredited program and satisfied the minimum length of time as an apprentice, and after passing the national examination, one then is allowed to legally practice in the state where the candidate has obtained licensure.

Examination and Becoming a Licensed Professional

In countries where an examination is a requirement before becoming a professional landscape architect, the examination[8] is generally a national examination administered by an organization with each state being an affiliate member. In the United States, the material contained in the examination is selected to test for minimum competency to practice landscape architecture. The purpose of the examination is not to exclude qualified individuals from practicing their profession. The examination is to assess an individual's understanding of the minimum knowledge necessary to protect the health, safety, and welfare of the public. In other words, the goal of having licensure for individuals to practice the profession is to protect the public from harm as a result of poor or inadequate design. Similarly physicians receive a license to practice medicine after having passed an examination. Lawyers and other professionals have an examination requirement before being allowed to practice law or their professions.

The concept of first passing an examination before being allowed to practice one's profession is closely adhered to in the United States but not followed in many other countries. Other countries place a greater reliance on university preparation and work experience. In the end, reputation is what ultimately establishes one's capability to perform landscape architectural services. The operative legal system in any given country is what identifies qualifications to practice one's profession.

While much of the work landscape architects do is in their office or on site, gathering field information, they often make presentations of the work in public forums. These forums are scheduled as an integral part of the design process and serve to inform and educate the public and client, as well as seeking their input and later approval. Figure 1.5 shows a landscape architect making a public presentation.

Figure 1.5 A professional landscape architect presenting a design proposal to a public audience as part of a larger process of engaging the public and interested stakeholders in project approval and later construction.

Notes

1 The City Beautiful Movement was an influential architecture and urban beautification movement that began with the building of the Chicago World's Fair of 1893 and that flourished in North America during the 1890s through to the early years of the twentieth century. Proponents of the movement believed that city beautification could promote a more harmonious social order that would increase the quality of life for urban inhabitants.

2 Peter Schjeldahl, "Take Your Time," *The New Yorker*, Jan. 5, 2015, p. 78.

3 Charles Eames, Carla Hartman, and Eames Demetrios, *100 Quotes by Charles Eames* (The Eames Office, 2007).

4 Elbert Hubbard, *Little Journeys to the Homes of Great Teachers* (Wm H. Wise & Co., New York, 1916).

5 Bruce Brooks Pfeiffer, *Frank Lloyd Wright on Architecture, Nature, and the Human Spirit* (Pomegranate Publishing, Portland, OR, 2011).

6 People also become educators for other reasons: to teach, to engage in creative work, and to pursue their own unique interests that best align with an academic career.

7 Foundation courses include design studio, plant materials and design, landscape technology, history, professional practice, and some programs in horticulture, soils, and land surveying. In the United States, course requirements for determining accreditation are established by the Landscape Architecture Accreditation Board.

8 In the United States, a national organization—the Council of Landscape Accreditation Boards (CLARB) with representation from each state that requires licensure to practice landscape architecture—develops and administers the Landscape Architecture Registration Examination (LARE).

Further Reading

A few good references to further satisfy your curiosity about the profession of landscape architecture:

James Corner, *Recovering Landscapes: Essays in Contemporary Landscape Architecture*, Princeton Architectural Press, New York, 1999.

Kellean Foster, *Becoming a Landscape Architect*, John Wiley & Sons, Inc., Hoboken, NJ, 2009.

Charlotte M. Frieze, *Private Paradise: Contemporary American Gardens*, The Monacelli Press, New York, 2011.

Robert Holden and Jamie Liversedge, *Landscape Architecture: An Introduction*, Laurence King Publishing, London, 2014.

Walter Rogers, *Professional Practice of Landscape Architecture: A Complete Guide to Starting and Running Your Own Firm,* 2nd edn, John Wiley & Sons, Inc., Hoboken, NJ, 2010.

Bruce G. Sharky, *Ready, Set, Practice: Elements of Landscape Architecture Practice*, John Wiley & Sons, Inc., Hoboken, NJ, 1994.

Simon Swaffield (ed.), *Theory in Landscape Architecture: A Reader*, University of Pennsylvania Press, Philadelphia, PA, 2002.

Roxi Thoren, *Landscapes of Change: Innovative Designs for Reinvented Sites*, Timber Press, Portland, OR, 2014.

CHAPTER TWO

THE LANGUAGE AND CONCEPTS OF DESIGN: PRACTICAL PRINCIPLES AND DEFINITIONS TO BE THINKING ABOUT

Why dedicate a life to art? What is art? Why is there Art? Art, in all of its forms, exists to help us find meaning for those emotions and feelings which are not easily put into words . . . art is vital to our lives, and however we use the gifts that we have been given, we should use them courteously.[1]

Introduction

It would be helpful to tackle early on some words and terminology involving design that might best be dubbed slippery. They are slippery in the sense that they may have different meanings from more common usage. While students may be familiar with and use the words in their everyday life, their meaning as used by designers may cause confusion. It would be useful to review them at the outset to avoid unnecessary confusion that can arise when design faculty and landscape architects talk about design and theory.

Is Design a Verb or a Noun?[2]

Each profession has its terminology, theories, and knowledge base often uniquely its own. Designers communicate easily with each other. Sometimes as a layperson listens in on a conversation, they may walk away not fully understanding what they heard. The words, while having dictionary definitions commonly understood by the general public, may, when used by designers be puzzling to non-designers. For instance, the word "design" has a dictionary definition that when read is quite clear. What is interesting is that this word "design" as used in landscape architecture and other design professions can communicate multiple concepts or ideas. The simple answer to the question of whether design is a verb or a noun is: it can be both depending on how or in what context the word is used. For example:

> Gertrude Jekyll was a designer (noun) of some of the most memorable public and private gardens in late nineteenth- and early twentieth-century England. She designed (verb) over 400 gardens in the United Kingdom, Europe, and the United States. She was a prolific writer whose design (adjective) theories had wide-ranging influence, particularly when she design (adverb) processed spatial sequences and created imaginative palettes of color and texture for her visually exciting plant combinations for which she was internationally renowned.

In some countries, such as Portugal, the word design is used as a noun and refers to a drawing: the design. In America and elsewhere, design can mean a process, it can be used to infer the creative act of making as in making a design. And it can mean the product of a creative process such as "the design." To further complicate the matter, the word design may have additional meanings when used by other cultures. What the intended meaning is depends on the context of how the word is used and how the specific meaning is generally understood when designers talk to one another.[3] When design is used in a sentence to mean design as a process, the intended meaning is the process one goes through in understanding and solving a problem. The problem requiring a design solution might be a spatial problem. That is, searching to find the best approach for designing (creating) a space or the design of an facility such as a children's play structure or a fountain for an entry.

When Is Dirt Soil?

Is dirt soil, is a bush a shrub, and is blue sky blue? Well, the immediate answer to all three questions is perhaps, it depends on who is using the words and what might be at stake. The meaning of the words also depends on whom one is addressing. The word soil in landscape architecture refers to a specific composition of ingredients and other desired physical properties (grain size, percentage of organics, pH, nutrient content, etc.) that are specified for specific plants (one type of soil may be required for a proposed lawn area while other types of soil are specified for trees and shrubs). More detail on soils will be reviewed in Chapter 8. While a client might refer to certain types of plants as bushes, a landscape architect refers to them as shrubs. Shrubs and bushes have the same meaning, it just depends who is talking. The issue of what is considered soil or not crops up when a landscape contractor brings a load of dirt (or soil) to the construction site. If the material is full of rocks, roots, and maybe bits of broken concrete or pieces of metal, can the landscape architect stop the contractor from using it? A soil specification is the basis for accepting or rejecting whatever is in the truck. The landscape architect will describe what constitutes acceptable soil and the basis for rejecting soil as outlined in the written technical specifications that accompany the drawings. Without the technical soil specification, the contractor can pretty much bring on site soil or dirt.

The term "blue sky" is used with two parallel meanings. The term is used when discussing the value of a business, such as a landscape architecture consulting firm.[4] Blue sky refers to non-physical values or worth of a firm, such as reputation. The reputation of the firm grows as clients and potential clients view the quality of a firm's designs, the value added of these designs contributing to the increased worth of a built property, due to the quality of the landscape design. Blue sky can also include how reputable and ethical are members of a design firm (the owners and principals). Are the word and ethical conduct of members of a firm reliable? Is the firm to be trusted? The question of trustworthiness is particularly important when the landscape architect takes on the responsibility of representing the client during the administration of a construction contract or appearing before a government board for some legal or administrative matter such as a zoning application.

Other words and terms and their meaning will come to your attention as you advance in your academic studies and continue in the profession. Words are important and one learns that choosing the right or best word can make a difference in achieving effective communication skills, both in writing and speaking.

Landscape Architects as Stewards of the Land

Those who choose landscape architecture as their profession, generally have an affinity with, certainly an appreciation of, nature. This appreciation of nature is manifested in two ways: (1) valuing the natural environment; and (2) assuming a professional responsibility caring for or acting as a steward for the land and its natural elements. Stewardship is a basic tenet that has been institutionalized by landscape architects in America through their national professional organization: the American Society of Landscape Architects. The mantle of steward of the landscape is a legacy that can be attributed to Frederick Law Olmsted. Olmsted was instrumental in persuading the U.S. Congress to designate Yosemite Valley and Mariposa Big Tree Grove, located in the Sierra Nevada Mountains in California, as public reserves. The action of setting aside and therefore preserving large tracts of wild lands later resulted in establishing the U.S. National Park Service. For Olmsted, his agrarian roots reinforced by his altruistic endeavors early in his career,[5] guided his later work of creating public parks and designing new communities. These works, beginning with the design of New York's Central Park, were informed by his sense of improving the lives and health of people these places served. His approach to design began with what we today call a site analysis: a thorough investigation of site conditions, including topography and land form, soils, vegetation, and other physical features of the landscape. His understanding of a site gained from the site analysis served as the framework for subsequent design decisions. Olmsted was greatly influenced by the works of early landscape designers in England such as Capability Brown and Humphry Repton, whose works he visited during his travels in England prior to his commission to design Central Park in New York with his partner, the architect Calvert Vaux.

Stewardship is the commitment to the responsible overseeing, management, and protection of something considered worth caring for and preserving, such as riparian streams, cultural landscapes, and lands crucial to maintaining the integrity of open space and wildlife habitat. In the United States, landscape architects have formalized a variety of stewardship tenets through policies adopted and promulgated through the American Society of Landscape Architects (ASLA). One of the organization's stated policies that reflects the stewardship responsibility inherent in the profession is a policy on the preservation of landscapes associated with wildlife and wildlife habitat.

Landscape architects, as a profession, extend stewardship concerns and responsibilities to urban, rural, and natural areas. Cultural and historical sites and landscapes are acknowledged to have an intrinsic value and require a stewardship stance, as the ASLA does in its policy on historic and cultural resources of the nation, state, and local jurisdictions.

By logical extension, one way that landscape architects can carry out their stewardship responsibility is by applying lessons learned from the process advocated first by Frederick Law Olmsted in the nineteenth century and later in the mid-twentieth century by Ian McHarg. McHarg elegantly argued in his book *Design with Nature* (1970) for a systematic approach to assess the suitability of land resource allocation to accommodate human uses and development.

Design with Nature

Landscape architects often derive inspiration for their designs from their experiences and observations of nature. The nature-inspired designs are rarely a direct appropriation of forms and compositions experienced in actual nature. Naturalistic landscape designs seem to move in cycles of favor and relevance among landscape architects, or from the way one landscape architect "works" as opposed to other forms of artistic expression (formal or abstract, for instance). Designed landscapes informed from nature are often referred to as naturalistic designs. This is a term with a broad meaning with many variations. Naturalistic designs are composed with forms (compositional arrangements) and materials (the use of materials taken directly from nature such as native plant species and building materials). Landscape designs appropriated or inspired from nature are rarely direct copies but rather are abstractions, symbolic, or interpretations although artistic intent may result in some ambiguity. The viewer might be compelled to ask: "Is the landscape natural or not?" The designs of traditional gardens of China and Japan were created with the intent of realizing an abstraction, even a miniaturization of nature. While natural-looking, these gardens are filled with symbols composed of plants and arrangements of rocks placed to represent other places (sacred or admired) or animals such as birds. The creation of naturalistic gardens is a tradition steeped in Western culture, including the Romantic gardens of Northern Europe and North America. Nature became the fountainhead of theory and approach to landscape planning and design in the latter half of the twentieth century in an approach referred to as design with nature.

Ian McHarg, Professor of Landscape Architecture at the University of Pennsylvania, emerged as the charismatic proponent of a systematic approach to landscape design and planning. He was the author of the landmark book, *Design with Nature*, published in 1970. McHarg recognized that a reconciliation of human and natural systems could be achieved through the systematic sifting and layering of geo-formatted data in the form of maps. The aim of his pioneering approach was to identify suitable landscapes for development that would reduce the negative impacts caused by the mismatched or unsuitable location of human development and activity. His work was further developed by others exploring regional landscape planning theory, and this has led to identifying designs for site development, community development, and resource management that could be more sustainable while achieving a quality and healthy environment, economic advantages, and social equity goals.

The book immediately proved to be popular with a diverse readership. Its message gained wide acceptance and its publication coincided with the passage of the U.S. Environmental Protection Act of 1970 that established the Environmental Protection Agency (EPA). The basic tenet of the book argued for a systematic approach of designing with nature. The approach considered the underlying processes of nature as a basis for planning and designing places for human activities, while considering the historical and cultural context. McHarg's message was that incorporating what we know about natural phenomena and processes could help us to make better land use and design decisions. McHarg's assumption was basically that past decision-makers and designers of land use did not understand the value of nature, nature for its own sake and for human survival. This assumption was generally the case, witness the plethora of environmental disasters that have made headline evening news with great regularity since the 1970s. Later, McHarg began to incorporate human considerations in parallel to natural factors. Professor McHarg became an influential advocate for making better-informed decisions regarding environmental resources. He was widely sought after as a speaker for his systematic approach to making land use and resource development decisions. His message resonated with those active in the environmental awareness movement of the 1970s through the 1990s, not only in America but elsewhere throughout the world.

McHarg's design with nature process has evolved over the years, incorporating the use of GIS (geo-spatial information software) to rigorously document and analyze an extensive variety of mapped information such as soils, topography, vegetation, hydrology, demographic data, and a seemingly unlimited range of information about the Earth and human physical conditions. The systematic processes for analyzing information about a project site and its surrounding context have become an intrinsic process approach by landscape architects, informing their design and planning decisions. Suitability maps are often generated from the GIS information to indicate the optimum locations for various design elements (program activities, functions, and facilities). The mapped information can also be used to suggest resource management decisions, resolve land use conflicts, and lead to inspired design decisions. The Landscape Institute of the

UK describes what is a very basic principle of landscape architecture: the design process:[6]

> Landscape architecture is rooted in an understanding of how the environment works and what makes each place unique. It is a blend of science and art, vision and thought. It is a creative profession skilled in strategic planning, delivery and management. Landscape architects bring knowledge of natural sciences, environmental law and planning policy. And they create delight with beautiful designs, protecting and enhancing our most cherished landscapes and townscapes.
>
> (Landscape Institute, 2012)[7]

> The more we study the major problems of our time, the more we come to realize that they cannot be viewed in isolation. They are systemic problems, which means that they are interconnected and interdependent.
>
> (Capra, 1996)[8]

Sustainability

The underlying and contemporary foundation of landscape stewardship for environmental and cultural resources is to protect these resources for future generations through a rational planning and design process. The concept of protecting these resources for future generations is referred to today as sustainability. Sustainable landscapes are of sufficient integrity where the processes and support systems necessary for the plants and animals are able to continue functioning and to survive. Stewardship provides the underpinnings for sustainable thinking and well-informed land and resource management principles. The goal of achieving sustainable wild, rural, suburban, and urban landscapes while accommodating human development depends upon the application of environmentally responsible strategies of land management and land development. The application of responsible design and planning strategies would seek to achieve a mix of human spaces and healthy land, water, and wildlife systems across the landscape. Landscapes where humans dwell, work, and play, whether they are urban, rural, or wild landscapes, are a complex mosaic of earth, water, and sky. Sustainable designed landscapes are created by applying an array of independent design interventions and making comprehensive land use decisions. The accumulation of each design and land use decision of the past eventually has created fragmented landscapes, such as isolated slivers of wildlife habitats. Eventually these fragments have eroded a landscape to the point that they no longer serve as viable, self-sustaining habitats. In fact, they have eventually disappeared altogether. The small residual patches no longer are capable of functioning as robust and healthy natural systems. A forest may over time be subdivided with roads, utility lines, and other built structures so that eventually what remains of the original forest no longer has the capacity to support wildlife in a sustainable manner. Fragments of native forest and other ecosystems that once were of an extent and level of health to sustain themselves and wildlife can no longer do so and are no longer capable of protecting or conserving the water quality of a site or region as well.

Incremental habitat modification over time leads to changes and losses in ecosystem diversity. Landscape architects, with their academic training, approach planning and design with the intent of preserving native landscapes as much as is feasible. This approach to design thinking is considered early in the development process of a project. Landscape architects are often the only profession in the process who are taught and trained to apply sound ecological and land management principles and therefore serve as the voice of reason for a more sustainable approach to planning and design. Working toward maintaining biodiversity by preserving functioning ecosystems has the most realistic chance of promoting positive change. The integration of ecological information with the design process can create a healthier union between land use and the natural environment. The protection and maintenance of healthy and functioning natural systems, even in urban and suburban areas, have gained increasing acceptance in the twenty-first century. Achieving sustainable landscapes through development is an approach that is now understood to build in economic value to new neighborhoods and infrastructure. Sustainable design, together with responsible stewardship, creates economic value, with the result that these environments are considered desirable places to live and work in the marketplace.[9] Sustainable design can provide a competitive advantage in a competitive commercial or residential market.

McHarg was a twentieth-century pioneer, whose own work and similar work by his contemporaries raised the public's understanding of landscape architecture from garden art to making landscape architects into significant players in sustainable design. Their work has contributed to creating more livable and disaster-resilient urban settlements and more responsible resource development. Topics that are now an integral aspect of the academic training and professional practice of landscape architects include the following:

- Site analysis and site suitability:

  - systematic approach to site planning and design, incorporating natural factors
  - greenway planning and design
  - design within zones of wetlands, floodplains
  - design in harsh environments, such as deserts and dry areas, permafrost, hillside slope erosion and slope failure
  - microclimate moderation to improve energy efficiencies and reduce negative impacts, such as the reduction of heat islands in cities.

- Landscape design contributes to better health:

  - healing gardens
  - livable and walkable communities
  - smart growth and other community planning strategies to create more livable cities.

- Landscape design contributes to a healthier environment:

  ○ water conservation and water quality
  ○ best management practices
  ○ reduction and mitigation of flooding
  ○ increase in biodiversity
  ○ bio-remediation.

- Landscape design has become an integral component in the route selection, planning, and design of various infrastructure systems, including transportation, public works, utilities, and others.

Collaboration

Earlier in this book the question was raised whether landscape architecture was an art or a science. Considering the art half of the answer, the romanticized notion of the lone artist working in his/her loft studio may not fully characterize how one might actually practice the profession.[10] The complexity and broad potential impacts of most design and planning projects that landscape architects are involved with today have come to require multiple disciplines working together in transdisciplinary or interdisciplinary teams. While the landscape architect might work alone in an urban loft, nowadays working collaboratively, perhaps electronically connected, has become the norm. Regardless of where one works—an office loft or any workplace environment—the designer is required to have the capability to communicate and interact with others either in person or electronically.

It is common for landscape architects to work with other design professionals on projects, with each having their defined areas of responsibility. Generally the landscape architect is responsible for the areas outside the building or other structure footprint that require coordination with the building architect. A project might also have roads, parking lots, storm drains and sewers, and electrical requirements, thus requiring coordination with various engineering disciplines, such as civil, electrical, structural, and geotechnical engineers. Depending on the project type, other consultants may be involved, for instance, biologists or water quality specialists for projects with wetland and habitat renewal requirements. Just as in the field of medicine, the growth of specialization is creating niche professionals. Landscape architects find themselves establishing niche areas of specialization in the contemporary and globalized practice of planning and design.

The ability to effectively communicate and collaborate with other specialist and allied professionals is a valuable skill. Working with others can be rewarding professionally and personally. Working effectively with others is a highly desired attribute and those who do well are highly sought after. There is the opportunity to learn from others that ultimately will increase one's professional influence.

Scale: Another Word with More than One Meaning

Another word worthy of some clarification at this time is "scale." A ruler is called a scale after you enter college to study landscape architecture. The word "scale" can be used to communicate three very different ideas in the design professions. The wooden or plastic instrument we knew as a "ruler" in kindergarten is referred to as a scale in landscape architecture, engineering, and architecture. In its first meaning, the word "scale" refers to the device used for measuring (determining the dimensions) to guide the designer in creating a plan or detail on paper or with a computer. For drawings created on a computer, there is a measuring function in the program to guide the designer. The second meaning of the word "scale" refers to proportions—that is, a means of representing the actual dimensions of a building, object, or project property site by a drawing that fits on a sheet of paper. This second meaning of the word refers to the scale of a drawing or map. In order to make a drawing of a large property, a space, or object, it is drawn not at its actual size but drawn at a size to fit on a piece of paper. For instance, in a drawing that is produced at 20 scale or 100 scale, one inch drawn on a piece of paper would be equal to 20 feet or 100 feet. All objects delineated in plan or section would be drawn using the same relative scale. In the case of a tennis court with dimensions of 60 feet by 120 feet, it might be drawn where one inch equals 20 feet in order to fit on a design plan. Using a scale (ruler), the designer would draw the tennis court at 20-scale so that the drawing would be 3 inches (or 60 equivalent feet for the width) by 6 inches (or 120 actual feet for the length). Keep in mind that the drawing on the paper is representing the tennis court but drawn so that every 1 inch on the paper is equal to 20 feet on the ground. Metric scales have corresponding equivalents drawn to represent the actual size on the ground.

A third meaning of "scale" refers to the size of an object relative to the size of a person. In this case, when we use the word "scale," as in "the wall height is in scale with people," we mean that the height of the wall is not overwhelming relative to the space and the people using the space. A designer uses the word scale to characterize the height of the wall to mean the wall is a comfortable height relative to a person standing next to it. Or the paved area of an urban plaza is of a size that would make people feel comfortable in the space relative to the buildings that surround the plaza.

The pattern of the campus walkway shown in Figure 2.1 is located in the central quadrangle on the UCLA campus.[11] The early twentieth-century Californian landscape architect Ralph Cornell designed this heavily used walkway. His intent was to aesthetically relate the pedestrian circulation systems and the spaces defined by the buildings by incorporating selected architectural details and materials. The buildings are all faced with brick, using both standard ($3\frac{5}{8} \times 2\frac{1}{4} \times 7\frac{5}{8}$) and Roman ($3\frac{5}{8} \times 1\frac{5}{8} \times 11\frac{5}{8}$) sized bricks. The basic module that underlies the size, shape, and pattern of the walkway is based on the Roman brick. The walkway was designed with a sufficient width to comfortably handle the traffic of large numbers of students. The

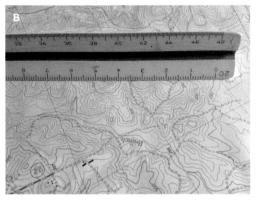

Figure 2.1 A: A pedestrian walkway on the UCLA campus in Los Angeles, California; B: An engineer's scale used to measure distance on a USGS topographic (or quad) map.

walkway was subdivided into units representing individual personal space. The larger intersection that can accommodate 16–20 students is given a personal scale by subdividing the width of the walkways into smaller units. The designer for the original drawing used an engineering scale, prepared at 20- or perhaps 40-scale. One can critique the design by saying that the designer brought the scale of the expansive walk built to carry a large number of people down to the individual human scale by establishing a detailing module that roughly approximates the personal space of a single student. So the word "scale" can be an object: a ruler or it can be a term that refers to proportions of space in relation to a person or group of people. And it can refer to the proportional scale used to create the drawing of the walk.

Landscape architects in America use two scale systems: engineer and architect. An engineer's scale divides units into tens or multiples of 10. 10-scale means one inch equals 10 feet. 20 scale means one inch equals 20 feet. In the case of an architect's scale, units of measurement are in fractions. For instance, 3/4 scale means 3/4 inch equals 1 actual foot. 1/8th scale means every 1/8th inch equals 1 foot on the ground. An architect's scale is used for almost all drawings involving buildings. Drawings that involve primarily earthwork such as grading, drainage, and road design would use an engineer's scale. A landscape architect and landscape contractor need to be equally conversant using both scales. A landscape architect would prepare drawings in a construction package that included both scales. There are conventions that professionals follow that dictate which scale is appropriate for each type or subject of a drawing. While earthwork and associated elements would be drawn using an engineer's scale, and buildings and other structures would use an architect's scale, details, such as for a deck, wall, or fountain, are typically drawn using an architect's scale. Confusing, yes, at first, but eventually the type of scale used becomes second nature. Landscape architects who practice in countries that use the metric system have it much easier: one measuring system, one set of scales: metric.

Agent of the Client

The word agent used in landscape architecture identifies a role quite different from Agent 007 of the James Bond character in the movies. Once students graduate, they advance to their professional training as interns or entry-level employees. Gradually the students (who are now part of the office professional staff) gain more contact with clients with whom the office is contracted to work. As they begin to interact with clients, the question of whether or not a project solution is a good or appropriate solution ultimately is the decision of the client, while the landscape architect will have his or her own assessment of what constitutes a good solution. The client is the person who must approve a proposed design if the project is to advance to the construction phase.

It is at the construction phase that the role and responsibility of the landscape architect shifts. The landscape architect now represents the interests of the client and it is the landscape architect's responsibility to ensure the contractor builds in accordance with the construction drawings, technical specifications, and contract. The landscape architect's role is that of agent of the client, whose responsibility is to ensure the contractor carries out the orders of the client. The role of agent gives the landscape architect the responsibility of ensuring that the contractor installs materials at a level of craftsmanship and in conformance with construction documents and applicable laws and standards, within the contract budget, and in a timely manner. The landscape architect observes the materials installed and the workmanship of the contractor to determine if they conform to the construction documents. The landscape architect then approves the work and determines the appropriate levels of payment in situations when a contractor can request partial payments. Throughout the construction process, it is the landscape architect who interacts with the contractor, makes decisions, and provides responses to the contractor's requests. The landscape architect carries out these activities as the representative of the client and therefore has the responsibility of maintaining the interests of the client. This is a special relationship and much of the success of a landscape architect is based on having established their professional integrity and gained the trust of clients. Being fair with the contractor is another area where a landscape architect can achieve success. When contractors feel the landscape architect was fair in carrying out their responsibilities as the client's representative, the contracting community will have greater confidence in knowing what to expect when developing contract bids for a project prepared by that particular landscape architectural firm. Often contractors working with landscape architects whom they deem treat them fairly will submit lower bids. This compares to situations where contractors will submit higher bids when they feel their risks are higher working with landscape architects whom they feel do not treat contractors fairly.

Elaboration of Further Design Topics

Plants Grow and Change, over Time

The universe can be understood in terms of space, energy, matter, and time. It is the dimension of time (among other subjects) that distinguishes landscape architecture from architecture. While not 100 percent the case, once a building or any other structure in the landscape is built, it more or less remains static with few physical changes that are as dramatically evident as the changes plants undergo in their life span. The architect's building is a fully realized object once completed. The landscape architect's work after installation of the plant materials can be anticipated to physically change over time.

Small (young) trees grow into large trees. When small trees are planted in a space, the intended impact of the space is minor, compared to when the trees approach maturity and fill in and grow into a canopy, shading the space.

Many plants undergo changes with the seasons throughout the year. Deciduous trees and shrubs lose their leaves in the fall in anticipation of the approach of winter. Before the leaves drop, they change color in autumn from shades of green to multitude shades of yellow, orange, red, purple, and brown. With the onset of spring, the leaf buds on bare brown branches swell, gradually turning from pale, light shades of green to increasingly more intense shades of the leaf color they eventually will achieve on maturity by early summer. All these changes are part of a continuum or natural process and it is the knowledge of this process of change that is understood by a landscape architect. This palette of change is considered when specific species of plants are selected and placed in the designed landscape. Landscape architects also consider the metamorphic changes of plants over the span of time when designing spaces and places.

As the installed plants mature, the spatial qualities and scale of the designed landscape evolve. Planted spaces become more in scale to the visitors of these spaces, perhaps as spaces where there is a more comfortable feeling. Comfortable in terms of scale and more agreeable spaces to be in as the shading aspect of the trees is realized. Landscape architects will select and place plants to moderate the effects of wind, sunlight, and views. Deciduous trees planted along the face of a south-facing building will shade it and reduce heat gain from the summer sun. These same trees will lose their leaves in the fall, reversing the effects of sun, allowing for heat gain into the building. Plants can serve to screen undesirable views. As the plants grow, their potential for blocking or reducing undesirable views increases over time, eventually providing visual privacy. The physical permutations of change that plants undergo in a year's time or over tens or even hundreds of years are challenging to learn and for a landscape architect to master. To add a further dimension to the challenge is that each region of a state, provenance, country, and continent has unique aspects of time-related changing, that must be learned and understood. The physical changes from season to season or year to year have aesthetic implications to be learned as well. Horticultural knowledge of the plants and their time-related changes can enhance or moderate some of these changes. The landscape architect at the outset of the design process must account for the ramifications of soil, climate, longitude, and hydrology when developing a plant design palette. With the sound understanding of these factors, more informed decisions will be made with respect to plant species selection and their impact on the designed landscape.

Circulation

Circulation (both vehicular and pedestrian) is an element in the landscape that provides the organizing structure for a plan of a new neighborhood, the site design of open space, a campus plan, and any project that has a variety of program elements requiring access, the internal connection between facilities and use area, and way-finding requirements. One of the steps in the process of developing a site plan for a park or neighborhood, for instance, is to organize various program elements in a bubble diagram, then connect the various elements to the park programmed elements with vehicular and pedestrian circulation (Figure 2.2). A continuation of the site design process discussion can be found in Chapter 3.

The walkway in Figure 2.3A connects the upper central quadrangle on the UCLA campus to the lower athletic fields through the use of a terraced flight of stairs. The walkway extends the bilateral symmetry of the upper academic quadrangle making up the dramatic change in elevation with the stairway system. The lower axis has as its terminus the distant hills while the upper axis is aligned with a grouping of academic buildings that provide the peripheral frame of the central activity area of the original campus. The pedestrian and bicycle path in Figure 2.3B skirts along the edge of one of the

Figure 2.2 *Park master plan diagram with circulation. Courtesy of Reich Associates, landscape architects.*

retention ponds at the Water Ranch Park in Gilbert, Arizona. The path allows the visitor access to several wildlife viewing locations and connects several ponds, each having vegetative habitat to attract a great variety of visiting bird species. The walk in Figure 2.3C is an example of the concept of conceal and reveal. The idea is to align the walkway to provide a glimpse of what is ahead, creating an element of surprise and hence interest for the pedestrian. The planting of a vegetative screen further enhances the concealment effect. An "S" curve in the walkway alignment is often used to create a concealed then revealed experience as shown in Figure 2.4. Notice how the movement of the walk draws your eye in the direction of the circulation as well as creating a dynamic visual composition within the space.

Figure 2.3 *Examples of three very different pedestrian walkway design concepts: A: Simple lineal; B: Serpentine; C: Bilateral symmetry.*

Figure 2.4 *Curved pedestrian path at the San Antonio Botanical Garden.*

Figure 2.4 *Curved pedestrian path at the San Antonio Botanical Garden.*

Where Do Design Ideas Come from?

During a class field trip to the office of Lawrence Halprin in San Francisco, one of the students asked Mr. Halprin what was the inspiration for his landscape designs. Halprin, who was an avid hiker, including making many visits to Yosemite National Park and the Sierra Nevada foothills, replied with one word: Nature. Then he went on to elaborate that design was 99 percent perspiration and 1 percent inspiration. In other words: hard work.

Sources for inspiration in design can come from many places, often originating from the unexpected. The music heard in a concert can inspire a design. Art seen in a gallery or on a page of a magazine has been the source of inspiring landscape designs. Experiences on an outing, particularly natural settings located within the context of a project site, can be the basis for a design.[12] Design inspiration generally draws from one's experiences: experiences involving listening and seeing and to a lesser degree drawing from the other senses. Inspiration can also come from reading: reading for pleasure or reading when conducting research. Inspiration, when it does come, usually reveals itself somewhere in the early process of a project when the landscape architect is absorbing what can be learned from the project site, gathering information on the locational context of the project site, and certainly at the stage when considering approaches to organize program elements. Design ideas may reveal themselves in the process to resolve design issues. In the following pages various sources of design inspiration through examples will be presented.

Inspiration from Nature

We will start with nature as a source of design inspiration; the source that Lawrence Halprin and others have said has often influenced and guided their landscape designs.

Let us begin considering nature as a source of design and inspiration. The scene in Figure 2.5 is located in Bandelier National Monument in the state of New Mexico. There is little doubt that this is a natural space with a pathway, perhaps with minor alterations (such as some clearing the path of rock and other debris) made by the early Native Americans who lived there.

Next, look at the three landscapes in Figure 2.6. They look like scenes taken from nature. However, all three are photographs taken of designed landscapes visited by the author. They were not designed as copies of actual natural scenes but inspired by what the designer saw and experienced. After some research and detailed field observations, the landscape architects returned to their office to develop what you can observe as their resulting designs.

Planting Design Inspired by Nature

The images in Figures 2.6A and 2.6B are two created landscapes at locations in the American Southwest. Figure 2.6A is located in a residential subdivision in the foothills above the City of Albuquerque, New Mexico. The vegetation you see was all planted using species native to the area as a part of an extensive landscape restoration plan. The plan also included the creation of a new storm-water drainage scheme, complete with surface water detention areas. This restoration work was required after a major earth-moving operation transformed a previously natural landscape for

Figure 2.5 Bandelier National Monument, New Mexico.

residential development. Native plant species endemic to the area were selected and in a few years naturalized to achieve full coverage of what was bare earth after site grading was completed. Figure 2.6B is a residential garden located in Scottsdale, Arizona. Steve Martino, the landscape architect, chose native plant species, arranging them in a composition to enhance the views and provide seasonal changes in the garden. The image has a natural appearance; however, the plant

Figure 2.6 Three landscapes: A: New community storm-water basin with native plants in Albuquerque, New Mexico; B: Residential garden using native plants in Scottsdale, Arizona; C: Imperial garden in Kyoto, Japan: a garden design inspired by nature.

groupings and arrangements in space were the result of the artistic intentions of the designer based on his experience walking the trails in the surrounding high desert landscape. The image in Figure 2.6C is of a garden in Kyoto, Japan. The landscape was a fabrication, the result of the designer's vision to create a symbolic rather than an actual recreation of nature, of a particular scene, or an amalgamation of a variety of scenes inspired from the many travels of the designer and client. Tree species in particular were selected for their sculptural form and how those forms would enhance the views from various locations of the living quarters in the residence as well as during a stroll through the garden itself.

The designer of each landscape pictured in Figure 2.6 used basic art and design composition guidelines, including creating visual cohesion in the selection of the color, texture, and forms of the plants and other materials. The landscape architects balanced the various elements in the composition, creating a dynamic movement through space for the eye to follow, as an artist would organize a composition on a canvas. In the following sections we will review other concepts where a landscape architect might find inspiration and be guided in the development of a project design.

The Poetics of Sunlight and Shade Patterns

Sunlight and its absence can make a significant visual difference in a space and impact the physical features arranged there. Fountains, for instance, specifically the water, are far more dependent on the play and presence of sunlight (and artificial light in the evening) than on the actual physical fountain design. Consider a fountain as a stage composed of a vessel containing water. The water can be manipulated various ways by the handling[13] of water by a mechanical system and light (natural sunlight or artificial lighting). To a large extent, light is required for the water to be animated and produce the dramatic visual and sound effects that water movement can create. Access to direct sunlight during the day and light fixtures at night use light to show the play of the water (see Figure 2.7).

Figure 2.7 A: Residence fountain, Scottsdale, AZ, by Steve Martino, FASLA, landscape architect; B: Evening view of water curtain in Las Vegas, Nevada.

The presence of light and shadow on plants, paved surfaces, and walls adds drama, creating layers of visual interest, to animate objects such as plants, landforms, and built objects in landscape spaces. In Figure 2.8 are two images of a garden wall at a residence in Scottsdale, Arizona. Steve Martino, FASLA, designed the walls and garden. Figure 2.8A shows the wall without direct sunlight on the side facing the viewer. While still an engaging composition, the image relies on form, color, and texture to provide visual interest. The same wall viewed on the opposite side is facing into the sun (Figure 2.8B). The sunlight not only intensifies the color but casts a tree shadow onto the wall, adding visual interest to the otherwise plain surface. As the sun travels from east to west during the day, the shadow pattern is altered, changing the overall composition. On an overcast day the landscape appears flat, lacking depth or three dimensions, and absent of shadows.

In Figure 2.9 is a view of exposed structural roots of a live oak. The strong light and shadow washing over the roots in the image in Figure 2.9 produce very rounded, three-dimensional forms.

The nuanced nature of sun and shadow patterns in the landscape is more highly variable as the sun moves across the sky from dawn to dusk and through the seasons. The amount of cloud cover and moisture in the air affect the variability of the sun's appearance and effect in the landscape. The low angle of the winter sun creates long shadows

Figure 2.8 Garden wall, residence, Scottsdale, AZ, by Steve Martino, FASLA, landscape architect.

Figure 2.9 Live oak structural roots exposed above ground.

Figure 2.10 A: Tree branching pattern of sunlight and shadow cast across open lawn; B: Tree branching pattern washed on courtyard walls, Scottsdale, AZ, garden by Steve Martino.

whereas in the summer the sun is high in the sky, resulting in sharp, crisp shadows but not as long as in the winter. Landscape architects should consider the presence of the sun in all its daily and seasonal variability and harness the variable effects in their designs. Consider how a design might take advantage of sunlight and shadow for their visual effects in creating a spatial design with poetic qualities.

Consider the dramatic scenes in Figure 2.10 and the visual nuances that sunlight creates in producing tree branching shadows on the ground and walls. Most people walking through the spaces most likely are aware of the plants, the wall, and the steps in the space, not realizing the exciting visual interest contributed by the pattern of shadow and sunlight.

Look at Figure 2.11 and you can see by example how happenstance can add to a designed landscape. In this situation visual interest is enhanced by the combination of low-angle sunlight on a winter day washing across the modular paved surface accented by a long tree shadow. The pattern of the Palo Verde[14] flower petals sequestered in the concrete voids further increases visual interest with the serendipitous addition of color and texture. Beautiful, perhaps unplanned, but then again, the image should suggest a design element that may have been anticipated and even considered by the designer. You hear clients complain about leaves or the seeds that trees drop on the ground. Consider educating them so as to see the aesthetic merits of leaf, seed, and flower gifts that literally fall out of the sky adding interest and variety to the landscape.

Figure 2.11 Palo Verde flowers increase the visual drama of the low angle winter sun and the shadows that wash across the walk.

Sunlight and shadow are employed in the design of golf courses to enhance the strategic challenge for the golfer. The landscape architect will shape the topography of the green area especially the sculpture forms of the earth mounding to create shadow patterns that can trick the golfer's eye and judgment of distance. The resulting patterns and forms created by the play of sunlight and shadow washing across the ground surface adds an aesthetic dimension to the game of golf. Golfers appreciate and favor courses that are aesthetically pleasing as well as challenging.

The Changing Quality of Night and Day Lighting

The linear park built on an abandoned elevated train structure in New York City is shown in Figure 2.12. The park promenade is shown in daytime (2.12A) and the evening (2.12B). This popular elevated urban park is reminiscent of the Viaduct Promenade in Paris, France; an elevated park also built on an old railroad structure. Views of the High Line Park in Figure 2.12 show the dramatic differences that the presence or absence of sun has on the structure and landscape. On a sunny day the paving and outdoor furniture appear animated with sharp contrasts of shadow and sunlight. In the evening the view is more dramatic backlit by a setting sun with a darkening sky. At night, the sculptural elements of the seating and raised curbs and landscape are made more dramatic from the light cast by outdoor lighting. The colors of the plant materials can appear more intense and vibrant just after sunset as compared to midday.

Figure 2.12 High Line Park, New York City, by James Corner Field Operations; A: In daytime; B: In the evening.

The Age of Context[15]

While ideas about beauty and what constitutes good landscape design are a subject meriting interminable attention—and can be further described as a moving target—they are something that will continue to occupy designers into future millennia. The notion of Context[16] has emerged in recent years as a valuable frame of reference for assessing the merits and informing landscape design. The plethora of global issues associated with climate changes that we can see eroding the natural environment—literally right before our eyes—with the loss of biodiversity, forest cover, wetlands, etc., and the impacts on public safety, regional economies, health, and quality of life—a holistic position on evaluating the intrinsic merits of a design—are increasingly gaining importance in discussions of what constitutes a good landscape design. The contextual dimensions of aesthetics seem more easily communicated, understood, and valued than ideas about beauty and what makes one design more attractive or not so. Parameters that fall under context are presented here in quite broad terms and include a number of dimensions including:

1. function and ideas about efficiency, convenience, comfort, accessibility, social justice;
2. safety, including floods, landslides, earthquake, concern for public health and welfare;
3. economics equity, risk, short- and long-term costs, value-added impacts;
4. ecology, including biodiversity and ideas about sustainability and water conservation, concern or responsibility for addressing issues of the biosphere such as global warming and rising ocean levels;
5. culture (traditions, religious beliefs, cross-cultural considerations) and history of the area of project concern;
6. aesthetics, including beauty, harmony, cohesion, proportion, balance, and, of course, scale.

Another way of understanding context is as a frame of reference or simply the surroundings. The considerations that go into thinking about a project to be designed generally involve a particular location and piece of ground, such as a city lot, neighborhood, or street corridor. Contextual thinking would involve considering not only the piece of ground of the project but also its physical, social, cultural, economic, and environmental surroundings. A proposed project where context informed the design will more likely be accepted, certainly understood and appreciated by the client of a private project or the stakeholders of a public project.

Putting It All Together

The experienced landscape architect develops over time an approach to problem solving followed by a process that they have found to be reliable in arriving at good, if not inspired, design solutions. Often the designer works through the process, not thinking about "process" but unconsciously following one. While the designer may identify design goals and objectives for specific projects, most often they draw from an unconscious list of design tenets[17] developed over years of experience. These design tenets allow the designer to identify workable design solutions that, for the most part, result in good, if not outstanding, design solutions. Roger Trancik in his book, *Finding Lost Space*[18] (another book that should be in your personal library) developed a list of design tenets that together can be reasonably applied in most design projects, and, if nothing else, could be used as a checklist of sorts for the landscape architecture student to refer to.

1 Create an Organizing Framework or Structure

One of the considerations in the early stage of a project when a landscape architect is developing a design is to organize the various activities and activity areas so that circulation (pedestrian and vehicular) movement is efficient and conducive to ease of visitor movement and way finding. The various activity and use areas are also organized in groups where shared facilities such as parking are possible, clustering activities that are passive together and possibly separating them from active, noisy activities. Other spatial organization considerations in addition to facilitating way finding or arranging uses by desirable proximity relationships are topographic and climatic preferences of the project program's functional elements and activities.

A design that creates well-organized spatial relations and carefully considers the circulation system greatly contributes to achieving a successful design. Spatial organization is also a contributory factor in achieving art that is admired. Landscape architecture that is well organized can be aesthetically pleasing as well. Designs that are aesthetically pleasing but not well organized or lacking in a carefully considered structural framework may be viewed as problematic and not judged favorably. For example, the design of the picnic pavilion may be stunning but if the pavilion is not located convenient to the designated group picnic area or parking, then the overall design may be viewed a failure.

2 Foster a Distinctive Identity

Creating a unique design is often in the minds of landscape architects as they approach their work. The intended meaning of *fostering a distinctive identity* can mean shifting the emphasis from creating a unique design to the idea that the designed landscape should visually relate to the region or its surrounding context (the neighborhood). The idea of distinctive is not so much a matter of being unique but ensuring that the design has visual qualities that resonate with the context. A designer who carefully considers the context surrounding the project site, including its climate, native or dominant plant species, selection of building materials and styles of architecture, or detailing of structures, will make better design decisions. Better in that the design incorporates what was learned and valued from studying the site context or region. The design visually "feels" like it belongs in its surroundings and nowhere else (a site-specific design).

3 Create Variety and Interest

The underlying theme in the academic training of landscape architects is to make beautiful and brilliantly functional, humanly comfortable, and healthy environments. The balance sought is to create places that solve functional requirements and offer an experience to the user or the persons passing through the spaces that is satisfying to the senses and is memorable. This may seem a daunting task given all the pulls and tugs from clients, economic restraints, governmental regulations, and from other realms that weigh into our lives as designers. Spaces designed with a variety of forms, colors, textures, and visual interest can be experienced as successful spaces. Controlled variety accented with points of interest or focus is a hallmark of a critically successful designed landscape.

4 Ensure Visual and Functional Continuity

Visual variety and interest alone will not necessarily result in achieving high-quality or skillful landscape design. While visual continuity is an important goal, it must be provided within a structure and organization where logical circulation and appropriate functional relations between spaces and activities are achieved.

5 Maximize Convenience

Achieving convenience in design requires the landscape architect to carefully identify and understand the important spatial relationships of program activities and use areas. In its essence, convenience means program elements are in their right place and that the use areas are arranged so that their functional proximities facilitate logical access or the sharing of common use areas or facilities. Ease of access would benefit program elements that require close proximity to parking for users and visitors. For recreation and sports facilities, the landscape architect should consider arranging the activity areas to be convenient to service-related facilities, such as a restroom or parking. Providing common use areas and logical circulation and access in commercial and residential projects are other examples where consideration of convenience will contribute to achieving a successful design.

6 Provide for Comfort and Safety

Comfort is achieved when the designer implements a range of desirable dimensional design considerations (such as heights of walls and benches, for example) and environmental moderation considerations (such as providing shade in sunny locations, buffering undesirable wind and noise, and moderating surface glare are a few examples where design can produce comfortable places). The placement of deciduous trees along south-facing building with windows can moderate heat gain inside the building during the summer when the trees are in full leaf. Conversely, deciduous trees and other plants allow for heat gain in the winter when the trees lose their leaves. Color and texture selection of materials can affect comfort. For example, the selection of matte-finished earth tone colors for large expanses of pavement can reduce reflective glare at the same time as reducing the high surface temperature that highly reflective surfaces tend to create.[19]

Safety includes creating designs that neither cause harm nor create dangerous conditions or structures, and is one of the primary bases for licensing professions such as landscape architecture. Protecting the safety, health, and welfare of the public is a requirement of professional practice. A landscape architect must consider the regulatory and administrative design standards when developing design solutions. Walkways and paved surfaces must meet an array of design standards, including maximum slope, non-skid surfaces, and the absence of potential design flaws that could cause tripping or other unintended mishaps, resulting in bodily harm to the public.

7 Emphasize Quality

There are several ways of thinking about the idea of quality in landscape architecture design and practice. The first has to do with providing quality design services. This first consideration has business and marketing implications. The landscape architect who provides a high degree of service and product (such as design and construction drawings and construction administration) and follows business practices that attend to customers' and users' needs and satisfaction will achieve in the long run greater market share, healthy profits, and thus stay in business. The second way to consider quality in design is creating designs that are safe, comfortable to be in, and facilitate the requirements of the activities and uses. Quality design also suggests the selection of quality materials and developing construction details that result in fewer mistakes, lower long-term maintenance costs and problems, and enhance and retain the economic value of the project and built work.

Cultural Differences in Design

Globalization has had an effect on the landscape architecture profession as it has on architecture and engineering. Landscape architects are crossing borders to provide design services in greater numbers to work in countries other than their own. Firms are opening up satellite offices or establishing partnerships with local firms as new markets for design services open up globally. It would be an unfortunate oversight if the notion of the cultural dimensions in landscape design were not mentioned here. While it is convenient to think that there are universal design concepts that can be applied from one country to another, there exist cultural differences that must be recognized in order to practice successfully in other countries and cultures. Basically, the idea is that what one culture may think is a good design may not be so in another culture. Having taught and lectured in China on several occasions, I have found the statement to be all too true. Teaching design to Chinese landscape architecture students, I have learned to be more careful about how to communicate with the students. The quizzical looks I would get during a desk critique were not a matter of language differences but different ideas about design. For instance, I might suggest to a student to consider organizing their site design, considering certain ideas about creating harmony and cohesion. They might have a different notion of what constituted a cohesive layout from the one I was suggesting. Further, I might suggest developing a more naturalistic arrangement of plant materials and spatial organization and they in turn would give me another puzzled look. Puzzled not because they did not understand the words I used but the concepts. This does not mean that the Chinese would not agree to the use of a naturalistic approach in developing the design of spaces and arranging plants materials. Rather, we would need to better understand what would be a naturalistic approach based on their experience as opposed to my experience.

In Figure 2.13 are two images: one is a traditional landscape design of a residence in Shanghai and the second a contemporary street landscape in Hangzhou. Most Westerners think of the garden in Figure 2.13A when considering Chinese garden design. This and similar garden designs in China are a blend of naturalistic forms and arrangements of materials and heavily pruned or modified natural materials (plants and stones, for example), showing the hand of human intervention: man and nature. Quite a different approach to landscape design in China is currently in vogue as shown in the street landscape in Figure 2.13B. Current landscape design in China typically incorporates human intervention and arrangement of plants and other materials. Heavily pruned and clipped trees and shrubs characterize the sensibility of contemporary Chinese landscape design preferences. While stylization is evident in both traditional (Figure 2.13A) and contemporary (Figure 2.13B) designs, asymmetry and use of natural forms and symbolism best describe traditional landscape design. The heavy use of symmetry with the employment of layering is the desired approach today, as I found from working with Chinese landscape architecture students. The students and practitioners expressed their preference for an approach shown in Figure 2.13B. This landscape design along the street presents China to the world as a modern advanced nation similar to their Western contemporaries.

To continue, we should understand what we mean when discussing culture and cross-cultural differences in design. Culture is a set of shared characteristics such as thoughts, values and behaviors and, in the case of design, design sensibilities that are unique to any one culture (country). Design theories and concepts are understood and talked about differently within each culture. There are defined sharp lines along which cultures differ, in terms of what is desirable and which characteristics describe good design or design relevant to any one culture. The first layer to understand cross-cultural differences would be in communication: language. Assuming that language translation

Figure 2.13 A: Yu Garden, Shanghai, traditional garden; B: Hangzhou typical street landscape currently in vogue throughout China in cities and along highways.

is not an issue, there are elements in language in the realm of concepts—design concepts—that might make communication difficult for a visiting landscape architect to present his or her design ideas in the host country. For instance, Western cultures often use metaphors to describe design concepts. It is quite possible that metaphors do not translate from one language and culture to another and may simply not be understood. Wise advice would be not to assume your words and their meaning are easily understood and that extra effort may need to be taken to ensure your ideas are understood correctly. There are of course psychological and social differences from one culture to another. Dimensions of personal space, for example, vary by culture. How close you are to another person can cause discomfort. Seating arrangements can cause discomfort in one culture if the space is too close, while that same spatial dimension may seem comfortable in other cultures.

While the Chinese are very interested in learning about Western landscape design, it does not necessarily mean that they think Western design is good in their eyes. One intern from my university in America who was doing her internship at a Beijing office was told by her project manager that her designs were not Chinese enough and she was asked to redo a design assignment several times. It was not a matter that she was a bad designer. It is just that she interpreted the design directions given by her supervisor in a very different way than her supervisor had in mind. I gave a lecture on contemporary American landscape design at the same office. Afterwards, there were lots of questions and some excellent and lively discussion. It came out that, while they appreciated the presentation, they had trouble seeing the projects I used in my lecture as something they would do in China. It was a matter of cultural differences. The design sensibilities from the American experience would not transfer well to the Chinese one. Basically it boiled down to this: they like to see plant materials clipped and pruned into nice layers and shapes. They do not like the unruly look of plants allowed to grow without being re-shaped, as we generally prefer in America. The thousands of miles of new roads and streets in China have been heavily planted. These plants are routinely pruned and clipped. The Chinese would find the landscaped freeways in California planted with native, drought-tolerant plant materials an approach they would not favor or find attractive. They might say the landscape looked unruly and not very beautiful. They would have the same criticism of the planting design, for instance, of the High Line in New York.

There is always the opportunity to learn from others and, in cases involving cultural differences, the learning curve can be rich as well as perplexing. Keeping an open mind would be good advice when practicing one's profession in another country. Keeping an open mind while working in another region of one's own country which has different climatic and other environmental attributes would be advisable as well. Think of the differences between the tropical conditions of southern United States and the arctic conditions in Alaska and Canada. An approach that would lead to a good design in Florida may lead to a disaster in Alaska. The differences can be as much environmental as well as cultural.

Figure 2.14 Residential street scene in Mexico City, D.F.

Finally, Make Room for Serendipity

As a designer, you would like to think you have complete control over your creations and have considered all possibilities before making your final design decisions. To some extent it is possible to have considered all possibilities and conditions that could impact a design. But then complete control could mean missing the unexpected, the unprogrammed from falling into your life, resulting in something extraordinary that makes what you designed very special, sublimely beautiful, and a lasting memorable experience. See Figure 2.14 for an example how a single plant (Bougainvillea) can produce an exuberant visual display created by the contrast of natural and built elements. The Bougainvillea was planted well inside one property but managed to "invade" an adjacent property, producing an exuberant display of contrasting colors. The color combination was a happenstance result, greatly admired by passing motorists and pedestrians.

Notes

1 Taken from the program notes by the directors Patricia O'Neill and Richard Baker for the play: *Master Class*, Theatre Baton Rouge, May 15–24, 2015.
2 Design can also be an adjective as in design firm or adverb as in design processing.
3 I taught a design studio in Portugal and remember the confusion of both the students and myself when I first talked about and used the word design. The Portuguese students understood that I was talking about a physical drawing, as in a construction drawing and not the meaning I had intended: design as a process and the resulting creation: "the design."
4 Goodwill is a term that also refers to the non-tangible assets of a business.
5 Such as establishing what eventually became the Red Cross during the American Civil War.
6 The process of design is not one-dimensional nor necessarily linear. A student first learns initial design process in the classroom then later adapts and alters that learned process to better meet the unique set of environmental and jurisdictional conditions of individual projects. The process of design is a process that landscape architects develop for themselves based on their own experiences, knowledge, and understanding of how best to make and then communicate their design recommendations.
7 Landscape Institute, *Landscape Architecture: A Guide for Clients* (Landscape Institute, London, 2012), available at: www.landscapeinstitute.org.
8 Fritjof Capra, *The Web of Life: A New Scientific Understanding of Living Systems* (Anchor Books, New York, 1996).
9 It is perceived that sustainable design builds in competitive advantage and provides value. The result is that these projects command a higher price in the marketplace than comparable projects developed without sustainable design and planning features.
10 Compared to other design professions, such as architecture and interior design, landscape architecture offices are quite small in numbers of staff. In America, the average size of a private practice office is two or three. A large landscape architecture staff might be 30–50 with just a handful in the neighborhood of 100. A 100-person office is considered a modest office size in architecture and engineering. There are multi-disciplinary firms employing a few thousand professionals, many with offices located in multiple cities as well as in numerous countries.
11 University of California at Los Angeles.

12 I recall the explanation that the designer Angela Danadjieva gave as to what inspired her design for a fountain in a park her firm was commissioned to design in downtown Anchorage. She answered: "Admiring the form of ice and play of sunlight of the face of the Portage Glacier where it met the lake gave me the inspiration for the Town Square Fountain in Anchorage."

13 The mechanical system of a fountain produces the many ways that water can be moved, such as in a spray, circulating and moving up and down over fountain surfaces, dripping, bubbling, splashing, and even remaining still.

14 *Cercidium parkinsonia.*

15 Tom Turner, *City as Landscape* (Spon Press, London, 1996).

16 Context with a capital C.

17 The word tenet is used here to suggest a list of beliefs or principles that may be used as initial design principles to consider but not as doctrines to be rigidly followed.

18 Roger Trancik, *Finding Lost Space: Theories of Urban Design* (John Wiley & Sons, Inc., New York, 1986).

19 The feeling that the air temperature is somehow lower may be a psychological response rather than an actual physical difference.

Further Reading

A few good references to further satisfy your curiosity on landscape design principles:

Travis Beck, *Principles of Ecological Landscape Design*, Island Press, Washington, DC, 2013.

Michael Boylan (ed.), *Environmental Ethics*, Wiley-Blackwell, Oxford, 2014.

Catherine Dee, *Form and Fabric in Landscape Architecture: A Visual Introduction*, Taylor & Francis, London, 2001.

J.B. Jackson, *A Sense of Place, A Sense of Time*, Yale University Press, New Haven, CT, 1994.

Aldo Leopold, *A Sand County Almanac*, Oxford University Press, New York, 1968.

John M. Marzluff *et al.* (eds.), *Urban Ecology: An International Perspective on the Interaction Between Humans and Nature*, Springer Science + Business Media, New York, 2008.

Ian L. McHarg, *Design with Nature*, 25th Anniversary Edition, John Wiley & Sons, Inc., Hoboken, NJ, 1995, originally 1970.

Anne Whiston Spirn, *The Language of Landscape*, Yale University Press, New Haven, CT, 1998.

Ervin Zube (ed.), *Landscapes: Selected Writings of J.B. Jackson*, University of Massachusetts Press, Amherst, MA, 1970.

CHAPTER THREE

THE DESIGN PROCESS AND THE LIFE OF A PROJECT

Introduction

One of the attractions of landscape architecture—and there are a great many—is that those in the profession find themselves in the forefront of diverse design and planning endeavors. This diversity includes everything from a stream restoration and garden design to planning a new community for hundreds of families or college campus. Because of this diversity, there is not one approach to working that can be followed for all project types. There is not any one single process or way of working that meets the needs of everyone.

When talking about design, the terms process and tools of working come to mind. The two terms are integrally linked. One develops a process that works best for them to guide them in successfully carrying out their work. Second, one has a set of tools to employ during the process. In the case of landscape architects, their tools are the graphic methods of drawing and communicating their design ideas and solutions. Practitioners have a tendency to work with a wide array of digital and analog drawing systems throughout all the phases in the life of a landscape design or planning project. Computer aided design (CAD) systems have been used for years to produce construction drawings and are an essential part of every design and planning activity in today's office. Building information modeling (BIM) is a relatively new computer application used to generate coordinated plans, sections, and elevations as well as 3-D models and material quantities. Hand drawing continues to be an important skill, particularly in the formative stages of the design process. Once the landscape architect has identified a preliminary design, the process switches over to the use of computer programs, although, depending on the office or individual, a combination of analog and digital applications is used. Each person or office develops a set of graphic representation tools to effectively generate concepts, develop ideas, and communicate design solutions. Figure 3.1 shows a landscape architect's desk.

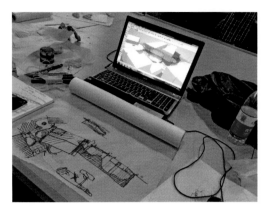

Figure 3.1 The tools of the design process: hand-drawn sketches followed by visualization with computer representation software.

Notice both hand-drawn and computer-generated graphics are being used simultaneously to arrive at a design solution.

In this chapter we will focus on the design process. Landscape architects employ a process to systematically deal with all the steps and complexities that even the smallest project requires. The process presented here roughly parallels the phase of work in a professional services contract between the landscape architect and the client. The steps are more or less universal in the design professions, including engineering and architecture.

Design

One can design following a "wait until lightning strikes" or when "an idea or the mood comes to me" approach. Waiting for lightning or the mood to strike may work for some people. However, as design projects reach a threshold of complexity in terms of program, site characteristics, government requirements, and the number of stakeholders involved, a more systematic and analytical process may be necessary. Of course, whether or not one needs to follow a systematic approach is not solely a function of project scope and complexity. One can just as effectively approach the design of a residential garden following a systematic process as a much more complex project, such as the design of a regional park. Just because one approaches the design process systematically does not mean there is no room for inspiration. Inspiration is not something we can turn on or turn off. Nor is it advisable to ignore it just because it appeared while analytically engaged. The designer engaged in a systematic approach is laying the groundwork that may have an enabling effect for inspiration to seemingly appear out of nowhere. The systematic process is a process starting out with activities that lead to discovery, then this is followed by understanding. In the process, one grasps important relationships and patterns. In other words, one becomes smarter as the significance of various facts and relations becomes apparent. The designer arrives at a point where the project and its complexities are understood and clarity emerges. The coming of clarity produces the conditions conducive to solving the problem and knowing what to do.

The Design Process

The intended meaning of the word *process* refers to the steps a landscape architect follows in executing a design contract with a client. The steps described here are the steps contained in a professional services contract between the landscape architect or professional services firm and a client. In the United States, the steps or phases of work in a professional services contract have been formalized into a standardized agreement, universally adopted in the design professions, including architecture, landscape architecture, and civil engineering. While a professional services contract may contain any number of steps, depending on the project scope and the needs of the client, five steps or phases are most common. Phase I begins with preliminary research and investigation, site analysis, programming, and finally the preparation of a preliminary design solution or in some cases the preparation of two or more alternatives. Presenting a client with several alternatives is a strategy that is similar to comparative analysis used in literature courses. The presentation of alternative design solutions allows the designer to show a range of possible design options and then compare the merits of each. This allows the client to better understand not only what is possible but more importantly to better understand why one solution best meets the project's objectives. Often the alternatives represent a range of potential costs from the less expensive to the more expensive alternative. While cost is not always the basis for selecting one design over another, the client can better appreciate the more costly solution and perhaps be willing to go with that solution after seeing the relative benefits, compared with other less costly alternatives. Sometimes, the client may not be so clear what they want and therefore may not sufficiently articulate their project desires. So the landscape architect may respond by developing alternatives as a way of helping the client see the potential of the project and in the process make a final decision.

For the design student, a valuable lesson to be learned by being required to develop more than one solution to a design assignment is that there are, in fact, many possible good, if not outstanding, design solutions. This is an important lesson to learn at an early stage of one's design education, a lesson that can help students to be more critical of their own designs. Exploring alternative design solutions allows the student to be more open to look for other, and hopefully, better solutions than the first one that comes to mind. Being open to other possibilities can be the basis for arriving at a very good, if not outstanding, design proposal. Closing one's mind and being too quick to accept the first design solution without being critical often limit a designer's problem-solving process: a process that should in fact lead to a better and hopefully creative and appropriate design solution.

As with architecture and other design disciplines, landscape architecture generally follows a more or less particular procedure to bring a project from initial research through subsequent steps until construction is ready to commence. This process is common to the design professions, certainly so when multiple professions are working together contractually under a professional services contract. There are five phases in the typical process:

i. Schematic Design (SD)
ii. Design Development (DD)
iii. Construction Documents (CD)
iv. Bidding and Negotiations (B&N)
v. Construction Administration (CA).

We will now briefly review each of the five phases.

Phase I: Schematic Design

Schematic design consists of several components, beginning with early meetings with the client, initial research (due diligence), site analysis, programming, and the preparation of one or more schematic design proposals.

Pre-Design: Background Research, Inventory, and Evaluation

The first phase or step of the design process comprises gathering information and gaining familiarity with the client's project aspirations, the site and its physical and historical context, and the legal landscape. At the outset of a new design project, the landscape architect must first become familiar with four important factors of the project. The process of gathering information for the four factors has two components: (1) gathering or inventorying the information; and (2) interpretation and evaluation of the information collected. The aim is to gather what will be useful information that will later inform site planning and site design decisions. That information is:

1. Research concerning the client, users, and stakeholders including:

    a. Program elements including activities and uses, facilities and other structures.
    b. Likes, dislikes, and desires of client.
    c. Project aspirations of the client.
    d. Area and other dimensional requirements of each program element and structure.
    e. Optimum relational diagram of program elements.
    f. Circulation requirements including: vehicular, pedestrian, bicycle, service vehicles, and parking.
    g. Climate, sun exposure and prevailing winds.
    h. Hydrology analysis, particularly general direction of surface water flow patterns.

2. Knowledge and understanding of the physical attributes of the project site: the landscape architect must understand the site and its context[1] (neighborhood and region), including the topography, climate, soils, vegetation, sun and seasonal variations, and myriad of other physical and temporal site-related characteristics including:

    a. Topography, landform, and slope analysis (Figure 3.2).[2]
    b. Aspect[3] or topography-climate (Figures 3.3 and 3.4).
    c. Soils and geology.
    d. Vegetation (Figure 3.5).
    e. Climate, including seasonal rainfall, air temperature, and wind direction and speed.
    f. Sun angles (summer and winter).
    g. Views and landmarks.
    h. Existing man-made features.
    i. Utilities and infrastructure (on- and off-site).

j. Historical and physical context in which the project site resides, such as cultural and historical records of activity and legacies (such as structures) and physical features such as vegetation, and architecture styles and building types.

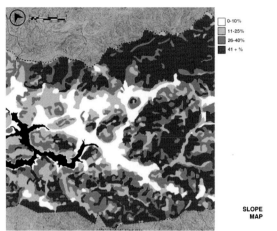

Figure 3.2 Slope map showing categories of slope from level to steep.

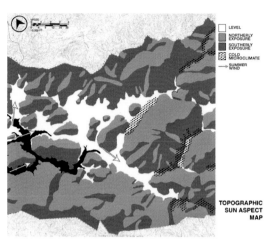

Figure 3.3 Sun aspect map based on topography.

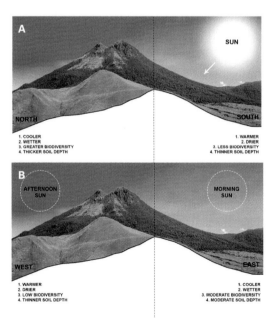

Figure 3.4 Sun aspect diagram: A: North–South sequence; B: West–East sequence.

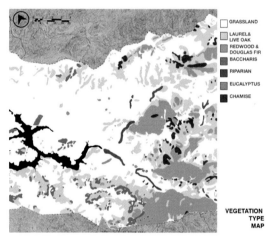

Figure 3.5 Vegetation map often created using aerial photography in combination with on-the-ground field studies.

3. Knowledge of applicable laws and governmental regulations and procedures, issues of safety, and environmental regulations. The information researched here is referred to as *performing due diligence*, a term that indicates the requirement that any professional must undertake to fulfill required professional responsibilities. For instance, the need to determine the applicable zoning requirements and restrictions, fire and safety requirements, flood plain limits and restrictions, and permit requirements. The landscape architect must identify all applicable laws and regulations and permit requirements to insure the project design conforms. Each design discipline understands the importance and necessity of performing due diligence as a professional responsibility.

The designer as part of a professional service contract will investigate the local and governing laws and administrative requirements that are enforced in the jurisdiction(s) where the project is located including:

1. Land use zoning.
2. Building and other structure setbacks.
3. Rights-of-way, servitudes.
4. Building codes.
5. 100-year flood elevation.
6. Setbacks from wetlands and waterways.
7. Storm and surface water management requirements such as best management practices. Floodplain constraints and design elevation requirements (FEMA[4]).
8. Wetlands management and mitigation.
9. Health, safety, and welfare administrative guidelines and requirements.
10. Environmental Protection Agency requirements: clean water, clean air, and environmental impact assessment.
11. Government permit requirements (local, state, and federal agencies).

Other areas of knowledge include an understanding of the construction industry and available contracting companies, including:

1. Availability and sources of landscape and construction materials (vegetation, soil, building materials).
2. Construction methods.
3. Contractor expertise and capabilities.

Schematic or Preliminary Design: Establishing Design Intent

Now that the landscape architect has researched, gathered, and considered the relevant background information related to the project, the preliminary design phase of the process begins. That is not to say that the designer has not already been thinking about design until this point. Often ideas about design begin emerging almost at the first hearing of the project and even before a contract with the client is signed. Design is not something one can necessarily turn on and off. Ideas "pop" into one's head virtually of their own accord, as designers, by their very nature, live with the design switch turned on. But at this point in the process the designer will turn their full attention to developing design concepts while digesting and applying the background research.

Developing initial design ideas depends on the nature of the project. In the case of a community park, the designer might first focus on organizing the physical relations of the various park elements (the program), followed by considering the circulation sequence from entry to passage from area to area. Functional relationships of the program elements consider which activities are best clustered together in order to share such things as entry, parking, and support elements (such as restrooms). Clustering of program elements might be based on separating active from passive activities, organized and unorganized sports, and topographic features that might support and enhance the park visitor experience.

In addition to functional considerations the designer would consider the experiential possibilities for the park visitor. For instance, the design goal might be to create a naturalistic environment or to set the park elements within a cultural or historical theme, based on background research discovered about the site's history. The schematic design phase considers function, the physicality of the project site and the program, and the experiential potential that will together create a sense of place or a unique character.

A Bit of a Digression on Design

One of the dilemmas of taking a naturalistic approach, that is, developing a design that fits in with and incorporates the physical attributes of the site, is that it may result in a highly used and thus successful park design, but it may not appear that a designer was involved. The park looks natural, that is, its design does not make obvious the human hand. This approach to design is sometimes referred to as *light-handed* design. For clients like national park or historical property agencies, fitting in and looking natural (or appearing as if nothing or very little has been changed) often are the goal. For the landscape architect, a more *heavy-handed* design makes the touch of the designer more readily apparent. For some individuals, this is an approach that seems (not necessarily always) to garner design awards and other forms of recognition.

Contemporaneous, avant-garde designs make clear the hand of a designer was present, unlike designs that blend in with their surroundings. Some clients seeking unique and more highly visible built[5] projects want this approach. The issue is not one of right or wrong but is an issue designers sometimes find themselves confronted with. Each landscape architect approaches the matter as fits their design sensibilities and professional goals. And also, marketing is often part of the discussion. Some landscape architects and their firms strive to create unique designs that are readily associated with the firm. The term branding comes to mind, where one's designed built works have a consistent and recognizable style or aesthetic that clients may find desirable, and this means they will seek these designers out for their projects. I cannot say for sure that Louis XIV's minister Jean-Baptiste Colbert admired the design of Versailles (an earlier design by André Le Nôtre) when making the decision of selecting André Le Nôtre to design his Parc de Sceaux. Le Nôtre was hired to design the grounds of Parc de Sceaux, located south of Paris, and the resulting design shares many physical features with Versailles. This example should serve to demonstrate the notion of branding in design and its potential importance to landscape architects in marketing their services. Other factors, besides design style and aesthetics, are considered in response to a range of different circumstances where environmental, social, and economic issues must be addressed. Scarcity of water, loss of biological diversity, increased flood hazard, and a reduction in long-term maintenance funding are growing influences in landscape architectural design. These tugs on the attention of landscape architects and their clients do not necessarily mean that design aesthetics is no less important. On the contrary, landscape architects are being challenged to continue their creativity, but still considering other factors in the matrix of influences and considerations that go into creating an appropriate design.

At the completion of the research, the site and program analysis, and following through on the investigation of due diligence, the landscape architect will then prepare one or more preliminary or schematic designs to review with the client. In the case of government projects, the stakeholders and the general public will also have a chance to review the schematic design proposals and weigh in during the discussion. The drawings, models, and other means of representation produced in the schematic design phase are illustrative and more diagrammatic and not heavily detailed. They include three-dimensional and sectional representations and may be accompanied by a well-reasoned narrative outlining the design intent, the goals, and the critical considerations (site, economic, government, social, and environmental). The results and recommendations of alternative studies and designs may be included, outlining the logic and reasoning that support their consideration and clearly make a case for the preferred design. At the basic level, schematic design is a problem-solving exploration that relies on coherent and logical reasoning to help guide which design decisions will be made and demonstrate the justification of these decisions informed by the research, site analysis, client and stakeholder input, and other pre-design subjects investigated.

The typical elements included in the schematic design package are: a site design plan, sections, perspective drawings, 3-D models, and other visual materials used by the landscape architect to communicate design intent, benefits, and how the design meets the program and budget objectives of the client. The plans, sections, and other drawings contain sufficient detail without elaborating on the specifics of material selection and construction details. The plans, sections, and other drawings should be drawn to scale so that they are measurable. The site design plan is often referred to as an illustrative plan, but lacking the detail necessary to construct the project. The landscape architect will also prepare what is called an estimate of probable cost to construct the project based on the schematic design. The landscape architect will consider the budget established by the owner when developing a design solution and generally will arrive at a design that is within the budget. If the designer, in the course of the schematic design phase, sees desirable opportunities that might result in a budget higher than established, the design will be presented to the client following the strategy of first showing a design that is within budget, then making the case for an increased budget while arguing the benefits of the additional and more costly design elements. One never knows when a client might be enthusiastic for the more costly design but the savvy landscape architect will either alert and discuss the possibility of a more costly design with the client beforehand or organize the presentation of the schematic design so there is a logical and acceptable fallback design that is within budget.

Figure 3.6 is an example of the kinds of schematic design-level images and drawings for a proposed river restoration and greenbelt park project, the Xin Jin Baihetan National Wetland Park.[6] Figure 3.6A is one of several hundred photographs taken by the landscape architect to document the initial visit and field investigation to the project site. During this initial field trip, the team identified important physical features, land use activities, problems, and other attributes of the area in order to gain an understanding of the site and its context. Figure 3.6B shows work in progress after field studies and the kind of diagrams used to analyze information from field studies and develop initial diagrams of desirable program element relationships. Evolution of a design scheme from initial concept doodle is shown in Figure 3.6C. Further development of site design diagrams are shown in Figures 3.6D and 3.6E, further evolving into a more carefully worked-out site design shown in Figure 3.6F.

Figure 3.6 Design process drawings for Xin Jin Baihetan National Wetland Park, a greenbelt and river restoration project in central China; project team: Sichuan Agricultural University, Landscape Architectural College, with Bruce Sharky, FASLA.

Phase II: Design Development

The purpose of the schematic design phase was to establish the design solution for a project as well as gain client acceptance for the preferred design alternative. With the acceptance of the schematic design submittals, the landscape architect begins the next phase: Design Development. As the name implies, the goal of Phase II is for the landscape architect to develop the approved preliminary design in greater detail. During this phase the landscape architect will carefully study and prepare plans for the various systems that will go into the final design package. These systems include: grading and drainage including storm-water management; plant species or material types; circulation and parking layouts, materials such as for paving, walls, and structures; lighting and way-finding; site furniture and specialized equipment such as children's play structures; and other elements included in the design, for example, paving materials such as brick, concrete, or modular pavers; tree types such as deciduous or evergreen; and examples of various equipment such as lighting and fountain items. The landscape architect will include supplemental materials with the Design Development plans such as catalogue samples and photographs of all materials and equipment. Critical decisions in this phase include the shape, size, systems, and materials in sufficient detail to more accurately estimate probable construction costs. For instance, an entry sign will be drawn to scale, indicating materials of construction, letter style, logo or art to be incorporated in the sign, lighting requirements, and suggested finish colors. Basic dimensions of the sign might be included but not to the detail required in construction drawings.

The Design Development package submitted to the client would include plans rendered to scale and with greater detail than the illustrative plans in schematic design. The sections are more complete and drawn to scale with supporting notes. More refined three-dimensional drawings, such as perspectives, are also submitted along with estimates of probable cost with a supporting narrative. The landscape architect might also identify in the narrative any special or unique circumstances in the construction industry that might impact construction costs, including availability of materials and lead times for delivery of special items. Mention might include possible timing alternatives when seeking bids, depending on the known current workloads of area contractors.

At the Design Development phase it may be necessary to submit a preliminary package of the project to appropriate government agencies and begin the application process towards obtaining design review acceptance where required, and preparing the necessary documentation required for various permits such as a wetland permit. The government design review and permit process have become more complicated, often requiring long lead times from the start of the application process, through the review process, including both public and agency review input, and finally the execution of the actual permit. Some 30, 60, and in some cases even more days are becoming the norm for securing permits and various government approvals. Landscape architecture firms are divided in terms of taking the lead of shepherding the permit and design review processes. Those that take the responsibility rather than hiring consultants will devote the time to learning the permit procedure. Those firms which learn the permit review procedure then can offer the service and benefit financially. Perhaps more importantly these firms will be in a position to be more directly involved in any discussions that could impact the design. Where a firm wishes to retain design control, direct involvement in the permit process can assure a better design result.

An example of an illustrative plan is shown in Figure 3.7A, which is a refinement based on a client review from the Schematic Design Phase (Figure 3.6F).[7] Figure 3.7B is an aerial perspective of the same area. The perspective drawings depict the proposed museum entry (Figures 3.7C and 3.7D). The perspectives provide a view looking at the restored wetlands from a proposed visitors' viewing deck. An illustrative drawing such as Figure 3.7A would be reviewed with the client together with sections and perspectives to gain approval with a follow-up client review adding Figures 3.7B–D. A preliminary estimate of probable costs and other supplementary information (material and equipment alternatives and potential suppliers) would also be submitted for review by the client.

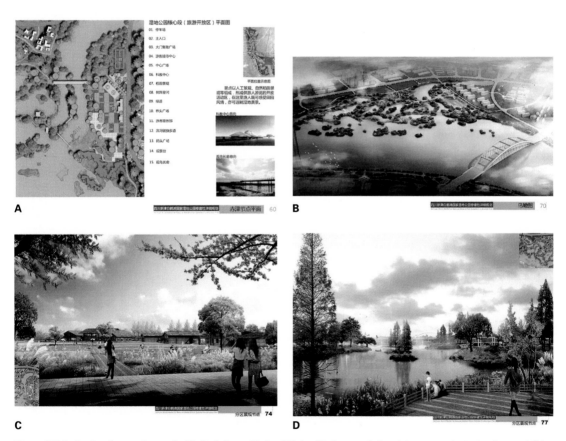

Figure 3.7 *Design Development images for Xin Jin Baihetan National Wetland Park, a greenbelt and river restoration project in central China; project team: Sichuan Agricultural University, Landscape Architectural College, with Bruce Sharky, FASLA.*

Phase III: Construction Documents

Construction documents are the graphic and written directions prepared by the landscape architect and used to secure bids from potential contractors. The same documents will be used to guide all work of the selected contractor to build the project. The construction documents consist of three main components prepared by the landscape architect:[8]

1. *Graphic drawings*, consisting of plans, details, technical sections, notes, material schedule.
2. *Technical specifications.* In some cases, for instance, a geotechnical investigation and report with soil testing results and recommendation would also be included.
3. *Construction contract* (between owner and contractor) and *bid documents* including various bid forms and related insurance documentation materials.

The construction drawings show "the what" is to be built, installed, and where (see grading plan, Figure 3.8). The technical specifications describe the quality of the materials, the general methods of construction, and how the built and supplied elements will be evaluated for their conformance to the intent of the drawings for acceptance and payment as recommended by the landscape architect to the owner. The drawings are prepared in sufficient detail describing the size and shape, quantities, and locations of physical elements compared with one another. The drawings should not describe building products or quality standards on drawings; this information is included in the technical specifications. For example, the drawings will indicate the size, color, and type of brick in addition to the pattern for the bricks to be installed. The technical specifications will describe the quality of

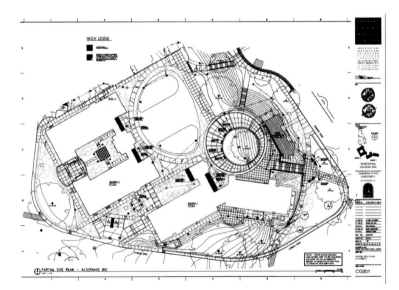

Figure 3.8 *Site plan with grading. Courtesy of LSU Facility Services Planning & Design, and Dennis Mitchell, LSU landscape architect.*

the brick material (formed or wire-cut and the strength testing standards), and the quality control criteria to be used by the landscape architect to evaluate the workmanship of the brick installation.

For the student interested in learning more details on the requirements and what is included in preparing a professional set of construction documents, Design Workshop have produced a very useful text.[9]

The drawings, technical specifications, and bid documents have three purposes: (1) to secure final government approvals where required; (2) to secure bids from potential contractors; and (3) to guide the construction of the project.

Phase IV: Bidding and Negotiations

The construction documentation package[10] is provided to prospective contractors (by the landscape architecture firm or client) in order to prepare a construction bid. The contractors then analyze the package to determine the quantities of materials, considering the plans, details, and the information included in the technical specifications as well as the bid forms, construction agreement, and insurance requirements. Using the bid forms provided in the bid package, the contractors submit their bids (in sealed envelopes) by a specified time and date. Prior to the date, one or more meetings may be held in an office or at the project site for prospective contractors to ask questions. The landscape architect, after conferring with the owner, will transmit written answers to all registered contractors after the meetings. At the specified date, time, and place, the bids are opened. Typically anyone is permitted to be present at the bid opening. The procedure of which contractor's bid will be selected can vary. Generally, the lowest bid from a qualified contractor will be selected. Bid selection is not always based on the lowest bid but may be determined by other factors described in the bid documents. Assuming the selected bid amount falls within the project budget of the client, an award is made that includes a signed agreement between the owner and contractor. This also assumes the contractor has duly executed and provided the insurance and other forms required to be included with the sealed bid.

Once the construction agreement has been signed, a construction start date is established. The agreement will also include a specified number of days for the satisfactory completion of all work. The landscape architect will determine a convenient schedule for a project start-up meeting and will reiterate the other scheduling requirements specified in the contract. The contractor will need to submit, for example, sample construction materials, shop drawings, and other pre-construction and installation requirements for approval. It is the responsibility of the landscape architect to review these submittals and determine if they meet the intent of the drawings and technical specification. For instance, the contractor will submit the plant material suppliers and their location. The landscape architect has the right to visit the suppliers to determine if the plants and other contractor-supplied materials meet the technical specifications. If they do not, the contractor is given the opportunity of resubmitting or may request substitutions of materials for the landscape architect to consider.

Phase V: Construction Administration

During the construction implementation period, the landscape architect serves as the construction administrator in place of the owner. The designer assumes the responsibility for carrying out the interests of the owner and makes decisions on the owner's behalf. There are instances where the owner will be given the opportunity to weigh in, particularly when a decision may have a significant impact on the budget and may possibly extend the time to complete construction. The landscape architect reviews the documentation provided by the contractor for periodic payment and will recommend or deny progress payment requests submitted by the contractor based on what has been actually constructed and accepted.

The role of the landscape architect during construction is that of administrator. In this role, the designer's main responsibility is to evaluate the adequacy of the materials and workmanship of the contractor and to provide guidance when questions arise (Figure 3.9). The responsibility is not to direct the work of the contractor but to determine the quality of the work and the acceptability of the materials and equipment (such as irrigation equipment or site furnishings) provided by the contractor. There is a well-defined protocol and relationship between the landscape architect and the contractor. It is not the landscape architect's responsibility to tell the contractor how to build and install the required work but rather to determine if the work and materials are acceptable and meet the intent of the drawings and technical specifications. If the landscape architect determines if it is in the interest of the project to change the location, materials, shapes and dimensions based on actual conditions found in the field; the role of the landscape architect is not to direct the work involved in the changes but to discuss the changes, allowing sufficient time for the contractor to respond. If, for instance, the landscape architect were to ask one of the employees of the contractor to shift the location of a tree to another location and the employee does so but in the process damages a water or electricity line, causing harmful results, the landscape architect will be responsible for the cost of repairing the damage. If the landscape architect wishes to shift tree locations, they would advise the contractor's foreman. The foreman will then follow a prescribed protocol that would include requesting the appropriate utilities locations to assess if underground lines or pipes are in the new location prior to digging the tree planting pits. If damage occurs, the responsibility for repair and resulting costs will be borne by the contractor.

As you can see, there is a close relationship and interaction between the landscape architect and the contractor. Having good communication and people skills are important attributes for the landscape architect tasked with administering construction in progress. There is an art to effective communication as well. Not all people are good at interacting with contractors. The skills indispensable to being an effective construction administrator can be learned for those willing

Figure 3.9 *Construction site with rough grading with early stages of structural fabrication in the background.*

Figure 3.10 *Landscape architect taking field measurements to be used in resolving wood dock detail condition identified during construction.*

to learn. For some designers, the art of construction administration can be as satisfying as design. It is during construction that many design decisions are made and the designer can have the satisfaction of being involved in the process.

Often unforeseen situations come up that were not contemplated during the design process (Figure 3.10). Being present in the field can result in a decision that turns the unanticipated into a significant design opportunity. Case in point: A boulder the size of an automobile was uncovered during grading for a new middle school in Anchorage,

Alaska. The presence of the boulder was not anticipated during early fieldwork and during the design process. The potential additional amount that the contractor asked for to dispose of the boulder was significant. The project landscape architect when confronted with the boulder came up with a decision to leave the boulder where it was uncovered at the building front entry. The boulder would serve as an informal sitting and waiting area for students. The presence of the boulder proved popular with the students. Not removing it did not require any additional costs to the project.

Phase VI: Post-Construction Evaluation

The landscape architect has the opportunity of including time and fees for evaluating the success of a project after it is built in a professional service contract with an owner. Not all owners are willing to include this additional service; however, those who do have much to gain that might result in cost savings for subsequent projects. The landscape architect can use the information obtained through a post-construction evaluation to avoid future design flaws or oversights. The landscape architect would also be able to offer suggestions to the owner on how to make necessary maintenance adjustments, for instance, or correct other deficiencies identified during the post-construction evaluation.

The purpose of a post-construction evaluation is to reaffirm the successful design elements of a project. Success is measured by how well the design has met the needs of the client or users, how well the materials and construction details and methods have held up in use over time, and to identify design flaws that became apparent after construction was completed. Many landscape architectural firms will, in their own time and using their own money, conduct a post-construction evaluation and use what was learned to inform future design decisions and material selections. The reward for doing so will be the ability to offer better and more informed design services to future clients. The reward will also improve a designer's capacity for attracting clients. While receiving payment from clients has its own reward, there is nothing more professionally satisfying than a happy client, one who returns requesting your services on future projects.

A Real-Life Project: Design Process

The following figures demonstrate the process from initial site visit investigation (Figure 3.11) and the subsequent design sequence beginning with Figure 3.12. Figures 3.12 to 3.15 show the design sequence from early design concept to the completed built work of an actual project at Arizona State University on the Polytechnic Academic Campus. The project involved the redesign of grounds around existing classroom buildings, the construction of a new classroom structure, and converting existing parking into a series of outdoor classrooms and gathering areas. Additionally, the landscape architect proposed a site design that managed storm water for use on site (for irrigation purposes, for instance) and to percolate into the soil and recharge the underground aquifer. The design eliminated the installation of a

Figure 3.11 Existing project site before new design by Christine Ten Eyck landscape architect. Courtesy of Christine Ten Eyck.

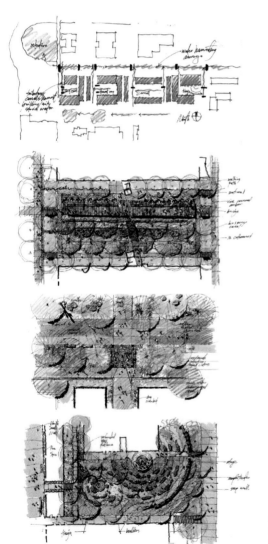

Figure 3.12 Types of drawings prepared by the landscape architect in the early stage of the design process. This drawing and others are presented to the client for feedback for eventual definition of final design.

Figure 3.13 Schematic Design
master plan drawing for Arizona
State University: Polytechnic Academic
Campus landscape.

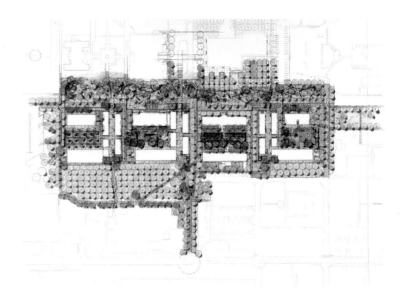

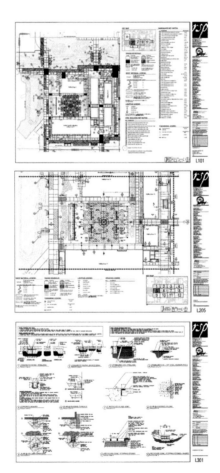

Figure 3.14 Three sheets from
a set of construction drawings for
Arizona State University: Polytechnic
Academic Campus landscape. All
images courtesy of Christine Ten Eyck,
landscape architect, Austin, Texas.

traditional, costly storm-water catch basin system. The approach to storm-water management gave the university the opportunity carry out a long-term goal of reducing water consumption and costs by installing an emerging design strategy that represents responsible steward-ship of precious water resources. The landscape architect applied low impact storm-water management principles (to be discussed in Chapter 4).

Figure 3.13 is the final site design. After this stage in the process the landscape architect prepares the technical drawings (Figure 3.14) and specifications that are used to secure bids from contractors and then used by the contractor to construct the project. Figure 3.15 shows the completed project after construction.

Figure 3.15 Views of completed built project, Arizona State University: Polytechnic Academic Campus landscape. All images courtesy of Christine Ten Eyck, landscape architect, Austin, Texas.

Notes

1 Variations of climate, soils, and other physical factors from one geographic region can impact a whole variety of design decisions. For instance, soil conditions in one region may be such that plant selection and manner of installing plants require specific knowledge to insure survival. Hardpan soil conditions in one area and the presence of highly acidic, organic soils in another will require very different methods of planting, even for the same plant species.
2 Figures 3.2–3.5 were drawn by Jidapa Chayakul, a master's degree student in landscape architecture and graduate assistant working under the direction of the author at Louisiana State University.
3 Aspect refers to the compass direction a slope faces with respect to the sun. A south-facing slope is a topographic landform that is oriented to face due south toward the position of the sun at noon (in the Northern Hemisphere and facing north in the Southern Hemisphere).
4 United States Federal Emergency Management Administration.
5 And hence more desirable on the marketplace relative to the competition.
6 Design competition team: Bruce Sharky, LSU; Drs. Guo Li, Pan, and Pang of Sichuan Agricultural University (SAU), Chengdu; Justin Kim, a landscape architect of Dongbu Engineering in Seoul, Korea; and graduate and undergraduate students from SAU.
7 See note 6.
8 In the case where multiple disciplines are involved on a given project, each discipline is responsible for preparing the appropriate drawings and technical specifications for the work they contribute. These materials are incorporated into one comprehensive package through which competitive bids are obtained and a construction contract is executed. The landscape architect may be the prime consultant of a team and will be responsible for organizing the comprehensive construction documentation package or may be a sub-consultant that submits their respective drawings and technical specifications to the prime consultant.
9 Design Workshop, *Construction Documentation: Standards and Best Practices for Landscape Architectural Design* (John Wiley & Sons, Inc., New York, 2015).
10 Sometimes referred to as the bid package.

Further Reading

More to explore about the design process in landscape architecture:

Norman K. Booth, *Basic Elements of Landscape Architectural Design*, Waveland Press, Long Grove, IL, 1983.

Leonard J. Hopper, *Landscape Architectural Graphic Standards*, John Wiley & Sons, Inc., Hoboken, NJ, 2007.

James A. LaGro, Jr., *Site Analysis: Informing Context-Sensitive and Sustainable Site Planning and Design*, John Wiley & Sons, Inc., Hoboken, NJ, 2013.

Thomas H. Russ, *Site Planning and Design Handbook*, McGraw-Hill, New York, 2009.

Bruce G. Sharky, *Ready, Set, Practice: Principles of Landscape Architecture Professional Practice*, John Wiley & Sons, Inc., New York, 1994.

Barry Starke and John Ormsbee Simonds, *Landscape Architecture: A Manual of Environmental Planning and Design,* 5th edn, McGraw-Hill Professional, New York, 2013.

CHAPTER FOUR

HISTORICAL CONTEXT OF LANDSCAPE ARCHITECTURE: FROM THE GARDEN OF EDEN TO THE NEW YORK HIGH LINE AND SUSTAINABLE DESIGN

Introduction

Nowadays, landscape architects enjoy professional recognition and benefits similar to architects and engineers. Much of this recognition can be attributed to the history and traditions of those who came before us. Landscape architecture as a distinct profession has not always been recognized as such. While landscapes of garden scale to regional parks and new communities have been designed or built throughout history we live in an era where a growing number of people, companies, and governmental institutions value the work of those practicing landscape architecture; not the case one hundred years ago or less. The pioneers who actively influenced and laid the groundwork leading to the acceptance of the professions, at least in North America, the United Kingdom, and Northern and Western Europe, practiced as landscape architects in the waning years of the nineteenth century. The history of the profession is a fascinating one, so we shall begin.

The study of history has many useful benefits that, among other possibilities, help us better understand and perhaps better appreciate who we are in the present and imagine our trajectory into the future. The history of landscape architecture does not require us to look too far back in time, as the profession is a recent one, compared to our allied design professions such as engineering and architecture. We can see the profession in the context of a continuum that is not so much a direct line but rather a legacy from those who created gardens and cultural landscapes before us but were not known as landscape architects. On this legacy and body of experience and knowledge practitioners today base much of their work and can draw inspiration. For instance, the cultural artifact of Stonehenge, England, was not the creation of a landscape architect. We can assume the civilization that constructed Stonehenge carefully analyzed information about the site, its physical features, and ultimately decided the placement and arrangements of the stone elements in the same way that landscape architects would analyze a site today in advance of creating a design. We can today study the forms and the arrangement of the stone pieces as a source of inspiration for a fountain, plaza, or other design feature. The study of history, when learning about art, music, and natural sciences, is useful in helping us to realize the potential of a work of art or piece of music that could inform our designs. The sources of design inspiration rarely are found in a vacuum but are based on our experiences.

The early gardens and public spaces of Egypt, Moorish Spain, Renaissance Italy, Japanese gardens, or the estate gardens in Europe were the creations of individuals whose practical knowledge of horticulture and experience guided their creative efforts. The creations of landscape architects are in large part derivative of what we have learned from the past and what we see and experience in our daily lives. Therefore, the study of garden and spatial design history is an important component of the academic training of a landscape architect. History is not only a source of design inspiration but also provides a grounding to and reaffirmation of our design ideas. The study of history, the history of gardens, art, and other cultural enterprises will not only serve to inspire our work but will also enrich the work and our lives. Design inspiration does not always come easily when we seek it. During those moments when design ideas are not forthcoming, a review of history may provide just the spark to ignite our creativity.

This chapter presents an overview of landscape architecture from a historical perspective. Frederick Law Olmsted toward the end of the nineteenth century was the first to use the term "landscape architecture" in America. The term "landscape gardener" or "garden designer" was used in the early part of the nineteenth century in England and before Olmsted in America. The tradition of garden and estate design can be traced back to earlier centuries of Europe and Islamic North Africa. Many different labels including gardener, architect, and even poet in ancient China referred to the people who designed the early gardens, parks, and public spaces of European cities and other regions of the world. The Renaissance gardens of Italy are attributed to specific designers or horticulturalists of those gardens; however, their training was based on practical horticultural experience or following in the footsteps under the tutelage of more experienced garden designers. It was not until the twentieth century that a distinct profession of garden designer, park designer, and designers of public spaces emerged. In America, it was only with the establishment of the American Society of Landscape Architects in 1899, by a group of 12 landscape architects,[1] in Boston, MA, that the profession gained professional standing comparable to architects and engineers. At about the same time Harvard University initiated the first university degree offering in landscape architecture in America.

Later, after World War II, in the 1960s, licensure to practice landscape architecture was established in a few states. Today nearly all states in America and the Canadian provinces require licensure to practice. One is eligible to take a state licensing exam in landscape architecture after meeting two requirements: (1) graduation with an accredited university landscape architecture degree; and (2) serving an apprenticeship period. Licensure is administered by individual states while the exam is a national examination administered by the Council of Landscape Architecture Registration Board. Currently there are approximately 80 university programs in North America offering bachelor's and master's degrees and certificate programs. Close to all 50 states and Canadian provinces require licensure for an individual or firm to offer professional landscape architect design services.

The profession as a distinct discipline was recognized in the United Kingdom and later France, Germany, and the Netherlands in the mid-twentieth century. Most other countries in the European Union have subsequently recognized the profession and established university degrees in landscape architecture. Several European countries (Spain and Italy, for instance) are still in the process of considering recognition of landscape architecture as a distinct profession from architecture or engineering. In these countries, architects and in some cases engineers (engineering agronomists) are required to perform the services legally while those who consider themselves landscape architects by education or training must provide their services under the supervision of an architect or engineer. The profession exists in other regions of the world with significant university programs in many countries, particularly in Asia and to a lesser degree in Latin America. While landscape architects are active in many parts of the world, each country and each region have their own history in terms of recognizing these professionals. Keep in mind landscape architecture is a relatively new profession, compared to architecture and engineering. Given the unique set of skills and knowledge base, particularly the emphasis on the incorporation of natural system thinking in the design process, landscape architects are providing a valuable contribution and thus finding acceptance in increasing numbers in other regions of the world.

At the end of the twentieth century with the launch of the Le Nôtre initiative, members of the profession in the European Union worked to establish a universal landscape architecture curriculum. The goal of this initiative is to allow anyone who successfully graduates with a degree in landscape architecture to practice in any of the member countries of the European Union. Similarly, other professions (architects, engineers, doctors, to name a few) have established a parallel initiative under the aegis of the European Union.

Historical Overview of Landscape Architecture

The term as opposed as to the practice of landscape architecture came into common usage in the twentieth century. The practice of garden, park, and public spaces design, irrespective of what the designers were called (gardeners, horticulturists, and the like) from a Western perspective began symbolically with the Garden of Eden in the regions bordered by the Mediterranean. The concept of a garden, a space created (designed) for some purpose other than the production of food developed as civilizations accumulated excess agriculture production and wealth and their economies and society structure diversified. Gardens with the embellishment of spaces served as the physical manifestation of one's power, role, and wealth in society. Gardens—so-called pleasure gardens—were for personal use and enjoyment as opposed to communal agricultural production. The predominant use of geometrical patterns in these gardens might suggest man's dominion over the Earth or simply an expression of an individual's or group's power and control over others. This expression of dominion translates into one's leadership role over others. Gardens as cultural artifacts were created to symbolize one's status and provide pleasure for the owner. The design of these gardens might be representational of another world, imagined or symbolic.[2]

The Garden of Eden or Paradise was the dominant model that was adopted in the Western Judeo-Christian-Islam ethos. The interpretation of the spatial organization of Eden with its four rivers (as described in the Book of Genesis) was expressed in the geometric forms organized using bilateral symmetry. In the West, gardens of paradise were laid out in geometric patterns while in Asia natural and asymmetric forms were adapted to create a composition filled with symbolism meant to represent their ideals of paradise. Paradise did not have the connotation of a working environment such as agricultural fields. Paradise was a place to enjoy oneself, not necessarily to labor in. Therefore, the concept of garden was that of a place of refuge, a place to find enjoyment, for pleasure, and to entertain. In some cases a garden was meant for contemplation as opposed to undertaking practical matters.

The Garden of Eden is one of the starting places representing one of the garden ideals that permeate throughout Western garden traditions. In this chapter we will survey the history of garden design with the later establishment of the landscape architecture profession and areas of practice that include urban and community design; management and restoration of landscapes, sustainable approaches to storm-water management; parks, including neighborhood, city, and regional parks; all types of sports fields, including golf courses; and special venues such as the London 2012 Olympic Park. Landscape architects are also contributors to large-scale infrastructure and land reclamation projects.

This historical overview will include periods of ancient, Islamic, Renaissance, Italian, French, and British garden design traditions, followed by an overview of the industrial period and the rapid growth of cities with the emergence of the Garden City movement, Modernism in the early twentieth century, and post-WWII urban expansion developments. The profession gained increasing influence as concerns about the reduction of environmental quality and biodiversity created emerging areas of emphasis. Increasingly landscape architects apply scientific-based principles of sustainability and best management practices[3] as an important aspect of their professional contributions.

Dawn of Early Human Habitation on the Land

A history of designed landscapes begins with human adaptive habitation and activities on the land. Early human modifications of their environment to better accommodate agriculture and basic living activities were minimal with no appreciable legacies such as structures or land modifications. Early societies were composed of nomadic hunter–gatherers, engaged in the day-to-day survival of living off the land. As the populations of the early human societies outgrew a nomadic approach to survival, agriculture with its requirement to manage and alter the landscape created a new relation of people to the landscape. Agriculture led to permanent place-making and practical adaptations of the land, creating patterns of use to maximize agricultural productivity and accommodate commercial activities. The human–landscape relationship was one of humans working with the landscape (early application of environmental determinism) based on their knowledge and understanding of seasonal events and harnessing the productive capacity of the land to support agriculture and to meet other needs such as providing safe shelter. The Bandelier National Monument in the state of New Mexico was home to the ancestral Pueblo People from the twelfth to the early seventeenth centuries, situated in a deep river valley with agricultural activities located within the flood plain, where the presence of rich soil and water would support crops (Figure 4.1). The summer habitation of the residents was located safely in the higher ground above the flood plain. At the onset of winter, the inhabitants relocated in dwellings carved out of the side of south-facing slopes (an advantageous location for receiving heat gain). Human use and habitation of the landscape exhibited regional expression where a society's activities and methods varied according to the potential or limitations of

Figure 4.1 *Bandelier National Monument, New Mexico, an early Pueblo People settlement.*

soils, water, seasonal climatic events, and endemic flora and fauna in each region. The capacity of a society to survive and flourish in a region depended in large part on human knowledge, will, and ingenuity. It also depended on the collective body of knowledge a group acquired through trial and error, experience, and observation.

The role of plants is fundamental to human history. Plants were a central component of human survival as a source of food and means of providing shelter. Plants were used and also cultivated for medicine, clothing, and many other practical purposes. Societies approached selection of locations for settlement based on their understanding of the plants available, natural systems, and the seasonal variations of climate. The relationship between seasonal rains, position of the sun, topography, and plant cover was considered in the matrix of habitation selection and conducting daily life. Patterns of settlement were based on acquired knowledge of natural systems and temporal variations. It was not until advanced societies evolved that plants were selected and used to embellish their built environments. Embellishment was not only the creation of cultural artifacts such as gardens. Landscapes that were not intended to be solely utilitarian but rather embellishments of space evolved into designed landscapes that reflected the relationship of societies to nature and the very structure of a society itself. The designed landscape considered notions about political power, society hierarchy, defense, and eventually contributed to quality of life and economic value. Designed landscapes followed two basic manifestations: (1) landscape forms and building patterns that were based on geometry; and (2) patterns and forms that were found in nature. Eventually the combination of geometry and nature became an additional framework for landscape design. The built environments in the early advanced societies, such as in Latin America (Teotihuacan, for example, in the Valley of Mexico), the Mediterranean and North Africa, such as Luxor in Egypt and the temples of Greece, and the Middle East, such as Babylon (see Figure 4.2), were created to advance symbolic meaning (political power) or function as a celestial device, such as marking of the seasons for planting and harvest based on celestial positions.

Figure 4.2 A: The Hanging Gardens of Babylon; B: The Acropolis, Greece.

Early Southern and Northern European Garden Design Traditions

The Islamic Garden

The English word *garden* is *jardin* in Spanish and French, and *Garten* in German. The words share a linguistic origin. The meaning of the word can be traced to Hebrew origins, a contraction of *gan* or *gar* meaning to protect or defend (to fence or enclose) and *eden* meaning pleasure. The two words joined together came to mean pleasure garden, as an enclosed space not meant for agriculture production. A garden is symbolic in the form of a cared-for cultivated place for enjoyment. Garden also came to be associated with the biblical Garden of Eden or Paradise. The *gar* half of the word suggests to guard and this could be applied to mean the enclosing of Eden as a walled or private garden. Symbolically the Garden of Eden of Mesopotamia is a concept shared in the Judeo-Christian-Islam biblical traditions. In the biblical context, the Garden of Eden contains four rivers consisting of water, milk, wine, and honey: all symbols of sustenance. The Garden of Eden translates in the deserts of the Middle East and North Africa as an oasis where travelers would come to rest and be revived with shade, water, and nourishment; see Figure 4.3. The four rivers

A

B

C

Figure 4.3 A: A desert oasis in North Africa; B: The summer palace and estate of the Emirate of Granada adjoining the Alhambra Court of la Acequia (water channel court or water garden), an example of a medieval Persian garden constructed during 1302 to 1309; C: Public space in Madrid, Spain.

Figure 4.4 *Tivoli Gardens, Italy, are located in the hillside town of Lazio outside of Rome.*

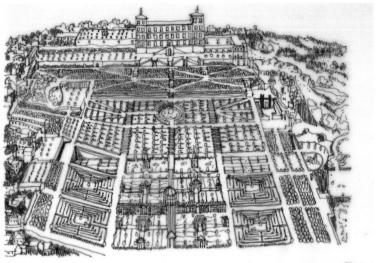

Figure 4.5 *A: Parc de Sceaux by André Le Nôtre, Paris; B: Luxembourg Gardens, Paris, France.*

or paths became the spatial organizing structure of Southern European, Mediterranean, and North African gardens and public parks and spaces

The biblical Garden of Eden and the desert oasis served as a paradigm for garden design in Mediterranean countries, particularly in Southern Europe during the period under Islamic influence (see Figure 4.3B). The arrangement of an Islamic garden as depicted in Figure 4.3C is organized spatially using bilateral symmetry. The four rivers of Eden divide gardens and later public parks into four or multiples of four spaces traversed by garden paths. The spaces in between the paths are typically planted with a dense pattern of trees to provide shade, in the same way that an oasis in the desert would provide. Typically a fountain or water feature would be placed in the center of the garden at the point where the four or eight paths would meet. Later during the Renaissance period, first in Italy and later in France, the bilateral symmetry and geometrical arrangements of the Islamic-influenced gardens were adapted in highly ornate and stylized patterns such as Tivoli gardens in Italy (see Figure 4.4), Parc de Sceaux (1662–1665) and Luxembourg Gardens in Paris, France (Figure 4.5), and even in Blenheim Palace estate (1705–1722) in England (Figure 4.6). The garden designers of Italy in the Renaissance departed with imaginative effect from the earlier Islamic gardens in response to the hilly and undulating Italian topography.

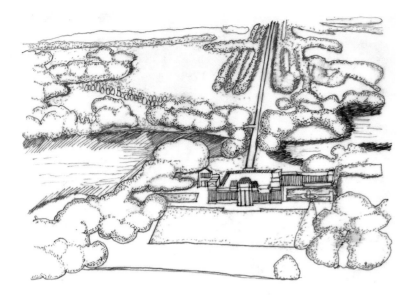

Figure 4.6 Blenheim Palace Estate, Oxfordshire, England.

Northern Europe

A comparable paradigm for the oasis as a place of refuge in Northern Europe was the opening in the forest. Openings in the forest translate in the garden as an asymmetrical pattern of interconnected open areas framed by trees and plants. The estates, public gardens, and parks in England, Germany, and other countries in the colder climates of Northern Europe were arranged similarly as a series of swaths of lawn framed by mixed tree species woodlots with understory plantings. One came into the open lawn areas for warmth or active pursuits. Access to the sun was desired, given the cooler temperatures, as opposed to the desire for shade in warm Mediterranean outdoor spaces. The basic structure of the garden estates of eighteenth-century England reflects the Northern European concept of sacred or pleasurable place of refuge. Beginning with William Kent in his design of Stourhead (1744) (Figure 4.7), in England, followed by Lancelot "Capability" Brown at Blenheim (1758), and Humphry Repton at Blaise Castle, the pastoral landscapes in rural England were created. The designers of these estates were proponents of the picturesque and pastoral garden or country landscape.

The estate and garden designs of eighteenth-century England traveled well to America. The public parks and country estates that Frederick Law Olmsted visited in England proved a significant influence on his work in America. New York's Central Park was an early Olmsted project in which he, in partnership with Calvert Vaux, translated the opening in the forest and picturesque English gardens into a series of outdoor rooms meandering through heavily planted forests as shown in Figure 4.8. The lush forest-like plantings bordered the openings of lawn areas and water features that weaved through the park. The openings in the forest became the activity areas such as sports fields, picnic areas, and gathering or event spaces.

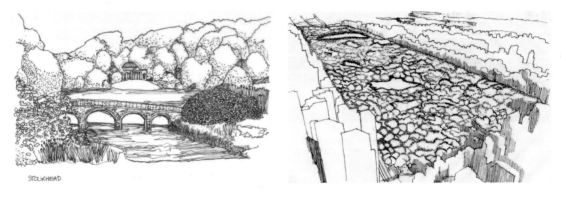

Figure 4.7 *Stourhead by William Kent.*   **Figure 4.8** *New York's Central Park by Olmsted and Vaux.*

Olmsted adapted English landscape design principles with the aim of attaining full use of the endemic features of a specific site. His designs are noted for subordinating individual details to the greater design concept so that the design does not call attention to itself. While he paid great attention to details and materials, they were orchestrated to produce an overall and particular effect: experience. In the case of Central Park, Olmsted and his partner Vaux created a refuge for residents to find relief and relaxation from the dense, noisy bustle of the city. Later, the ambition of his other public projects was to attend to other ills of rapidly growing and industrial cities. The system of parks that make up Boston's Emerald Necklace stylistically evoked the pastoral theme of New York's Central Park but with an added layer: The creation of the Emerald Necklace was, in fact, an integral component of the new storm-water management infrastructure. The underlying purpose was to manage storm water and its attendant flooding problems within the designed context of a generous park system. The pastoral style of the design included vast expanses of green with varying size lakes and groves of trees with a built-in pedestrian trail network. The built project produced a soothing, restorative effect for visitors and the surrounding residences and commercial districts. An added and now much understood benefit of constructing expansive parklands adjacent to residential and commercial land uses is that it generally increases property values and thus the tax base of a community. There is economic as well as social value when implementing parks and landscape beautification for adjacent neighborhoods and the larger community. Cities known for supporting a robust park and public beautification system enjoy a competitive advantage in attracting economic development. The perceived value of having a healthy park system is compounded with the support of other public infrastructure initiatives, including good schools, public transportation, and active art and cultural venues.

The City Beautiful and Other Idealistic Movements in Urban Planning

The firm Olmsted established continued to work into the twentieth century and his influence in North America is evident today. Other influences emerged at the end of the nineteenth century, notably the City Beautiful movement. Olmsted's legacy is the celebration of nature: the natural forms of nature and the health benefits that places of beautiful refuge can provide. The legacy of the City Beautiful movement was to infuse cities with symbols of beauty and monumentality with architecture and equal formation of open green space. The movement saw the potential of promoting civic and moral virtue by creating beautiful, well-organized, and ordered urban patterns that together would produce—it was believed—harmonious social order. The movement began with the planning and construction of the 1893 World's Columbian Exposition in Chicago. The architect Daniel Burnham directed the planning with major contributions in the development of the public and landscape spaces by Frederick Law Olmsted. The exposition was intended to be a model of what cities could be. The influence of the exposition continued well into the early twentieth century in such cities as Cleveland and Washington, D.C. The movement was the precursor of urban planning. The City Beautiful movement was, more importantly, a response to the crowded tenement districts and poor quality of life that the rapidly growing, industrial-fueled cities produced. Other movements followed, each with their idealistic beliefs as to what a city could or should be.

Town and Land Planning

Frank Lloyd Wright entered the urban planning conversation with his plan for Broadacre City (see Figure 4.9A). It was both a sociopolitical scheme and a planning statement of a particular vision of a particular life style that hearkened back to the American ideal of the pioneer spirit and the self-sufficiency of the family unit. Each family in the development would have a 1 acre (4047 square meters) plot of land. The community would be built from scratch, relying on individual transport, absent of public transportation. The scheme celebrated rural values not at all attuned to the trends of a country rapidly heading toward becoming a dominantly urban population. Figure 4.9B represents another concept of urban planning, one of many new towns planned and built after World War II in England. The towns were built, in part, to provide housing for the large numbers of people who had lost their homes during the war. The new developments were located in open areas beyond the limits of London and other large cities. The towns included car-oriented layouts and often with variants of a grid arrangement. New towns found their way later in Scotland and Scandinavian countries.

Figure 4.9C is an example of an abundance of planned communities constructed at the beginning to mid-twentieth century in America to meet the demand for new housing that occurred in the flight from urban centers to the suburbs. The designs of these new communities were laid out without regard for public transportation,

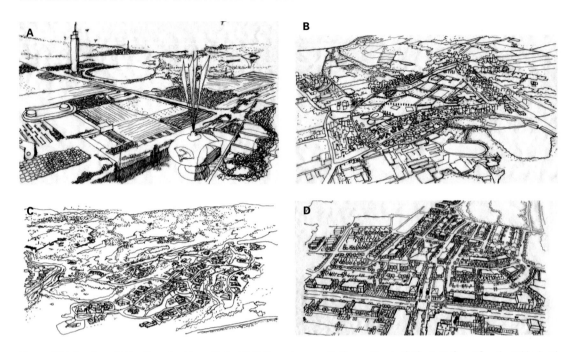

Figure 4.9 A: Broadacre; B: New Town development in the UK; C: Planned community, Orange County, California; D: Smart Growth neighborhood.

favoring instead individual automobile transport. The streets followed a non-grid, more serpentine, curvilinear layout featuring cul-de-sacs. Limited access into a neighborhood often included gated access, thus restricting connectivity to other neighborhoods and town centers. Each neighborhood, if large enough, included schools and parks. The higher-end (real estate price range) developments might feature a golf course and recreation center accessible primarily to the individual community. With the rise in energy costs, the rising demand of urban citizens for healthier living options, and the growing popularity and need for more responsible uses and conservation of natural resources (air, water, and land), land planning shifted emphasis. This shift in thinking on how cities should develop (or even be re-imagined) saw the emergence of Smart Growth, and similar land development theories such as New Urbanism and Sustainable Development emerged late in the twentieth and into the twenty-first century. Smart Growth and New Urbanism (Figure 4.9D) were a late twentieth-century approach to land planning that concentrated urban and suburban growth to achieve public transit-oriented, compact, walkable, and mixed-use communities. Proponents of Smart Growth planning understood urban growth would continue but should be accommodated in a comprehensive way with a more healthy and sustainable approach as opposed to unchecked, urban sprawl.

Modernism and Contemporary Themes

Modernism was a movement that permeated the full spectrum of the arts in the twentieth century. In general, proponents of the modern movement felt that traditional forms of art had become outdated in the new economic, political, and social environment, in what had become an industrialized world that was rapidly proliferating. Followers of Modernism in architecture, art, literature, or music reacted to the past, deeming past design sensibilities outmoded to fulfilling the needs of modern life. The past was discarded in favor of the exploration of more meaningful expression in the arts that addressed current experiences and trends. The idea in architecture and landscape architecture was to "make new" and to create new forms of expression such as was occurring in the studio arts, beginning with Impressionism followed by the experiments of Cubism, Dadaism, and other forms of non-representational expression. In America, Modernism came to landscape architecture during the mid-1930s with Garrett Eckbo, Dan Kiley and their classmates at Harvard. They, in essence, rebelled against the formalism of the Beaux Arts as taught in landscape programs at the time. They looked to what was happening in art (painting and sculpture) with the work of Picasso, Braque, Duchamp, Hans-Hoffman, Miró, and others, believing the work of these artists was much more relevant to society and the times. Figure 4.10 presents three examples of the Modernist expression in landscape architecture. Landscape architects explored new forms of expression (essentially finding new ways to organize and create landscape spaces without relying on the bilateral symmetry and the formalism of Beaux Arts that had been prevalent in the past). The landscape Modernists sought to employ new materials to better

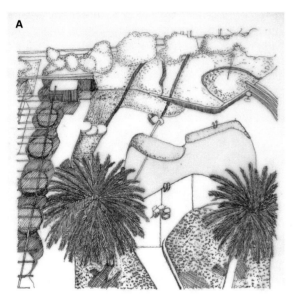

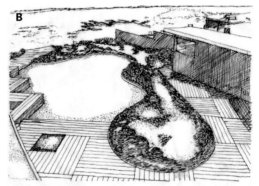

Figure 4.10 Work by Modernist landscape architects: A: Garrett Eckbo; B: Thomas Church; C: Robert Zion.

realize their built projects. The Modernist movement in landscape architecture found a welcome home in California, coinciding with the return of Eckbo to his home state. Firms of landscape architecture and the hiring of landscape architects in government also grew, particularly as urban growth and expansion of cities in the suburbs occurred throughout America in the 1950s and 1960s. In addition to Garrett Eckbo, other practitioners established robust practices including Thomas Church, Robert Zion, Robert Royston, Ruth Shellhorn, and many others.

The Modernist movement evolved with the next generation of landscape architects exploring new approaches that, in essence, gave greater emphasis to interpreting sense of place design issues and emerging environmental awareness concerns. To some extent, this exploration into new design forms and materials paralleled the environmental movement that emerged and gained influence not only in the form of governmental policy but also the arts. Lawrence Halprin's work such as Ira's Fountain (Figure 4.11), a public plaza in Portland, Oregon, Seattle's Freeway Park, and Richard Haag's Gasworks Park, also in Seattle, are examples of the new aesthetic in landscape architecture. Also at this time, use of native plant species was becoming popular as landscape design theorists wrestled with concepts of authenticity, regional expression, and sense of place.

In 1970, President Richard M. Nixon signed into law the Environmental Protection Act and with that Act the establishment of the Environmental Protection Agency. Coincidentally, at around the same time, Professor Ian McHarg, Chair of the landscape architecture program at Pennsylvania University published his influential book: *Design with Nature*. The basic tenet of this work argues that planning and design of new projects should consider matching land use with appropriate land resources suitable to accommodate the uses, within a

Figure 4.11 Ira's Fountain, Portland, Oregon, by Lawrence Halprin.

Figure 4.12 *Sea Ranch, California, by Lawrence Halprin.*

density of development that did not burden the holding capacity of the landscape. The residential development Sea Ranch (Figure 4.12) on the Northern Californian coast was one of the early projects paralleling McHarg's *Design with Nature* approach to land planning. Lawrence Halprin's firm was responsible for the planning of the project, following a process using a system of thematic overlays (soil, geology, land form, plant species cover, weather and sun patterns, etc.) to find the optimal locations on the property for proposed land uses and siting of specific building footprints. Closely following this successful project was the Woodlands Community planned by the firm Wallace, McHarg, Roberts and Todd. The Woodlands was a master planned bedroom community located north of Houston, Texas. It featured a comprehensive system of greenways that served to accommodate storm water, provide recreation amenities, including bicycle and walking trails, and conserve extensive woodland and other natural ecosystems. The project, as originally conceived, became a well-regarded example of the benefits of designing with nature.

Sustainable Design

During the past 15 or so years, landscape architecture has found itself one of the leading design professions in the discussion and practice of design and planning involving concepts related to sustainability, resilience, and best management practices. These movements have increased the breadth and depth of knowledge that landscape architects bring to the creation of new communities and cities, revitalization or re-imagining of failed or dysfunctional landscapes, and the rehabilitation of affected natural areas. Current trends in landscape architecture involve exploratory design and resource management strategies in response to globalization issues (global warming and sea level rise) and the search for healthier and livable cities. The future of the profession is bright and an attempt to foresee the part the professions will play in the future will be presented in Chapter 11. The new technologies and knowledge base for practicing the profes-

Figure 4.13 Brooklyn Bridge Park,
New York City, by Michael Van
Valkenburgh Associates.

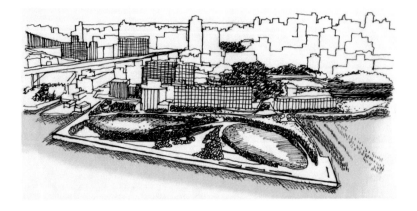

Figure 4.13 Brooklyn Bridge Park, New York City, by Michael Van Valkenburgh Associates.

sion in the future are currently being developed and applied. These are very exciting times for the profession. The Brooklyn Bridge Park, New York City, shown in Figure 4.13, is an example of the application of sustainable design strategies provided by landscape architects. The London 2012 Olympic site is another excellent example, showing the skill of landscape architects in restoring a derelict section of London. The planning and design team included landscape architects Hargreaves Associates. The team transformed a lost and a derelict post-industrial site containing a polluted, dysfunctional river channel into a healthy, attractive, highly desirable, mixed-use neighborhood and now heavily used greenway recreation system.

Boston's Emerald Necklace by Frederick Law Olmsted was an early predecessor of what is today referred to as "green infrastructure." Today the Emerald Necklace greenway system is enjoyed for its beauty and recreational amenities while its underlying intent was to manage the storm waters that had plagued the city prior to its construction. The Emerald Necklace can be seen today as a design strategy that provides both functional as well as aesthetic benefits to a dense urban area. The landscape architecture firm of Reed+Hilderbrand in Cambridge, Massachusetts, designed a green infrastructure system on the Clark Art Institute campus shown in Figure 4.14A. The system was created with the strategic location of buildings, parking lots, and other structures, considering the topography. Site grading was necessary to refine the direction of surface storm-water flow and to create an integrated system of water collection, redirection, and retention. On a larger, urban scale, the plan model shown in Figure 4.14B reveals a well-planned green infrastructure designed to manage the handling of storm water for a future community in the Netherlands.

The examples shown in Figures 4.13 and 4.14 provide a window onto work by landscape architects who apply best management practices (BMP) and low impact design (LID). The American Society of Landscape Architects, in partnership with the Ladybird Johnson Wildflower Center at the University of Texas-Austin and the United States Botanic Garden has established the Sustainable Sites Initiative (SITES). The Sustainable Sites Initiative is a voluntary system of guidelines and a rating system with the objective of promoting the design of sustainable landscapes in both the private and public

A

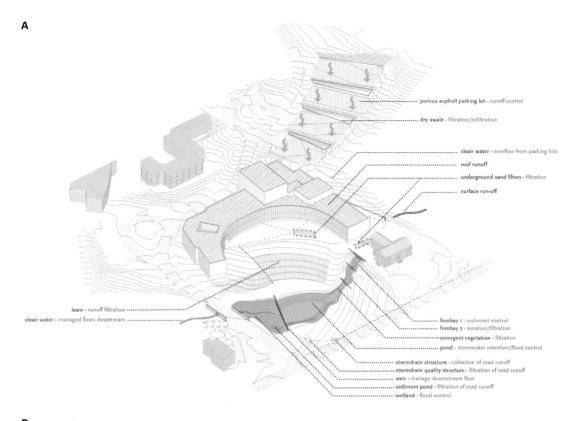

porous asphalt parking lot - runoff control

dry swale - filtration/infiltration

clean water - overflow from parking lots
roof runoff
underground sand filters - filtration
surface run-off

lawn - runoff filtration
clean water - managed flows downtream

forebay 1 - sediment control
forebay 2 - aeration/filtration
emergent vegetation - filtration
pond - stormwater retention/flood control
stormdrain structure - collection of road runoff
stormdrain quality structure - filtration of road runoff
weir - manage downstream flow
sediment pond - filtration of road runoff
wetland - flood control

B

Figure 4.14 A: The Clark Art Institute campus diagram. Courtesy of Reed+Hilderbrand Landscape Architects; B: Low impact storm-water management: towards sustainable design with green infrastructure for a new neighborhood in the Netherlands.

sectors. The SITES initiative was shepherded and is now managed by the American Society of Landscape Architects. The objective of this initiative is:

> [To] transform land development and management practices through the nation's first voluntary guidelines and rating system for sustainable landscapes, with or without buildings. The guidelines and rating system represent years of work by dozens of the country's leading sustainability experts, scientists, and design professionals and incorporate public input from hundreds of individuals and dozens of organizations to create this essential missing link in green design.[4]

Other areas of current practice that engage the design skill and experience of landscape architects include river channel and wetlands restoration to increase the biodiversity of damaged, formerly natural areas and improve the resilience of communities, mitigating the effect of natural disasters such as coastal storms. The legacy of our rich past greatly influences the areas of practice in which landscape architects find themselves deeply involved today. This legacy will be the foundation of the future contributions that professional practitioners will make in an increasingly complex set of challenges. Landscape architects will work in teams composed of scientists, other designers, and planners working together to forge functional and aesthetically enduring future built work for the health and enjoyment of future generations.

Notes

1 The group included one female: Beatrix Farrand, so that, unlike architecture and engineering, women have been accepted and significant contributors since the inception of landscape architecture.
2 Another world such as Paradise.
3 The term "sustainability" has, unfortunately, achieved a level of over-use to the point of being misused. It remains a vital concept, suggesting one should act in a responsible, stewardship role of taking actions and making decisions that preserve the Earth's natural resources for future generations. Best management practices is a term for the formalized process of controlling storm-water runoff and the handling of water-borne pollutants within the context of constructed projects such as roadway, subdivision, or other land use development types.
4 www.asla.org/sites.aspx.

Further Reading

More to explore on the history of landscape architecture:

Geoffrey Alan and Susan Jelicoe, *The Landscape of Man: Shaping the Environment from Prehistory to the Present Day*, 3rd edn, Thames and Hudson, London, 1995.

Elizabeth Barlow Rogers, *Landscape Design: A Cultural and Architectural History*, Harry N. Abrams Publishers, New York, 2001.

Elizabeth Boults and Chip Sullivan, *Illustrated History of Landscape Design*, John Wiley & Sons, Hoboken, NJ, 2010.

John Dixon Hunt, *Historical Ground: The Role of History in Contemporary Landscape Architecture*, Routledge, New York, 2014.

Norman T. Newton, *Design on the Land: The Development of Landscape Architecture*, Harvard University Press, Cambridge, MA, 1971.

Marc Trieb and Dorothée Imbert, *Garrett Eckbo: Modern Landscapes for Living*, University of California Press, Berkeley, CA, 2005.

CHAPTER FIVE

FUNDAMENTAL DESIGN AND SPATIAL ORGANIZATION CONCEPTS

Introduction

The world of design seems mysterious for those taking their first design course in landscape architecture. The words and concepts the professors use in their lectures can be confusing to students coming fresh from a high school education or transferring from a previous non-design academic major (we discussed this more thoroughly in Chapter 2). While some of the vocabulary is familiar, the intended meaning may not be obvious. Scale, balance, design continuity, contrast, form resolution, sustainability are words and concepts whose meaning may not be entirely clear when they are used in the early Introduction to Design lectures. To the consternation of new students, there does not seem to be such a thing as *the correct answer* in design as there is in other subjects. No mathematical formulas to learn and apply as in chemistry or mathematics. No problems to answer at the back of a chapter. Wrong answers seem to abound in the critiques of one's first design efforts. A whole new world of ideas and concepts and a new way of seeing unfold when one embarks on a landscape architecture curriculum. The design exercises are daunting and challenging at first, later becoming exciting challenges as understanding of the concepts and mastery of new skills lead to subsequent breakthroughs as one advances in the design curriculum.

The life of design is a continuous story, like life itself: one idea will lead to another and then another until eventually resolution is achieved. We find out very early in landscape design studio courses that there is no one, correct, or definitive solution to the design problems and exercises we are given. Instead we are instructed to explore the possibilities, ultimately arriving at a design solution by following the steps of something called a design process. The design process has several steps that we set out to follow in sequence, only to learn that the process of design is a reiterative endeavor. We learn that as we take each step forward, we may find that we have followed a dead end and will have to go back either to the beginning of the process or an earlier step to find our way in a direction which will yield good solutions. Finding a good solution to a design problem is not as linear a process as answering the odd problems in the back of an economics textbook chapter. We further discover that the process of finding answers in design continues after dinner and into the evening. We learn through experience that it is not the solution that is important or as satisfying as the search for finding a solution. It is in the journey of discovery that one finds satisfaction as a designer. The insights that seem to appear from nowhere as we work through the design process are a source of wonder. While our mass communication or biological science roommates seem to have time for a movie or hanging out with friends during the week, you and your classmates in design are in the studio grappling with the design problems at hand, then later making models and drawings, plans, and cross-sections in order to meet a deadline. The deadline does not entail *turning in answers* in a binder or on sheets of paper to be graded and later returned by the instructor. Rather, students are required to present their design solutions verbally to a gathering of faculty and sometimes invited guest critics who provide verbal critiques with time for questions and answers and sometimes a lively exchange. Looking around the room after all your classmates have presented their design proposals, we see that there are indeed many excellent answers or designs that solve the assignment.

Non-Linear Right Brain–Left Brain Thinking

What was just described is the reality of landscape architecture education. It is a form of education that has its roots in the ateliers or studios of the great Renaissance masters. Working under the guidance of a master, one learned one's craft not from books but by doing. There may perhaps be another way to more effectively or efficiently teach students how to design than what is sometimes referred to as *learn by doing*. However, to this day, the design studio and the atelier format successfully persist. It seems that one cannot learn design by simply reading a book. There is a process of learning that is hands-on and requires an unspecified amount of time for concepts and knowledge to mature before understanding is achieved. With understanding of the design problem, the designer can search for a good answer, an answer that meets the project program requirements. We find out through experience and going through the design process numerous times, the time required to find good if not inspiring design solutions decreases. Of course, the problems we are given to solve are increasingly more complex and larger in scale, so the design solving process may seem to take the same amount of time with little time to join our friends to hang out outside of class. But the process is an enjoyable one as we work with our studio classmates well into the night. A sense of camaraderie develops, resulting in many life-long professional friendships established.

Where Do Ideas for a Design Come from?

I don't have an answer to the question of where many of my landscape design ideas come from. I don't know if Mozart or Picasso could do any better in answering the question of where the inspiration for their music scores or paintings came from. More often than not when inspiration comes, it just comes. It is sort of like most serendipitous experiences: they just happen. But I do know where or how to look when I need to come up with a design concept or idea. Design ideas can come from many different sources or can be sought out in many different ways. Before we investigate the sources of design inspiration, we will consider another question: what is a design idea? That is a good question that might be easier to answer more directly than the question of where ideas come from and how. In this chapter we will explore many sources of design inspiration.

The Design Concept

So, where do ideas for designs come from or how do they come about? One could ask the same question of composers of where do the ideas for their compositions come from or where the images on the canvases of artists come from. A landscape design, a musical composition, or a painting is somehow derived by the mind processing stored knowledge and experiences. In Chapter 4, the history of landscape architecture was discussed. Certainly one's knowledge and understanding of historical precedence will be a source of inspiration, from which ideas for a design might occur. The experience of visiting built works of landscape architecture can be a source of design inspiration. Critically evaluating built works of landscape architecture that one has visited will build a body of knowledge and visual imagery that may provide an idea or concept that can lead to a solution for a current design project.

Tim Berners-Lee, the inventor of the World Wide Web, came up with an explanation to the question as to the source of design ideas or what is the process involved in creating new ideas. Berners-Lee suggested new ideas occur when a lot of random notions churn together until they coalesce. He described the process this way:

> Half-formed ideas, they float around. They come from different places, and the mind has got this wonderful way of somehow just shoveling them around until one day they fit. They may fit not so well, and then we go for a bike ride or something, and it's better.[1]

When the solution to the design problem becomes evident, the process of development and refinement of the initial ideas follows, finally evolving into the landscape design solution we present to the teacher or client.

Regardless of the explanation of how the mind works in processing and considering a plethora of information, it is from knowledge and experience that ideas emanate. That is not meant to suggest that one copies or replicates from the past. Rather, one is informed by the past and the knowledge accumulated suggests a new design or adaptation of ideas stored and processed in the mind.

Ideas that eventually lead to a concrete design proposal begin to emerge when we first start thinking about a project, visit the project site and gain familiarity with the surrounding context, and meet with the client. Early ideas may emerge during these three activities; often

Figure 5.1 *Use of historic precedents as a source of design inspiration: A: Parc de Sceaux by André Le Nôtre outside of Paris; B: A mixed-use residential neighborhood also in Paris.*

it is the site itself that may suggest a design concept, an idea that develops into a concrete design. Investigating the history of the site and its context and the people and cultures that were prominent during this history might suggest a design concept. An old street layout or historical landscape features such as an old irrigation canal or drainage swale might be the wellspring for a design solution.

Historical precedents (previously built examples) have been a source of inspiration down through the ages, perhaps beginning with the Garden of Eden. The two garden spaces shown in Figure 5.1 are a palpable example of where a historical precedent such as the great lawn at Parc de Sceaux in Paris (Figure 5.1A) and many similar gardens, designed with long vistas developed around a simple panel of lawn bordered by trees, has been adapted to other public and private gardens as shown in the contemporary public open space situated within a dense mixed-use neighborhood in Paris in Figure 5.1B. A discussion attempting to pinpoint where design ideas come from is a slippery, at best intellectual, enterprise. To understand the slippery nature of the topic we will review a number of design sources that have informed and been successfully applied by landscape architects.

Landscape as Narratives

People of all ages like a good story. Think about the evenings when bedtime stories were read to you. Sometimes at your insistence particular stories were read repeatedly evening after evening. The use of storytelling is an approach not only to convey information but also to generate visual imagery. The words in the hands of a skilled author can create visual images for the reader. The reader "sees" from the words put down on paper or told in the verbal reading of the text. There are many examples where the landscape architect has selected or derived a story that was the basis of a design. The story or narrative provided the organizing framework of elements contained in the design that when explained (told) can be seen and understood by the client and others. Following are some examples of design landscapes based on narratives.

Pershing Square, Los Angeles, CA

The office of the Olin Partnership in Philadelphia, PA, was the landscape architect for the design of the latest version of Pershing Square in downtown Los Angeles, California (Figure 5.2). The design is composed of an arrangement of interconnected spaces meant to symbolically showcase the cultural and natural history of the Southern California region, beginning with the Spanish Colonial period. Each space is meant to serve as a narrative of Los Angeles' past. For instance, one space designed as a gathering place for concert goers and large crowds hearkens back to the strawberry fields and other agriculture crops ubiquitous in the region prior to the early twentieth century. A second space containing citrus trees corresponds to the orange groves that the region of Southern California was famous for. The presence of water incorporated in a fountain and an elevated water trough suggests the water transport infrastructure that brought water to irrigate the area's agriculture fields. Southern California is situated in an active geologic fault zone and is represented in a sculptural piece integrated into the pavement depicting the San Andreas Fault. The architectural elements designed by the Mexican architect Ricardo Legorreta are meant to symbolize aspects of the

Figure 5.2 *Pershing Square in Los Angeles, California, by Olin Partnership, landscape architect, with Ricardo Legorreta, architect.*

Mexican cultural heritage of Los Angeles. For most people visiting Pershing Square, the narrative is not obvious. But the narrative was an important component during the design competition when the landscape architect Laurie Olin used the story to communicate his firm's design for the project. Like most designs based on a narrative, knowledge of the story is not necessary to enjoy the design. The elements of the story were carefully and thoughtfully woven to create a design with a solid organization, interesting and visually exciting physical elements, with arrangement of the program elements to facilitate visitors' enjoyment of the spaces and the park as whole.

Hayarkon Park, Tel Aviv, Israel

Gideon Sarig, a landscape architect with a private practice in Israel, designed Hayarkon Park located on the outskirts of Tel Aviv (Figure 5.3). The Mayor of Tel Aviv, during an early discussion about park design goals, asked Gideon to design a rose garden. There may be some roses tucked somewhere in the park in his ultimate design but, as you will, see Sarig's design took a direction different than the mayor's initial request. During an initial field study of the park site that is dominated by variable rolling, dry terrain, Sarig concluded that a rose garden did not seem appropriate. The narrative story and eventually the basis of the park design, was taken from the Bible (Joshua 4). Since a small stream ran through the property bordered by the hilly terrain, Sarig was reminded of the River Jordan and the story of the Israelites' time before crossing the river. The story goes: God asked Joshua, who was leading the Israelites, to ask each of the 12 tribal leaders to select a boulder and the next day to place their boulder in the river as stepping stones before crossing. This was done and the question one might ask on hearing the story is:

Figure 5.3 *Hayarkon Park, Tel Aviv, Israel, by Gideon Sarig, landscape architect.*

what happened, if anything, to the 12 boulders? Gideon's answer can be found in his design of Hayarkon Park.

The design and organizing framework of the park were a series of outdoor spaces. Each space had as either a central landmark or the primary construction material rocks and boulders taken from 12 different geologic formations found in Israel. The design was, rather than a collection and exhibition of roses, a walk through the geologic history of Israel. Plants selected were endemic to each region complementing each geologic region. The rocks that were selected for each space were arranged in a unique creation, in some cases sculptural-like and in others suggesting the terrain's endemic source where the rocks originated. Based on the telling of the biblical story during the presentation by Gideon Sarig, the design was accepted by the mayor. It has become a popular park because of its physical design with few or any visitors recognizing the biblical story of Joshua behind the design. They may wonder where all the rocks came from and for the curious, descriptive signage will provide an explanation.

Tezozomoc Park, Mexico City

In the mid-1970s, Mexico City completed construction of its first of many underground metro lines. The excess excavation material was stockpiled on a large parcel of land in the north quadrant of the city. The materials remained there in uneven piles. Among other results the site became a dumping ground for an assortment of debris, discarded materials, and refuse accumulated, to the consternation of adjacent neighborhoods. City government needed a solution of what to do with the area and the growing piles of debris. The idea of a park floated to the top of the discussion. The landscape architectural firm Grupo Diseños Urbanos of Mario Schjetnan, FASLA, was hired to develop a design solution. Initially the city assumed the mountains of excavated soil would have to be removed and transported at considerable cost to another location. Schjetnan's office eventually arrived at a design concept where the mountains of accumulated material became the basis of a design narrative. The narrative also saved the city a great deal of money in not having to remove the debris and soil. The story was a good one and guided a design that has resulted in a well-used and often-visited park, typically filled during weekend family outings and picnics as well as during the week by school children bussed to the park for outdoor learning purposes. The landscape architects reformed the unruly piles of earth, and molded them into an almost full-scale model of the Valley of Mexico where Mexico City is situated (see Figure 5.4A). Lakes were incorporated into the design representing the expanse of water and wetlands found in the valley at the time the Spanish arrived around 1520. Other areas were carved and molded to represent the communities where numerous native cultures inhabited the area along with the Aztecs. Essentially, a stroll through Tezozomoc Park is a pilgrimage to the communities who inhabited the valley prior to the Spanish. An extensive signage system has been placed, noting each village population and ecological zone that could at one time be found in the valley. While in the two previous examples, the underlying narrative is not evident, a story

Figure 5.4 Tezozomoc Park, Mexico City: A: Courtesy of Grupo de Diseño Urbano and Mario Schjetnan with Michael Calderwood; B: Courtesy of Grupo de Diseño Urbano and Mario Schjetnan with Gabriel Figueroa.

is celebrated and rewards the visitors who come to Tezozomoc Park for the family or school outing.

California Scenario, Costa Mesa, California

The Modernist artist Isamu Noguchi was commissioned to create a site-specific sculptural piece for a proposed sculpture garden located adjacent to the South Coast Plaza Mall in Costa Mesa, California. The site had previously been a lima bean field through the 1900s. Instead, Noguchi proposed making the garden of one piece: a narrative celebrating the many indigenous regions of California and the role water had played in the state's development. The aim was to also serve as a critique of man's destructive relationship with the California landscape. In Figure 5.5, water is revealed flowing through the stone surface of the plaza with gently carved stone forms in the background. The narrative is achieved through the lens of water movement in the landscape, passing sets meant to evoke specific iconic California landscapes created with rock and plant material. The garden has a Zen or contemplative effect, perhaps drawing from the Japanese cultural roots of the artist.

Figure 5.5 California Scenario, Costa Mesa, California, by Isamu Noguchi.

Landscape and Cultural Context

> I believe in roots, in associations, in backgrounds, in personal relationships.[2]
>
> Benjamin Britten

Imbuing a sense of place is a powerful design objective that has been used successfully by landscape architects as a source of inspiration for their designs. By incorporating iconic physical elements drawn from the context of a project site, landscape architects have created long-lasting and memorable landscape and urban design solutions, such as in the examples below. These design solutions are the result of the designer's investigation of the cultural and natural history of the site and its regional context as well as landmark or endemic features found in the immediate area or region. While the designs may be contemporary, the underlying organizing structure, materials, and forms instill a sense of belonging to the place of the designed project. The resulting designs feel right or appear to belong in their location. This quality of belonging is achieved by incorporating iconic natural or cultural materials taken from the location.

Examples of this approach include extending the street pattern of the adjacent neighborhood into the design as some other element, such as a pedestrian network, a paving pattern, a fountain or other special feature, and open landscaped spaces between buildings. The sinuous form of a nearby stream might translate into the flow of open space meandering between building groups (see example in Figure 5.6). The form and movement of this river might translate into the form of an open lawn area or system of created lakes and fountains. Using cultural references to inform design is a common approach by landscape architects. A further exploration of how designers have used their research and understanding of cultural and landscape context and reference to iconic features is provided in the following examples.

Figure 5.6 Dry stream garden inspired by stream canyon in nearby mountain, Upland California residence, by landscape architect, D. Rodney Tapp. Photograph courtesy of R. Tapp.

Inspired by Historical Precedent

Precedence studies have become an integral component of pre-planning and design research in landscape architecture. The idea of precedence is that one can learn and find inspiration from the built works of others. One can gain insight into alternative design approaches and considerations by critically assessing projects similar to the project at hand. Landscape architects also present the precedent information to their clients to communicate the design ideas they are considering. The saying that a picture—one or a series of well-chosen pictures—is worth more than one thousand words has become part of a strategy of educating or convincing a client of the merits of a design proposal. Historical precedent represents a trove of exemplarily built works to communicate and suggest ideas for a client to consider as well as inform the designer as he or she explores design solutions.

The detail of a parterre garden shown in Figure 5.7A is from El Escorial, Spain, north of Madrid. King Phillip II built it as part of a larger plan to commemorate his father by constructing the gardens. The use of clipped boxwood is reminiscent of Italian Renaissance gardens. The office of the Peter Walker Partnership in turn gained design inspiration from the sixteenth-century French garden estates for the forecourt plaza at the Orange County Civic Center in California, as seen in Figure 5.7B. The clipped boxwood shrubs commonly take geometric and often elaborate forms in contemporary design. The boxwood forms at the Orange County Civic Center have a sculptural quality, providing visual interest to viewers in the adjacent office towers and for the pedestrians on their way to buildings accessible from the plaza.

Chapultepec Park, Mexico City

Chapultepec Park was heavily forested land set aside by the Aztecs long before the Spanish Conquest in the sixteenth century. The forest served as a summer home or retreat for the emperor as well as a source of fresh water for the valley inhabitants. The water was transported by a series of canals to the surrounding communities. The existence of the canals was documented in historical records although they are no longer present in the twenty-first century. In 2005–2006, landscape architect Mario Schjetnan of Grupo Diseño Urbano was selected to investigate and design a more visually attractive and direct pedestrian connection between two major museums in the center of the park: the Museum of Anthropology and the Rufino Tamayo Museum. Artists and designers, such as Diego Rivera whose waterworks wall can be found in the

Figure 5.7 A: El Escorial, Spain; B: Orange County Civic Center, by The Peter Walker Partnership.

Figure 5.8 Chapultepec Park Canal Promenade, Mexico City, D.F., by Mario Schjetnan. Photographs courtesy of Grupo Diseño Urbano.

park, incorporated elements of the ancient water infrastructure in their work. Schjetnan was aware of the ancient water system and canals of the Aztecs. He developed a progression of canal-like fountains as the central design element with parallel walks to connect the two museums (see Figure 5.8). Along the walks he placed lounge-type furniture not only to provide seating but also to suggest lounging in reference to the original retreat purpose of the forest-park reserve.

Inspiration from Nature

Nature seems a tempting if not a fallback source, inspiring the designs of landscape architects. Many garden design traditions both in the East, such as in China and Japan, and the West, including North America and Northern Europe, contain natural elements and materials as well as designs informed by nature. Some of the nature-inspired landscapes are steeped in symbolism while other designs are attempts to create a stylized or—and some people might acknowledge—a reasonable facsimile. For a garden or landscaped space to look natural, such as New York's Central Park, it often requires that a romanticized interpretation of nature be taken.

Successful contemporary landscape designs are the result of creating new patterns and forms based on the natural patterns found in the landscape. Landscape architects attribute a significant influence to nature in their designs. They find design inspiration through observation and experience in their travels, hiking expeditions, and critically observing the surrounding project context (see Figure 5.9). Landscape architects also learn from nature and, for instance, select native plant species and their distribution and habitat when composing a new landscape. The regional landscape also provides clues to the astute and careful observer. They use what they learn about such factors as climate variability, wind conditions, soil composition, and hazard potential (potential for landslides and erosion), and hydrologic patterns when developing their design proposals.

Figure 5.9 A: Santa Barbara coastal mountain dry streambed; B: Dreamworks campus water feature in San Francisco, by Lawrence Halprin, landscape architect.

Donnell Residence by Thomas Church

The Donnell residence, located in Sonoma County, California, is one of the iconic Modernist landscape designs from mid-twentieth-century America (Figure 5.10). It was designed in the office of one of the early landscape architecture pioneers of California: Thomas Church of San Francisco. The design of the swimming pool is attributed to Lawrence Halprin, another well-known landscape designer who gained early experience in Church's office. The inspiration for the pool design came from the prominent pattern of wetlands coursing through the valley below the Donnells' hillside property.

Figure 5.10 Swimming pool, Donnell Residence, by Thomas Church, landscape architect, with Lawrence Halprin.

Levi Strauss Plaza, San Francisco, California

Lawrence Halprin took frequent walking trips in many landscapes of his adopted state, California. The Sierra Madre Mountains were a recurrent attraction for Halprin, so what he experienced, sketched, and wrote of his observations often found translation in his later designs such as the Levi Strauss Plaza in downtown San Francisco. Halprin greatly appreciated the geologic phenomena he encountered, in particular the rock outcroppings for their sculptural quality. One of his outings in the Sierras provided Halprin inspiration during the early design development for the Levi Strauss Plaza (Figure 5.11). He selected and tagged large granite boulders that were later transported to the plaza construction site. The boulders were incorporated into the central fountain and other elements found in the plaza. Incorporating specific materials taken from a natural landscape in creating a public plaza or landscape has been a successful approach for Halprin. He has created many of his memorable and most enduring creations after being inspired by his walks in natural areas. There is a more park-like section to the plaza located across the street. This second section was designed to have a more passive, pastoral quality in contrast to the dramatic and sculptural approach for the upper plaza. The contrast between the two halves is striking and intentional to provide the visitor an opportunity to experience two sides of nature that Halprin found in his hiking and sketching trips to the Sierra Madre mountains. His observations of nature in his travels to other regions and countries where he had clients served to inspire other of his designs.

Figure 5.11 Levi Strauss Plaza, San Francisco, CA, by Lawrence Halprin, landscape architect.

Taliesin West, Scottsdale, AZ

Taliesin West was the work of architect Frank Lloyd Wright and was his winter home and studio from 1937 until his death. Wright had a powerful

Figure 5.12 *Taliesin West, Scottsdale, Arizona, by Frank Lloyd Wright.*

visceral connection to and appreciation for the desert. He was inspired in the design of his residence to respond and somehow capture the long, low sweeping planes of the high desert landscape as well as the color and indigenous rock material. While the native landscape informed his design of the structure, the gardens and immediate grounds were organized and developed spatially as an extension of the architecture (see Figure 5.12).

Architectural Inspired Landscape Space

The symmetry of building architecture is often an expression of the modular nature of a building's structure. Windows and doors are arranged in a modular composition, as are other architectural features such as columns, mullions, and panels of a building's cladding or skin. Landscape architects either by their own choice and aesthetic sensibility or at the request of the architect will organize the outdoor space to project the visible modular building elements (windows, doors, and columns) out into the space and serve to organize the program elements. The extended building grid lines set the pattern for locating walkways, landscaped planting areas, gathering places, and other spatial elements programmed for the space between buildings and connecting to other functional areas such as parking.

Telefónica Headquarters Campus, Madrid, Spain

The Telefónica office campus is the headquarters of the national telephone company of Spain. The buildings are a glass and steel-clad contemporary architecture sited to form a large internal landscape space for employees and an ample entrance to the street welcoming visitors. The internal landscape open space follows proportions established by the extension of the architecture's modular structure. Walkways, gathering areas, and landscape planting beds align with this modular grid (see Figure 5.13). The grid is not always closely followed, therefore adding a layer of visual interest to a comfortably scaled variety of outdoor rooms. Employees can find individual quiet spaces to meet with others or informally conduct work. The positioning of trees also reflects the architectural module and at the same time allows the framing of views or provides shade where needed. The walks, walls, and seating elements are positioned within the module as well as a linear water feature that transects through the space.

Figure 5.13 *The Telefónica office complex, Madrid, Spain.*

High Line, New York City and Railroad Park, Santa Fe

Figure 5.14A captures one of the defining design concepts for the High Line in New York City by landscape architect James Corner of Field Operations. Just as its name suggests, the park was built on the superstructure of an abandoned railroad line built earlier in the twentieth century. Remnants of the original tracks were left or repurposed in establishing pavement patterns, site furniture, landscaped areas, and other elements of the richly layered design of this highly successful and popular urban public oasis.

A glimpse of Santa Fe Railroad Park by landscape architect Ken Smith is shown in Figure 5.14B. The underlying structure of the park is the railroad tracks and buildings of the previous railroad station. Left-over equipment such as switches, rail, and train parts were incorporated as visual elements suggesting the narrative of railroad functions from the past. Some of these same railroad remnants were incorporated into the design of the innovative seating and other site furnishings.

Canberra, Australia: National Capital Master Plan

The Chicago landscape architect Walter Burley Griffin and his architect wife Marion won an international competition for their design of the new national capital of Australia in 1912. Their solution employed a previous approach similar to Georges-Eugène Haussmann for Paris, France and Pierre Charles L'Enfant in Washington, D.C. At the heart of this approach is the creation of a network of organizing axes with each major street aligned to a significant building[3] or landscape feature such as a prominent mountain or series of mountains, as was the case in the planning of Australia's capital city, Canberra. What is remarkable about Burley Griffin's master plan was its

Figure 5.14 A: High Line Park, New York, by James Corner of Field Operations, landscape architects; B: Santa Fe, New Mexico, Railroad Park, by Ken Smith, landscape architect.

use of the street axes to resolve a political conundrum involving the desire for two established cities (Melbourne and Sydney) engaged in a heated competition to be the nation's capital city. The principal streets in the Griffin plan were aligned with major mountain peaks serving as landmarks for Melbourne and Sydney. The proposed plan for Canberra in essence stitched the country together by linking the mountain landmarks of the competing cities. The fact that the mountains were not visible from Canberra was not important. Conceptually the linkage of the mountains was made very direct

Figure 5.15 *Aerial view of Canberra, the Australian capital city. Courtesy of the Australian National Capital Authority.*

and in the end provided the resolution of what was a contentious debate between two competing cities. Looking at a recent aerial view of Canberra (Figure 5.15), one can see the axial framework for the plan. The layout of several of the major streets actually aligns to mountain forms visible and located near to Canberra itself. It is most probable that the reference to the alignment of the mountain features of Sydney and Melbourne is what gave the edge to the Griffins' competition submission.

Symbolism

Parliament Building, Canberra, Australia

As the result of another international design competition in Australia for a new parliament building, the New York architecture firm of Mitchell/Giurgola was selected with site work designed by landscape architect Peter Roland (Figure 5.16). The new structure would replace the temporary parliament building constructed at the foot of a hill facing Lake Burley Griffin. The original intention was to tear down the old building and replace it with the new structure. There was a public outcry when these plans were revealed as the public felt the old parliament building represented a valuable part of the city's cultural heritage. The Mitchell/Giurgola solution resolved the issue of maintaining the old building by positioning the new structure on the top of the hill above the old parliament with a roof garden or public park on top. This solution not only saved the removal of the historical building by placing a park above the new structure, much of which was buried underground into the hill. Building a park above the parliament building symbolically placed the *people* above their government.

In these two examples for Australia, we can see the power of a design. Two national political conundrums were resolved through design, the first being the 1912 master plan for the new capital city

Figure 5.16 *Parliament House, Canberra, Australia. Courtesy of the Australian National Capital Authority.*

of Canberra that resolved the competition by two cities to be the nation's capital followed later in the century by the clever approach that placed a people's park above the government housed in the new parliament building.

The Four Rivers of Paradise

One of the more ubiquitous historical references that has informed the design of private gardens and public spaces is the desert oasis and its manifestation: Paradise or Garden of Eden from the Bible. Whether or not there is a historical basis for its existence at all other than from biblical sources will not be discussed here. It certainly can be seen as a mythological or cultural construct that has influenced garden design in countries bordering the Mediterranean and in Southern Europe. The characteristic bilateral organization of spaces defined by the four rivers of the Garden of Eden can be found throughout regions bordering the Mediterranean, particularly Portugal and Spain and later exported to Latin America. Shade is provided by a dense planting of trees shielding visitors from the intense Mediterranean sunlight. Shade and water are also the basis and attraction of a desert oasis. The oasis metaphor embodied in the Garden of Eden substantiates the biblical origins of the garden as both a refuge and pleasure garden and originates—from a Western perspective—in the Tigris and Euphrates river valley.

In Figure 5.17 is a neighborhood public garden located in the Latin Quarter, Madrid, Spain. Note in the center of the garden there is a sculptural feature (standing in place of a typical fountain). A clipped boxwood hedge lines the walkways radiating from

Figure 5.17 *Garden of Eden, a small neighborhood park in the Latin Quarter of Madrid.*

Figure 5.18 *The Garden of Flowering Fragrance, Huntington Gardens, Pasadena, CA. Chinese garden designed by artisans from the city of Suzhou, China.*

the central feature. Often the central feature is a fountain or covered kiosk structure serving as a gathering place or stage, a feature common in Latin America. A dense canopy of broad-leaf trees shades the garden.

Chinese Garden of Paradise

Reference to paradise also informed the design of traditional Chinese gardens. The selection and placement of large boulders are a common refrain in these gardens. The boulders were selected from favorite locations of the garden owners and served as symbols reminding them of these landscapes of memory. The term "memory garden" is often used to describe the traditional Chinese gardens. In addition to the selection and placement of rocks and boulders, plants and water were carefully arranged to complement the story of a landscape of memory or paradise and an idealized vision of nature (see Figure 5.18).

Landscape as Art

Artists, those trained and/or who practice creating art, contribute to constructed landscapes either on their own or in collaboration with landscape architects. The examples presented here are landscape projects where the hand of an artist utilized the canvas of a landscape for artistic expression.

The Getty Center, Westwood, California

The J. Paul Getty Foundation constructed a new campus[4] in the hills above Westwood in Los Angeles, California. The site was developed in phases over a number of years with several landscape architects involved at each phase. The office of Laurie Olin designed the outdoor

Figure 5.19 *The Getty Center (1997), lower gardens, Los Angeles, California, by Robert Irwin sculptor with Spurlock Poirier landscape architects.*

spaces around the museum and administrative complex of buildings. The lower garden pictured in Figure 5.19 was designed by Robert Irwin, a Southern Californian artist in association with Spurlock Poirier landscape architects (1992–1997). The landscape design for this portion of the site approaches the spaces just as an artist would work on canvas. The artist approached the arrangement and the selection of plant species, the alignment of the walks and walls, and the lower fountain to create a piece of art. In this case, the art was meant to be experienced as well as to be looked at and appreciated. The artist used plants, stone, and water, as he would apply paint on a canvas. The resulting composition can be viewed from the upper exterior terraces as well as viewed from inside the buildings.

The design concept applied to the majority of the site reflected an approach where the outdoor gardens and space were intended to complement the building and serve as outdoor rooms. The materials selected for these spaces were meant to suggest a Mediterranean-like environment. This was an appropriate approach given the focus of the collection of art and artifacts housed in the museum.

Mesa Contemporary Arts Museum and Center, Mesa, Arizona

The design for the outdoor public spaces and gardens of the Mesa Contemporary Arts Museum and Center was the collaborative work of two landscape architecture firms, Martha Schwartz Partners and Design Workshop (see Figure 5.20). The architecture by Boora Architects of Portland, Oregon, is characterized as post-modern with an emphasis on an eclectic use of materials and forms reflected in the landscape design of the public spaces and garden areas. The landscape architect developed forms for fountains, raised planting beds, and sculptural walls as a conversation with the architecture. What would be defined as the landscape spaces were developed as a sculptural experience for those walking through the spaces within the campus composed of four performance venues, five exhibit galleries, and administrative support offices. Color and materials were selected to contribute to the idea of public spaces as a form of art.

Figure 5.20 Contemporary Art Museum, Mesa, AZ, by Design Workshop and Martha Schwartz, landscape architects.

Vertical Garden

The plaza in front of the Caixa Cultural and Museum complex includes a vertical garden, created by French artist and horticulturist Patrick Blanc (see Figure 5.21). Blanc has developed a system that allows the artist to install plants applied onto the face of buildings, as an artist would with paint on canvas. The vertical landscaped walls of Patrick Blanc demonstrate the potential of the vegetative media for artistic expression similar to many of the landscape works of the Brazilian artist and landscape architect, Roberto Burle Marx, where his canvas was the Earth.

Figure 5.21 Vertical garden, the Caixa Cultural Center and Museum, Madrid, Spain, by Patrick Blanc, artist.

Blanc used many walls, both interior and exterior, in buildings for his artistic horticultural installations in many locations in the world. Note in this work, located across the street from the Prado Museum, how much variety is achieved in terms of color, texture, and form in creating a remarkable three-dimensional composition similar to a bas-relief.

West End Skateboard Park, Albuquerque, New Mexico

Landscape architects have realized the potential for artistic expression in a wide range of situations where they have been commissioned

Figure 5.22 West End Skateboard Park, Albuquerque, New Mexico, by Morrow Reardon Wilkinson, landscape architects.

to provide design services. The potential canvases of course would include the ground plane and topography and vertical walls. The landscape architecture firm of Morrow Reardon Wilkinson and Miller realized the sculptural potential of a skateboard park they were selected to design in Albuquerque, New Mexico. The photograph in Figure 5.22 was taken at the pedestrian entry with the skateboard in the background. The entire ensemble was approached as a sculptural piece created using a palette of plain and colored concrete, rock and stones, plant material, and topographic modeling. The plants and hardscape materials used reflect the colors, forms, and textures of the high desert location in which Albuquerque is situated. To what extent skateboarders appreciate the artistic merits of this specialized athletic venue while doing their tricks has not been documented. Its high usage suggests the park has been a success from the users' perspective. The facility is attractive when not in use to park visitors as well to the neighbors with a view from their hillside vantage.

Plaza Salvador Dalí, Madrid, Spain

The reimaging of what was previously considered a public space to be avoided in the heart of Madrid has been a success and now Plaza Salvador Dalí has achieved great popularity as a place to relax, or to bring children to play while parents shop or visit with friends. The design by Mángado Architects included a strategy to support shade-providing vegetation and masses of color by the construction of large wedge-like polygon-shaped forms with sufficient soil depth to support large trees. Ample seating is incorporated in the sculptural concrete forms of the planters (see Figure 5.23). These same forms with their lush planting give the long grand space a comfortable feeling of human scale. The seating attached to the gray concrete walls provides a comfortable and warm-looking visual balance to the bare concrete forms. The plaza sits on the roof of an underground parking lot. A sculpture by Salvador Dalí was positioned at one end of the plaza with other sculptures and children's play equipment placed at other locations. A new system of paving was installed helping to bring the plaza to a more comfortable human scale. The paving was imbedded with LED lighting, adding visual interest as well as supplementing the light provided by pole lighting fixtures. Large bronze plates fit snugly within the grid-like pattern of the stone and concrete plaza surface. The bronze plates have been created with organic, bas-relief shapes, adding another visual element for visitors to appreciate and enjoy while walking through the space. Madrid's remodeled Palacio de Deportes

Figure 5.23 Plaza Salvador Dalí, Madrid, Spain, by Mángado Architects.

(Sports Palace) sits at one end of the plaza, serving as a backdrop and bookend for the space. The 1940s Franco-era architectural style is in sharp contrast to the contemporary wedge-shaped forms arranged on the floor of the plaza and the adjacent buildings that line the plaza.

Is it Art or Inspired by a Cultural Artifact?

The firm of Christine Ten Eyck was the landscape architects for the design of Steele Indian School Park in Phoenix, Arizona. The fountain and its garden shown in Figure 5.24 could be appreciated as a site-specific art piece where the designer incorporated cultural artifacts in creating the space with a central fountain water feature. The circular space built into a depressed landform was created with the eye of an artist and executed by the hand of a craftsman. The materials used to create the central space include native, drought-tolerant plants and rock (crushed and whole boulders) native to the area. The play of sunlight on the forms and surfaces of the hardscape and plant materials adds theatrical visual interest to the sculptural landform. The patterns of light and shadow change throughout the day and with the changing seasons during the year. The site-specific quality of this passive visitor space would make the same piece look like a foreign intrusion if it were constructed in any other environment in North America other than the Arizona high desert.

Figure 5.24 Steele Indian School Park, Phoenix, AZ, by Christine Ten Eyck, landscape architect.

A Garden Can Inspire Art

The photograph in Figure 5.25 was taken at Claude Monet's water garden in Giverny. This garden and the gardens of the family residence were the subject and inspiration for some of Monet's best-known works. The series of water lily paintings were inspired by Monet's water garden, but the garden was also his creation. Many of those paintings are now on permanent exhibit at the Musée de l'Orangerie in Paris, France. Landscape architects have also been inspired by gardens and landscapes they have visited. Lawrence Halprin found inspiration in visits to Yosemite Valley and the Sierra Mountains for several of his well-known works, including the Levi Strauss Plaza in San Francisco and Ira's Forecourt Plaza in Portland, Oregon. Capability Brown in England and Frederick Law Olmsted in America have works that were inspired by their visits to natural areas or gardens formed by their predecessors.

Figure 5.25 Water Garden at Giverny, by Claude Monet.

Figure 5.26 Garden at the Musée de l'Orangerie, Paris, France.

Musée de l'Orangerie, Paris, France

The art gallery of the Musée de l'Orangerie, located in the Tuileries Gardens in Paris, exhibits Impressionist and post-Impressionist artists, and is also home to the water lilies paintings of Claude Monet. The gardens, detail of one outside the museum is shown in Figure 5.26, may have been inspired by the art inside the museum. Certainly the colors and the very painterly manner in which plants have been arranged suggest the influence of the Impressionist art inside the museum. Try squinting your eyes while looking at the photograph in Figure 5.26, then the image takes on an Impressionistic quality.

Work of Practicality

The next works designed by landscape architects were the result of commissions to fix something, to improve water quality, to reduce flooding, to increase habitat and therefore biodiversity, or restore a river as a strategy of rebuilding a community from an abandoned industrial neighborhood. Restoration, improving water quality, mitigating hazards from natural disasters, rebuilding dysfunctional landscapes, and attendant improvements such as trail and park installations have become a significant source of work for landscape architects.

Baltimore Harbor, Maryland, was cut off from the rest of the city when the port, shipping yards, warehouses, and manufacturing were built along the water edge. As these once profitable economic uses fell upon hard times and were abandoned or underused, the city saw the revitalization of the harbor into a tourist and recreation destination as part of a larger strategy of transforming the harbor and downtown Baltimore from a derelict collection of abandoned buildings into a vital cultural and tourism center on the American East Coast. The previously derelict site of the London 2102 Olympics has a similar story to Baltimore's. Other examples of landscape transformations are described in this section, all examples of the type of projects landscape architects have become increasingly involved with; some in a collaborative role with others or as the primary designer.

Buffalo Bayou, Houston, Texas

It may be hard to imagine but the water feature in Figure 5.27 was a concrete-lined drainage channel a matter of only ten years ago. Buffalo Bayou was in a bad state, like so many rivers and water features in cities all over the world, that were not appreciated for their recreational, environmental, or aesthetic value and were either covered over, filled in, or cut off from the urban fabric. The city of San Antonio had a river that ran through the downtown that was once the source of flooding in the business district and was used as the service entrance to business lining the San Antonio River. The river is now a tourist attraction, contributing to the economic life of the city. The improved sections of Buffalo Bayou have now become popular walking, jogging, biking, and passive recreation attractions for adjoining neighborhoods. The improvements of the bayou became a catalyst for upgrading adjoining properties as part of a larger strategy for economic development. In addition to the extensive plantings, the landscape architects of the SWA Group widened the channel, increasing the water detention capacity to better accommodate the volume of water of heavy rains and thus contribute to the reduction of area flooding.

Water Ranch, Gilbert, AZ

Figure 5.27 Buffalo Bayou, Houston, Texas, by the SWA Group.

Water Ranch was a project of the environmental science firm of Jones & Stokes from Sacramento, CA (Figure 5.28). The firm had a staff landscape architect, who, with the firm's wildlife and environmental engineering specialists, conceived of a proposed wastewater treatment spreading grounds (infrastructure for water to recharge the underground aquifer) as a wildlife preserve (primarily for migratory birds), and regional outdoor education and family recreation facility. The project incorporated a city library, adding diversity to attract additional users to the park. A water treatment plant was also constructed on what was formerly an agricultural field. The designers developed a concept not originally considered by the city client. Previously constructed water spreading grounds in the region were composed of grid-like water-holding cells with earthen levees that contained the treated water. These facilities were designed without vegetation; a concept to reduce maintenance costs.

The firm of Jones & Stokes proposed the creation of ponds of irregular size and shape with variations in water depth. The irregular shapes increased the amount of edge that was then planted with a variety of endemic plants to provide habitat and nesting areas. With the varied water depth, different plant species could be supported in creating a varied habitat to attract a wide variety of birds and animals. The plantings also function to "polish" the treated water, adding another level of purification before the water infiltrates through the soil to the aquifer below. Along the edge of the park adjacent to the library, a children's play area was constructed with water features for the children's use such as a hand pump with a gravel-lined swale to carry the pumped water toward one of the ponds. Bird blinds were strategically located to afford viewing for birdwatchers without disturbing the birds. Educational signage was included along the pathway system. A community demonstration or outdoor education classroom was constructed where students and other visitors could learn about the wildlife in the area and water conservation.

Figure 5.28 Water Ranch, Gilbert, Arizona, by Jones & Stokes.

Figure 5.29 South (Zud) Park, Rotterdam, the Netherlands.

South (Zud) Park, Rotterdam, the Netherlands

South or Zud Park is located in Rotterdam, the Netherlands. It is a large multi-purpose green space comparable in size to New York City's Central Park. The original park was designed in the early twentieth century for passive recreation with great swaths of open lawn areas framed by dense forest trees cover. The park served a primarily middle-class residential population. Over the years the surrounding neighborhood population changed with the influx of Eastern European and Middle Eastern immigrant families. A few years into the new millennium the City Parks Department of Rotterdam sought to do a total make-over of the park with two primary goals: (1) to develop facilities and activity areas to better serve the new ethnic population; and (2) to increase the storm-water detention capacity of the park lands as part of a larger city-wide strategy to improve resilience to flooding.

There are several elements to observe in Figure 5.29. The park visitors can be seen strolling on a path built on a levee. The levee was constructed to contain storm water. This area of the park represents the potential storm-water detention capacity by increasing the level of detained water of the lake near the height of the levee as seen in the middle of Figure 5.29. The edge of the lake was planted with vegetative species having a water cleansing capacity so as to improve the quality of surface water runoff moving downstream. The forest cover in the background is a remnant from the previous park design. The forest serves as animal habitat, reduces water pollutants that come from runoff from surrounding roads and neighborhoods, as well as accommodating walking trails.

Frank's Valley near Muir Beach, Marin, California

Figure 5.30 Landscape erosion control and restoration, Frank's Valley, Muir Beach, California.

The area adjacent to Muir Beach and Muir Woods on the coast north of San Francisco is a popular day-hiking destination for Bay Area residents and visitors. The drainage swale in Figure 5.30 was recently repaired with an erosion control system consisting of netting and a matrix of deeply rooting native plants. Over the years, erosion in this upper area of Frank's Valley has resulted in siltation of the wetlands downstream (visible in the middle ground of Figure 5.30). Landscape architects and others developed a detailed design to reduce the erosion coming off the slopes along the drainage swale as well as replanting the wetlands below impacted by siltation from slope erosion. Medium-sized boulders were placed in the drainage channel to slow down and reduce the erosive force of rapidly moving storm water. In time, the plant material will take hold and fill in the slope so that the netting is no longer visible. Volunteer native species of plants from the adjoining undisturbed slopes will invade in the process of natural succession to further repair and reduce slope erosion. Assuming all goes according to plan, visitors hiking along the trail will see in as few as 10 years a naturalized landscape, unaware of the steps taken to get from heavily eroded bare slopes to recovery with native plant cover.

Sand Dunes Restoration/Protection, the Netherlands

The Netherlands has had to devise increasingly robust and sophisticated strategies to protect the country from winter storms and flooding since as long ago as AD 800. The Dutch are known for their system of levees, canals, pumping systems, including windmills, and other approaches to ward against winter-borne flooding. Much of the coast perimeter of the country is protected against storm flooding with the creation of sand dunes constructed over earthen levees. The dunes have been planted with a variety of plant species, mostly grasses, as shown in Figure 5.31. The dunes appear to be natural but are in fact a cultural artifact and

Figure 5.31 Storm protection sand dunes, the Netherlands

are appreciated as any native landscape feature. The plants and wildlife that inhabit the dunes have naturalized and, like any ecosystem, change and shift in composition over time.

Reconstructed Watershed Landscape

High Desert Water Harvester, Albuquerque, New Mexico

Designed by the landscape architecture firm of Sites Southwest of Albuquerque, New Mexico, in collaboration with Bohannan-Huston hydrologic engineers (Figure 5.32), this project is an example of a community-scale landscape watershed reclamation and water harvesting strategy. The aim of the project is to collect and detain rainwater, allowing time for it to percolate through the soil to the underground aquifer. In the process of constructing an adjacent sub-division, massive amounts of earth moving was necessary. The landscape architects devised a restoration plan, selecting native plant species to restore the disturbed areas, essentially recreating the natural habitat and biodiversity of flora and fauna. Storm water carrying pollutants drains from the adjacent residential properties and streets and then flows through the reconstructed watershed. In the process, the runoff water is cleaned of most pollutants as the water moves across the vegetated landscape. The water eventually is directed to an impoundment basin, lined with stone-clad banks in a formal

Figure 5.32 High desert water harvester, Albuquerque, New Mexico.

circular pattern with paths, and seating areas above. A large sculptural element was installed as a landmark that provides a way-finding function for trail users. The project functions as an integrated experience in which one can appreciate the rich visual attributes of a high desert landscape and interpret the movement of storm waters within the natural and built watershed environment.

London 2012 Olympic Park, London, UK

LDA Design, United Kingdom, and Hargreaves Associates, USA, collaborated in the final design for the 2012 Olympic Park in London, UK (Figure 5.33). The site selected for the Olympic Park was a previously contaminated industrial urban landscape. The design provides both new wildlife habitats and significant flood protection for East London. A tributary stream flowed through the site among discarded debris and carried a heavy load of toxic pollutants. In addition to having been selected for the 2012 Olympic

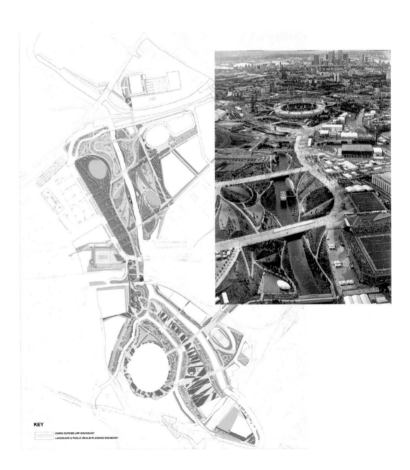

Figure 5.33 London 2012 Olympic Park, London, UK. Courtesy of Hargreaves Associates/LDA.

KEY

site, goals for the project included: revitalize and reimagine this NE quadrant of London as well as clean up toxic soil conditions, widen the existing river, increasing its water-holding capacity, improve water quality, and reconnect with the surrounding city. The master plan included a strategy where many of the Olympic facilities would be repurposed for later community use and where the surrounding property would support multiple land uses and functions. Strategies for clean-up were designed to restore water flows and habitat on the River Lee, while creating an accessible greenbelt with a system of walkways and trails, recreation venues, and other passive and active recreation opportunities.

Low Impact Development and Green Infrastructure

Landscape architects have increasingly incorporated storm-water management design services for clients. They employ what is referred to as *green infrastructure* in a variety of land and urban development projects. The application of green infrastructure in managing storm water has been adopted by public agencies under the term of *low impact design* (LID). The terms low impact design and green infra-structure generally refer to design systems and practices that mimic natural processes to infiltrate or reuse storm water on the site where it is generated rather than dispose of it off-site through an under-ground system of pipes. On-site collected storm water is allowed to percolate to recharge water aquifers and for onsite irrigation and other purposes. Green infrastructure can be used at a wide range of landscape scales and project types. The aim in employing low impact development is to replace or minimize having to construct expensive underground storm-water systems that collect water to be piped to a central wastewater treatment plant or directing the pollution-borne waters to a stream or other natural hydrologic feature. The concept is to treat storm water as a resource to be used on-site rather than as a waste product to be removed.

An example of low impact, green infrastructure is shown in Figure 5.34. The firm of Ahbé Landscape Architects of Los Angeles, CA, redesigned one side of an existing city street in Burbank, CA, with a bio-retention swale. The original street design followed a traditional approach to managing storm water, using curbs and catch basins to collect surface water, directing the captured water to an under-ground storm-water infrastructure. With the new design, surface waters are collected in a depressed planting strip that parallels the street. Surface waters are detained in the planted, linear basins and allowed to percolate to the aquifer below. The species of plants not only enhance the aesthetics of the street but take up some of the pollutants washed from the street, thus improving water quality.

Figure 5.34 *Bio-retention swale, Burbank, CA, by Ahbé Landscape Architects.*

Conclusion

The reader of this chapter should now have a better understanding of the breadth and depth of the landscape architecture profession. The work of practitioners can touch just about every aspect of people's lives, as well as the environment in which they live. The areas of practice that today's landscape architects find themselves in are challenging and at the same time provide practitioners the opportunity of making a significant impact on people's lives and their well-being. The work of practitioners also can improve the health of land, water, and other aspects of the environment.

Notes

1 Walter Isaacson in *The Innovators: How a Group of Hackers, Geniuses, and Geeks Created the Digital Revolution* (Simon & Schuster, New York, 2014), p. 408.
2 In a speech given in Aspen, Colorado, in 1964 referring to Aldeburgh, an area on the east coast of the British Isles where the English composer lived most of his life and where he stated his music came from. Alex Ross, *The Rest Is Noise* (Picador, New York, 2007), p. 448.
3 Haussmann's stated objectives were to improve traffic circulation, to provide space and light, to create views of the city landmarks, and to beautify the city. The widening of the boulevards also had a military advantage, including ease of military movement and making it more difficult for citizens to put up barricades.
4 The Getty Foundation first built the Getty Villa in Malibu, California.

Further Reading

Thomas H. Russ, *Site Planning and Design Handbook*, McGraw-Hill, New York, 2009.

Marc Treib, *Modern Landscape Architecture: A Critical Review*, MIT Press, Cambridge, MA, 1994.

Peter Valder, *Gardens in China*, Timber Press, Portland, OR, 2002.

Tim Waterman, *The Fundamentals of Landscape Architecture*, 2nd edn, Fairchild Books, London, 2015.

CHAPTER SIX

GARDENS, COMMUNITIES, PARKS, AND URBAN DESIGN

Introduction

Generally, people do not give a thought to the fact that the parks, gardens, urban public spaces, college campuses, landscapes that greet them when they go to work, arrive at an appointment, or the myriad of places they frequent during a day, were deliberately designed by someone. However, the designed places didn't just suddenly appear or fall out of the sky. They were the result of considerable thought over long extended periods of time, involving many people from many professions. Most people cannot imagine that so much thought, often involving a team of people, takes place before a project gets built and occupied. In previous chapters, discussion about the areas of consideration that go into the design of places people live, work, and play have been presented. Some of the areas of consideration include climate, functional relationships, safety, topography, views, traffic and circulation, horticulture, and much more. Most people do not think which professions were responsible for the design of places and spaces they encounter during their everyday life. The hand, mind, and artistic skill of landscape architects have played varying roles in the creative realization of many of these places. We will investigate the kinds of places landscape architects have been responsible for. The scale of the facilities and spaces can range from the very smallest parts of the built environment (see the stone vessel garden in Figure 6.1) to the extensive urban landscapes, such as the California Plaza in Los Angeles (Figure 6.23 on p. 129). Landscape architects have been involved in large infrastructure projects, such as the planning of interstate highways and their landscape installations, as well as the habitat and landscape restoration of land and river floodplains disturbed during the construction of the 864-mile-long (1390 km) oil pipeline that traverses the State of Alaska (Figure 6.35 on p. 137).

Categories are a convenient way to discuss a subject that has many subsets, as does the topic of landscape architecture design.

Figure 6.1 A: Stone vessel garden, Chinese Academy of Art, Hangzhou, China; B: Doorway garden, Vence, France.

A project type is the equivalent term for category and in this chapter we will learn about the common project types landscape architects design, beginning with gardens. While it is convenient to present the range of design work done by landscape architects under project type headings, the reader will quickly realize there is an unavoidable blur and much cross-over between project types. But nonetheless, we shall proceed.

Gardens

The word garden is freely used to cover a range of designed landscapes. In its narrowest sense, a garden is an outdoor space (open to the elements) for the display and enjoyment of plants and other natural elements (stone, wood, art, water). Specialized gardens are created to attract wildlife such as hummingbirds, butterflies, and dragonflies—yes, dragonflies. The activities of cultivation and care are associated with gardens, suggesting a degree of human toil in order for a garden to remain healthy and capable of functioning as intended. Cultivation involves systematic, routine maintenance and care. It takes work to care for and maintain a garden. The request by clients for a design that requires low maintenance does not mean no maintenance, as all gardens, regardless of the plants selected, irrigation system installed, and a variety of amenities, will still require maintenance if the garden is to survive, let alone flourish. One usually associates caring with a garden as opposed to a park or urban public landscape, where the personal activities required for caring for the garden are practical and not necessarily a personalized enterprise. A residential garden, for instance, might be created out of a love or appreciation for plants or for some utilitarian purpose such as a rain garden to collect and retain storm water. This is in contrast with a garden installed on the grounds of a commercial building where the need for a garden may have something to do with meeting a government requirement (landscape ordinance) or as an economic strategy for attracting customers, renters, and possibly investors.

Residential gardens are generally created for enjoyment. They are meant to be attractive to look at. They also make the surrounding residential structures more attractive and add economic value to the property and surrounding neighborhood. Gardens are used to entertain family and guests, to serve the outdoor activity needs of the owners, in some cases with specialized additions such as a swimming pool, game court (basketball, tennis), and children's play structures. They also can be designed to accommodate animals, such as a dog or even have an animal husbandry function, such as in raising laying hens. And, finally, gardens provide space for a hobby such as a bonsai collection, a greenhouse for propagation, or a studio environment.

Gardens are not permanent, installed to remain forever. Plants grow and mature. Some species proliferate either by seed or other multiplying process. Some species in a planting area proliferate, thrive, and in some cases take over, with the loss of other species not as successful in the garden environment where they were planted. Sunlight accessibility may change with the growth of one plant, such as a tree that shades out plants less tolerant to shade, while others are more tolerant of sunlight and will become aggressive to the detriment of shading-loving plants exposed to sunlight. For some gardens, the owner, in consultation with a landscape architect, will plan a garden to change with the season. Annual species are planned to be rotated or changed-out from season to season such as planting for showy spring display followed by summer, then winter performances. Annual and perennial gardens have a long history, particularly in northern climates where the changing seasons signal to garden enthusiasts the time to make their garden ready for the coming season.

Increasingly popular are gardens that incorporate food production in addition to their ornamental purpose. Kitchen gardens were once a necessity in early Roman times and the Middle Ages, then later during World War II, when victory gardens proliferated in urban, residential gardens. Fresh produce is the reward for those willing to commit to caring for a vegetable garden, as for the gardeners who plant and care for fruit trees and fruit-bearing vines and shrubs. Community gardens in the United States have been popular not only as a way to provide fresh produce,[1] but also to reclaim vacant or abandoned property as a strategy to reinvigorate a declining neighborhood.

Finally, most created landscapes we refer to as gardens are the work of home-owners. People with no specialized training but are do-it-yourselfers who install their garden over time, often without a plan or at best a rough plan devised after researching garden publications and magazines. A landscape architect or design-build landscape contractor designs a small percentage of residential and commercial gardens. For the most part, the gardens in this chapter are the creative work of landscape architects.

The stone vessel in Figure 6.1A is not intended as a garden in the strict definition of garden. The stone planter was set in an expansive rock-paved university campus space to provide enjoyment and limit vehicular access. As it turns out, there are several of these miniature "gardens" set in the space and they represent the only plant life in the immediate area. These miniature gardens are in some ways a symbolic gesture to infuse something living in what is otherwise a space dominated by paving and classroom buildings. In fact, these miniature gardens posses considerable power as they make a surprisingly formidable visual impact, much greater than their size would suggest. The power of a landscape for the human psyche is significant as can be seen in Figure 6.1B. The scene is of a long, continuous row of residences that bound a narrow street in the village of Vence, located in the hills of Southern France above Nice. While most residential streets in the town have no space for front yards as we know them in North America, the residents manage to make room for gardens consisting of potted plants that can be moved indoors during the cold winter months of the year. This is another example of

Figure 6.2 A: *Residential courtyard, Delft; B: Campus courtyard, Nijmegen, the Netherlands; C: Japanese garden.*

the visual impact that a few well-chosen and placed plants can have to infuse life and sense of nature in an architecture-dominated space.

Moving up in scale, there are three examples of gardens, shown in Figure 6.2, situated in spaces bounded by building walls and where trees are the dominant plant intervention signifying garden: a place to be enjoyed and to add visual interest to a space. The residential courtyard (Figure 6.2A) in a historic neighborhood of Delft in the Netherlands is composed of a single tree, more or less in the center of the space, planted in a panel of clipped lawn, and ringed by a cobbled walkway. The tree is a young horse chestnut, a handsome choice that will provide visual variety and interest in foliage coloration changes from season to season. In the winter the structure of the tree branching adds a sculpture-like element to the space. Two other examples in Figure 6.2 show how trees and their strategic placement in a space add visual interest and sense of life. Figure 6.2B shows how a largely paved open space bound by buildings can be brought to life with trees while Figure 6.2C suggests how a tree grouping adds vertical interest and structure in an enclosed landscaped public garden.

The open space defined by three classroom-buildings in Figure 6.3 is left-over space seemingly without thought of accommodating a garden in the sense we have been describing a garden so far. The space has the potential of being transformed into a garden and perhaps was intended to be developed as such at a later date. However, in its present state, it is reduced to grass, a few scattered trees and lonely shrubs, and stepping-stones. The space does afford circulation and perhaps access to one of the buildings. The space was treated simply as a flexible, multi-purpose place for students to hang out with friends between classes. By providing moveable chairs the space would attract greater use. The absence of plants (shrubs and more trees) could be interpreted that the space was intended for flexible use, including the display of student-built architectural structures constructed as part of a design assignment or informal recreation. The minimal landscape treatment complements the architectural style of the buildings.

The following images of gardens are contemporary designs, beginning with the Modernist garden icon, the Donnell residence by Thomas Church, located in the foothills above the Napa River, north of San Francisco (see Figure 5.10 on p. 95). The garden consists of several acres of linked spaces with a meandering pathway, allowing movement from one garden in a planned sequence to the next. What is considered the back garden or family activity area is dominated by the views of the adjacent Napa Valley landscape and the swimming pool with supporting deck and hardscape areas for family outdoor activities and entertainment. The shape of the pool is attributed to the young Lawrence Halprin who apprenticed with Thomas Church. The form of the pool was informed by the pattern of meandering wetlands along the Napa River visible below the property. The design of the water

Figure 6.3 In between space architecture: classroom building, Chinese Academy of Art, Hangzhou, China.

Figure 6.4 *Steele Indian School Park, Phoenix, Arizona, by Christine Ten Eyck.*

feature at Steele Indian School Park, Phoenix, AZ, by Christine Ten Eyck Landscape Architects was inspired in part from the ephemeral springs found nearby in the high desert mountains in the Phoenix region (Figure 6.4). The water is allowed to trickle down a series of stepped, rock terraces. The steps continue to the bottom of one side of the pool of water enticing park visitors to take off their shoes, get their feet wet, and cool off.

Steve Martino, FASLA, has practiced landscape architecture for many years in the Phoenix–Scottsdale, Arizona area, a desert landscape in Southwest United States. He organizes his garden spaces with contemporary architectural walls and building renovations of his own design and develops landscape compositions using native species to create visually exciting spaces of flexible functionality. His gardens have the important added quality of conserving precious water, by choosing plant species and preparing their planting beds with low water demand, similar to the natural desert landscape of the region. The two images of the entry garden shown in Figure 6.5 located in Scottsdale, Arizona, demonstrate the concept of "inside-outside." The concept was popularized in California, beginning in the 1950s, with the emerging emphasis in residential architecture design to create the feeling that the views of the adjoining garden could be an extension of indoor rooms. This was accomplished by installing large sliding glass doors that allowed viewing to the outside garden during colder weather, then allowing the garden to extend indoors during warmer weather with the doors open as shown in Figure 6.5A. Figure 6.5B is the same garden viewed from the entry gate.

Two very different residential gardens are shown in Figure 6.6. The garden in Figure 6.6A is an example of the use of native plants

Figure 6.5 *Two views of a residential garden in Scottsdale, Arizona, by Steve Martino, landscape architect.*

Figure 6.6 Two Scottsdale, Arizona, residences, by Steve Martino, landscape architect.

selected for their form, color, texture, and also for their low water use demands. The plant composition provides a soft visual contrast to the colored wall panels and concrete fountain. Note the absence of grass, a water conservation decision. The ground plane consists of densely packed crushed gravel that not only reduces the proliferation of unwanted weeds but also allows rainwater to penetrate into the soil and to further conserve water. The outdoor patio and garden in Figure 6.6B are as much an artistic composition as a setting for outdoors living. The walls were set at a height to allow views out into the surrounding native hills and landscape. The views of this landscape follow a Japanese concept of the "borrowed landscape." The designer considered incorporating the views of the outside landscape in the composition created for the

Figure 6.7 Residential garden, Escazu, Costa Rica, by Ana Pinto, landscape architect.

outdoor garden room. Native plants were selected for the garden extending the visual connection to the surrounding native landscape.

The residential garden in Figure 6.7 also uses native plant species. The garden is located in a highland tropical zone of Costa Rica. The plants are tropical species with lush green, shiny foliage in contrast to the fine-textured, dull gray foliage of an upper desert region shown in Figure 6.6. Concern for water conservation is not an issue since the garden and surrounding countryside experience heavy annual rainfall. Supplemental irrigation is rarely required. Routine maintenance is required to control the robust growth of the vegetation. Seasonal color adds further interest to this garden. Plants were selected based not only the color and leaf form composition but also the overall structural quality of the plants.

The view of the garden shown in Figure 6.8 is from the dining room looking out to the extensive grounds of the property. This is another example where the designers—the home-owners—achieved the visual effect of the garden extending into the home with the view

Figure 6.8 *Ross-Guevara residence, Escazu, Costa Rica.*

Figure 6.9 *Public garden at main entrance to the Rijksmuseum National Museum in Amsterdam, the Netherlands.*

reaching out into the garden background. The depth of the view is coaxed to the back of the garden by a covered entertainment shelter. Stepping-stones in the foreground lead the view toward the covered cabaña at the back of the garden.

Another type of garden, a garden for an institutional building, is shown in Figure 6.9. The garden is reminiscent of an Italian hillside garden, popular during the Renaissance. However, the garden is located in Amsterdam and is partially hidden from view from the street by walls. The charming garden provides a welcome relief of abundant plantings to greet visitors coming to see the art housed in the Rijksmuseum. It is meant for visitors to pause and enjoy the garden before stepping into another world of exhibition halls displaying the masterpieces by Rembrandt, Vermeer and others. The garden prepares the visitor for a more contemplative experience by providing a quiet vegetated space in sharp contrast to the bustle and noise of the streets outside the walled grounds. The sound of splashing water from the central fountain not only adds refreshing relief but also distracts the attention of the visitor from the sounds coming from the adjacent city street. The shiny green foliage tends to intensify the color of flowering plants dispersed sparingly throughout the garden. The sounds of water and layered plantings in the garden prepare the visitors mentally for their next spatial experience that awaits them in the museum interior.

Two different institutional gardens are paired together in Figure 6.10. Both provide a comfortable, human-scale retreat from their dense downtown locations. Plantings, shaded outdoor seating and moving water provide a pleasant ambience to meet friends and enjoy a meal in an outdoor setting of a popular market in Austin, Texas (Figure 6.10A). The garden is organized around the theme of an intermittent stream that winds through the main circulation space with a variety of seating—tables with chairs and informal garden seat walls—one needs to "cross over" to get to the adjoining seating areas. The winding path of stone pavers circulates through an outdoor garden for use of patrons and tourists to the Los Angeles Disney Concert Hall (Figure 6.10B). This is another example of a quiet garden retreat for visitors to relax and enjoy just a few steps away from heavy vehicle traffic traversing the government and cultural arts district of downtown Los Angeles.

The Yu garden (Figure 6.11) located in an older district of central Shanghai, China, was organized to facilitate visitor enjoyment of the garden by a carefully devised circulation system. The garden was originally created for a revered government functionary and later in the twentieth century became a city property opened to the public. The gardens were created as a retreat into nature for the family, following a traditional Chinese garden concept where the plant, water, and rock elements were composed as symbols of nature. While to the Western eye the garden would be described as "natural," the plants receive the heavy hand of the gardener to train and form the

Figure 6.10 A: Outdoor eating area, Whole Foods Market, Austin, Texas; B: Disney Concert Hall garden terrace, Los Angeles, California.

Figure 6.11 *Yu Garden, Shanghai, China.*

plants to achieve a stylized ideal of scenes found in natural settings. Much attention was devoted to the design of the path system. This attention to detail included the choice of materials so arranged to enhance the experience of the garden visitor and set the pace punctuated with walkway sections that caused the viewer to pause or walk more carefully. The designer of the garden had in mind to control both the elements of the garden and the experience of the visitor.

The Japanese garden located in the extensive grounds of the Huntington Garden is one of several specialty gardens that attracts visitors was originally an estate of the Huntington family (one of the early pioneers of the American railroad

Figure 6.12 *A and B: Stairs leading to Japanese garden exhibit, Huntington Garden, San Martino, California; C: Historical garden, Kyoto, Japan.*

dynasty). Americans as well as other Westerners greatly admired the gardens encountered in Japan, China, and Asia in general. Design elements have been adopted in part or in total from the Japanese traditional garden in creating private and public gardens in the West since the nineteenth century. The garden in Figures 6.12A and 6.12B is a fine example of the Japanese garden tradition with its collection and display of bonsai plants, a raked gravel Zen garden, and the larger, expansive garden that winds up and down a hilly slope of the Huntington Garden grounds. The extensive grounds maintenance program attests to the authenticity of this garden's origins. While to the freshman eye the plantings appear natural, they are anything but. Trees and shrubs require routine pruning. Guy wires and wooden supports serve a similar function to teeth braces to bend and cajole branches and trunks into a shapely ideal. The shapes of plants are not an accident, often their form is meant to represent a particular bird species or other significant element of nature. The garden in Figure 6.12C is a historical Japanese garden in Kyoto, Japan, once belonging to a family and is now open to the public as a cultural site. The garden was created as a place for contemplation and relief from busy urban life beyond its walls. It was a fabricated landscape, an artistic creation of the gardeners whose design was inspired by nature following Japanese design traditions for which Kyoto is well known. The garden requires continuous maintenance in order to retain its appearance of a natural scene frozen in time.

BIV or building-integrated vegetation has joined an alphabet of other initiatives to counter the environmental degrading impacts of urban growth and intense natural resources use of the past half-century. LID or low impact design and BMP or best management practices are two related initiatives to improve water quality and reduce the potentially destructive actions of storm water surface runoff. BIV (building-integrated vegetation) is a relatively new government initiative that makes use of old building technologies towards reducing the effects of rising air pollution, urban heat island build-up, reducing storm-water runoff, and loss of biodiversity and green spaces in urban environments. The increasing awareness of these health-threatening issues as well as the race among cities to improve their competitive advantage to attract individuals and business preferring to live in healthy, sustainable cities has compelled cities to adopt BMP, LID, BIV, and other sustainable development initiatives. The implementation of LID and the other more sustainable water management systems are realized primarily at the local rather than the federal level through the requirements of building codes, administrative directives, and financial incentives.

Examples of building-integrated vegetation are shown in Figure 6.13 and include green roofs and vertical gardens. Green roofs have been around for millennia and can be found in many cold regions of the world such as the sod roofs built in remote areas of Arctic North America and in the Scandinavian countries. Vertical gardens are a relatively recent phenomenon popularized by the French artist-horticulturist Patrick Blanc as well as visionary architects and proponents of green architecture (see Figure 5.21 on p. 101). Technological advances in building construction and horticultural innovations (new

Figure 6.13 Roof garden, Lake Merritt, Oakland, California.

soil mixes, automatic irrigation, soil moisture sensors, for example) have supported what amounts to experimental gardening on building walls and roofs. Product manufacturers have designed and marketed specialized support systems and products for building integrated gardens. In the case of Patrick Blanc, he holds numerous patents for his vertical garden innovations.

Gardens are generally spaces to be experienced passively for enjoyment or for their sensual inspiration and health benefits. They also enhance the aesthetic aspects of the space and surrounding built environment as well as increase the economic value for development. Gardens are often contemplative spaces to be experienced through the senses while parks are places to exercise the body by individuals, or places to visit when engaging in sports with others. Both can be places for socializing. In the case of parks, the process is, for the most part, socialization through activity while for gardens, socialization is a more passive interaction. Put simply, gardens are a special place for the mind while parks are places for the body. There are of course exceptions to this simplistic characterization of the two types of outdoor spaces.

Parks

Both the New York City Park Department and the US National Park Service contain the word *park* in the name of their organization. In the case of the New York City Park, parks have been established primarily to serve the outdoor recreation and in some case a diverse range of entertainment wishes of urban dwellers. The system of parks also supports specialized purposes, such as educational (botanic gardens and zoos) and social (community gardens for the production of fresh produce). The word *park* in the US National Park Service holds another meaning. The word refers to natural—in some cases, wild—landscapes or properties including historic sites and structures that have been set aside to conserve specific ecosystems, wildlife species, historical sites and property, memorials (for people or events), and other historical or culturally significant places. Other departments, including the US Forest Service and the National Wildlife Service, oversee large expanses of federal lands for purposes that include resource management of forests, minerals, and animal and fish conservation. These federal agencies also support human activities, such as backcountry hiking, skiing, hunting and fishing, wildlife viewing and education, and other outdoor recreation activities. The prime mission of the US National Park Service is not recreation as is generally understood in the establishment of city and municipal parks. That is not to say municipalities do not manage historically or culturally significant properties, as they most definitely do. The Emerald Necklace park system in the City of Boston primarily serves an outdoor recreation function for its citizens. The Emerald Necklace also was created to solve flooding problems in the city with lands set aside and developed to manage storm water, in addition to serving recreation uses, including organized sports, picnicking, boating, and trails.

Parks can be found in all sizes from small "vest pocket parks," a half-acre in size or smaller, created on slivers of leftover urban spaces and suburban areas to larger parks serving multi-purpose functions of 5–10 acres (2–4 hectares). There are large city or regional parks of 500–1000 acres (200–400 hectares) also containing multiple functions including nature trails, horseback riding, a golf course, a zoo, a botanical garden, and river-based greenways.

The reason city, state, and federal governments have established their park system was to meet the evolving needs of the citizens these organizations serve. Municipalities began establishing public parks a couple of centuries ago. The primary purpose was to provide passive recreation functions. Parks meant for passive recreation were for the pleasure of citizens in an outdoor, nature-dominated or garden setting. It was not until well into the twentieth century—primarily in post-World War II America—that specialized facilities for active sports, including team sports, were introduced into municipal parks. Children's play areas filled with swings, merry-go-rounds and other equipment were built at a pace barely keeping up with the families fleeing to live in the suburbs and planned communities associated with urban flight. The evolution as to what one might expect to find in a municipal park has followed the desire trends and the interests of the citizens served. Specialized parks such as skateboard and extreme sports parks have gained in popularity recently. Parks departments have reached out to provide educational opportunities in partnership with broader initiatives of other agencies charged with restoring wetlands, river greenways, and other once degraded and dysfunctional land resources.

The following examples represent the tip of the iceberg in terms of what parks are and how they function and serve the public. This is not an exhaustive review but should serve as a window view for those interested in a career designing parks.

Bryant Park in New York City is an example of a park that has had several different lives. It has been a part of the city's history, beginning in the mid-seventeenth century when the nearly 10-acre parcel was set aside as public use space. The park underwent numerous transformations, perhaps the most successful being its current condition. During the 1970s, the park was taken over by drug dealers, the homeless, and elements that made ordinary citizens feel uncomfortable and unsafe, and they tended to avoid it. In 1988, a team was selected to redesign the park using the opportunity for constructing underground parking and storage for the public library. The primary design goal was to open up the park to the streets and encourage diverse passive activities, including programmed events, such as concerts or evening showings of films. The photograph in Figure 6.14A is of the large central lawn area on a sunny day. The photograph in Figure 6.14B was taken hours later as a crowd of people filled the lawn prior to a planned late afternoon concert. A species of turf grass was selected with a specially designed soil mix and underground drainage system to survive the anticipated intense traffic of people. To achieve a feeling that this was a safe park to enter, the

Figure 6.14 *Main lawn area (before and after concert on the lawn performance) at Bryant Park, New York City, by Hanna/Olin.*

Figure 6.15 *Houtan River Park in Shanghai, China, by Turenscape.*

arrangement of plantings and outdoor seating considered creating unobstructed sight lines from the surrounding sidewalk and street into the park.

The paucity of useable or accessible open space for park purposes has led to authorities including park activity programming of river and wetland restoration efforts in urban areas. The examples in Figure 6.15 demonstrate how river and wetland restoration can successfully incorporate passive and educational functions. The site was a derelict and despoiled section of river passing through a neglected and underutilized industrial section of Shanghai, China. The restoration of the river, together with the planning and design of several outdoor education venues, provided the infrastructure to meet the heavy demand for an outdoor, green experience of city residents, especially families and school-aged children.

Amphitheaters such as those shown in Figure 6.16 are most always one of many facilities in a more extensive park, campus, or open space. The two in Figure 6.16 are very different and show the range of design possibilities and settings that can be created to serve outdoor performance or educational activities. The small amphitheater in Figure 6.16A is located on a historical property in the small border city of Hidalgo in the Lower Rio Grande River Valley of Texas. The facility is used primarily to present public education events. The much larger amphitheater located in a San Francisco city park is capable of handling large numbers of people for musical concerts and dramatic arts programs (Figure 6.16B). The design provides a variety of seating arrangements including stadium seating (stepped rows) of broad grassy terraces to accommodate picnics and groups wishing to socialize.

Children's play areas can be found in public parks such as in Figure 6.17 and K-6 school grounds. In schools, children's playgrounds generally serve an exercise function, a component of physical education. Playgrounds in public parks are provided as an outdoor recreation facility (Figure 6.18). They are constructed to serve as an amenity to attract families to condominium or apartment complexes as shown in Figure 6.20 on p. 127. Where there is adequate space or when the program demands, children's play equipment is clustered into age groups. The groupings can be as simple as toddlers, 5–7 or 8 years, and ages of 8–10. In America, where a litigious environment exists, great care and research are involved in the design of the play structures and the surface in which the structures are placed. Consideration of accessibility is also an important design criterion. With the litigious nature of American society, landscape architects rarely design the play equipment. Rather, they select equipment from catalogues from play equipment manufacturers thus shifting design liability claims to the manufacturer in the event of an injury. Fortunately the design of children's play equipment has become so competitive that the manufacturers are continually offering new products with greater variety with add-on items. In the example in Figure 6.17, the landscape architect selected the equipment from the play equipment catalogue, thus shifting his creative attention to the design of the surface and spatial environment that contain the play structures. This has become a common approach that limits the professional liability of the designer, allowing the creation of often highly inventive play spaces that receive heavy use.

Sport parks such as for team soccer and baseball can be found in the smallest community as well as large urban ones. Multiplexes of baseball

Figure 6.16 A: Amphitheater, Hidalgo, Texas; B: Stern Grove Amphitheater, San Francisco, California, by Lawrence Halprin.

Figure 6.17 Tongva Park, Santa Monica, California, by James Corner, landscape architect.

Figure 6.18 *Children's playground, Hangzhou, China, by Yuancheng Landscape Group.*

Figure 6.19 *West End Skateboard Park, Albuquerque, New Mexico, by Morrow Reardon Wilkinson, landscape architects.*

and soccer fields have been designed to host tournaments, attracting teams both nationally and internationally. The list of specialized park venues can be expected to expand as other sports become popular (Frisbee golf, for example) while the need for traditional passive or pleasure parks will continue and perhaps increase in popularity as urban growth and density increase. One example of a specialized park is the skateboard park shown in Figure 6.19. Designers have established consulting specializations for skateboard and water parks, extreme sports, dirt bike motocross, and competitive sports training complexes such as for Olympic kayaking. Landscape architects teaming with various engineering specialties have established practices of international scope for designing ski venues and zoos. The technology and construction detailing involved have come to support the establishment of specialized, niche consulting practices.

The parks shown in Figures 6.20 and 6.21 were designed to accommodate a great variety of functions for individual users, small and large groups, for hosting team sport events, and for specialized purposes. Grand Park in Los Angeles is situated in a government complex to serve daytime employees during the week. It is then transformed into a family-oriented or performance venue on weekends (Figure 6.20). The two parks in Figure 6.21 are large city parks, each with a unique aesthetic character with a design informed by historical or cultural precedence. The park in Madrid (Figure 6.21A) is organized with reference to the agricultural traditions of the location. The Parc Bercy in Paris[2] (Figure 6.21B) was constructed on what was historically a wine warehouse and distribution center with railroad and river barge transportation elements. Some of the historical artifacts were repurposed for passive recreation uses, such as the remnant canal in Figure 6.21B. The park in Santa Fe, New Mexico (see Figure 5.14B on p. 97) is aptly named Railroad Park and was a leftover portion of rail switching yards that were abandoned many years ago. Much of the layout and design used and adapted railroad elements in creating a railroad theme.

Figure 6.20 Los Angeles Grand Park, by Rios Clementi Hale Studio, landscape architects.

Figure 6.21 A: Manzaneras Park, Madrid, Spain, by West 8; B: Parc Bercy, Paris, France.

Urban Design

Urban design is another term with a broad definition with significant implications for the life and health of cities. It is the art and science of creating and giving shape to cities and towns—both large and small. Urban design, through the consideration of a complex range of subjects that work together, establishes a physical framework that organizes streets, blocks, and land uses. Urban designers also establish building groupings and densities, the location of public and private spaces, and all the physical elements that generate place-making or urban form where people live, work, or recreate. One can gain specialized academic preparation in the discipline of urban planning and design. The academic curriculum involves a range of subjects that includes economics, sociology, transportation planning, real estate development, government policy, and something broadly called urban design. In practice, urban design blends architecture, landscape architecture, city planning, and engineering.

A

B

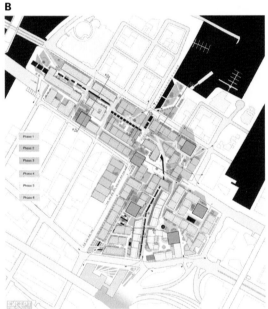

C

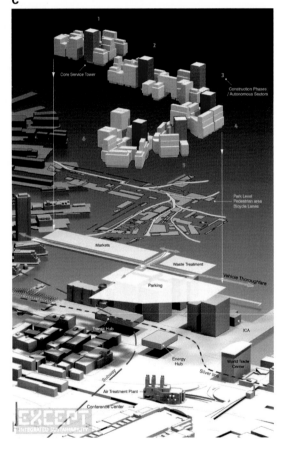

Figure 6.22 *Boston Fort Point Master Plan: A: Transportation planning; B: Layering of planned components; C: Master plan. Images provided courtesy of Except Integrated Sustainability.*

Landscape architects, by a combination of education, training, and experience, are major players in urban design projects, particularly in areas of the design or redesign of streets and public infrastructure, public use areas, or waterfront improvements for public use. Urban design now considers ecosystem restoration (such as wetlands), and emerging areas related to improving urban environmental quality. The aim is to develop urban plans that not only indicate the optimum layout for blocks, streets, and buildings but will also reduce energy consumption, improve air and water quality, and in general improve the health and quality[3] of living in urban environments.

The project in Figure 6.22 is an example of a typical, comprehensive urban planning project. The project was headed by the Netherlands firm of Except Integrated Sustainability and includes recommendations for the redevelopment of a historic section of Boston, MA, to improve the transportation network, introduce substantial public open space, and increase useable building floor space for the district, while considering sustainable strategies of construction.

Figure 6.23A is an example of an urban design project involving the design of a series of interconnected public use spaces for a dense office and commercial complex located in downtown Los Angeles. The public use spaces are accessible by a sequence of circulation routes and public spaces connecting to a nearby cultural arts district and a governmental complex. A dense high-rise residential development is afforded access by the same circulation system. Figure 6.23A is a central open space (Water Court) serving restaurants with public seating enjoyed at noontime by office employees in the neighborhood. The space includes a stage for music and other performance programs. The design includes several levels of terraces for circulation and outdoor uses. The terraces contain vegetation to provide visual interest and shade as well as reduce glare from the adjacent buildings. The stairway and ramps that provide access from the street are shown in Figure 6.23B. A fountain in the lower-level plaza greets pedestrians. This lower plaza by POD[4] and Sasaki Associates then continues through a breezeway lined with shops and restaurants between

Figure 6.23 California Plaza, Los Angeles, CA: A: Water Court; B: Lower plaza access, by POD and Sasaki Associates.

Figure 6.24 *Shinsaiwaibashi Office building and the inclusion of art in a public space, Tokyo, Japan.*

the office buildings to the Water Court. The design is a successful fabric of interconnected, comfortable people spaces and building levels. It is a popular destination for visitors and office workers from the surrounding complex of buildings with comfortable pedestrian access.

The two public plazas (see Figure 5.2 on p. 89 and Figure 6.24) are further examples of reimagined public park spaces created with the effective installation of art and imaginative water features. Both projects are makeovers of public spaces that had been transformed into heavily used open spaces serving adjacent dense commercial areas with design involvement of landscape architects.

Landscape architects design projects on undeveloped sites as well as work to create new designs to breathe new life into and enhance economic activity for existing built areas. The Shanghai office of SWA was asked by their client to reimagine and come up with a more pedestrian-oriented urban space in a dense residential and commercial neighborhood of Shanghai. Golden Street (Figure 6.25) is the result. A previous, heavily trafficked urban street was transformed into a pedestrian-friendly corridor of gardens, fountains, and event spaces with the removal of vehicles except for the occasional service vehicles that have access to make deliveries to businesses along the street. A dense planting of trees provides needed shade for the comfort of visitors. Great masses of shrub planting provide seasonal visual interest and serve to define and provide needed separation from various functional areas such as outdoor cafés, children's play area, and other spaces created for small groups to meet or evening dancers who come to exercise.

Figure 6.25 *Golden Street, Shanghai, China, by SWA Group.*

Figure 6.26 *Jin River Park in Harbin, China, by Harbin Institute of Technology, Design & Research Institute.*

As part of an extensive commercial and residential development for a section of Harbin, China, the Jin River Park was created over an underground commercial shopping mall and parking. The mall and parking serve the surrounding residential towers. The pyramid landforms seen in Figure 6.26 include skylights to bring natural light to lower underground levels. The geometric forms provide visual relief to what is otherwise an oversized and exposed, paved surface. The pyramidal forms (essentially sections of roof for the mall below) include sufficient soil depth to support plant growth, primarily shrub and perennial species.

Educational and Commercial Campuses

Telefónica headquarters is an office campus of high-rise buildings located north of the central historic district of Madrid. The buildings face onto an extensive central landscaped space used by employees and visitors. The space is divided into a series of large outdoor rooms made visually coherent by the extensive tree planting. Several spaces include a water element such as shown in Figure 6.27. In this example a canal appears to transport water from one basin of water to another. The canal and the large column of water visible in the background provide continuous movement and aeration of water. The sound of water provides background ambient noise to dampen the heavy street traffic outside the office complex. Group and individual seating arrangements are located throughout the space to accommodate informal office meetings or a quiet oasis for individuals to have a bit of solitude.

Figure 6.28 shows central open spaces on three different university campuses. All three function as gathering places for students to socialize, eat lunch or have a coffee, and as an outdoor study space. The landscape plantings in Figures 6.28A and 6.28B consist of primarily native plant species. The landscape character of the space at the University of the Algarve captures the spirit of the native upland pine forest of the region while the landscape plantings at the university space in San Francisco are arranged in panels of color, reminiscent of abstract paintings. An abstract painting is a two-dimensional composition that in skilled hands can communicate three-dimensional qualities. The essentially two-dimensional design of this central landscape confines the space to be dominated by the surrounding high-rise classroom buildings. The seating space at Rice University (see Figure 6.28C) is a smaller space than the other two examples. It was designed to be comfortable and intimate and this was achieved by the planting of a dense tree canopy. The canopy provides needed shade. A long, narrow trough of water adds an element of serenity complementing the intimacy and sense of refuge one feels being in the outdoor room.

Figure 6.27 Telefónica headquarters, interior courtyard, Madrid, Spain, by Rafael de La-Hoz Castanys, architect, and Marion Weber, landscape architect.

Figure 6.28 A: *University of the Algarve in Faro, Portugal;*
B: *University of California, Mission Bay Campus, San Francisco;*
C: *Brochstein Pavilion at Rice University in Houston, Texas, by the*
Office of James Burnett.

Waterfronts

As a project type, the design of a waterfront can be challenging as well as rewarding. Waterfronts are challenging for a number of reasons; first of all, they involve a dynamic, flowing element (a river or stream). Waterfront projects generally are initiated to transform and make the edge more accessible and pedestrian-friendly, which means removing what is often a tangle of commercial and industrial structures. The land use conversion includes creating a continuous park-like greenway with commercial, entertainment, and residential uses set back from the water's edge. An example of this transformation of a waterfront edge is shown in Figure 6.29. These transformations require consideration of hydrologic and seasonal water fluctuations and often-toxic soil conditions found on the sites. The complexities of the physical and dynamic conditions involved require a team approach, using the planning and design experience of a landscape architect, the scientific knowledge of a hydrologist, the professional experience of an engineer (of various specializations), and in the case of a coastal environment, other scientists and engineering specialists to arrive at a practical as well as a visually attractive solution.

The river waterfront in Bilbao, Spain, shown in Figure 6.29A was not previously accessible to the public as the river was considered a working river used for shipping and lined with warehouses and industries. With the construction of the Guggenheim Museum at the water's edge, the city began a cultural rebirth, as part of a larger process in the city's ambition to reinvent itself as a tourist attraction and more diversified economy. The boat mooring and warehousing functions were replaced by a continuous park and promenade connecting new visitor venues such as the Guggenheim Museum, residential living, and commercial establishments. Dramatic and extensive outdoor lighting extended the use of the river edge into the evening. Just about any city with a river flowing through it has traditionally turned its back to the river for recreation and cultural functions. The tide, so to speak, has turned and as the remnants of the industrial revolution have outlived their economic usefulness, cities now foresee new economic and social advantages by making their water edges more attractive and increasing the livability and health of the city. The Paseo de Santa Lucia River walk in Monterrey, Mexico, is a 1.6 mile (2.3 km) reconstructed drainage canal connecting the central downtown to a park and entertainment venue in what was previously an industrial steel mill plant (Figure 6.29B).

The water body in Figure 6.30 was once a nearly invisible flow of water buried in the urban fabric of a densely populated historical neighborhood in Beijing. The neighborhood was supplanted with the construction of the Beijing 2008 Summer Olympic venue. As part of the planning and design of the project, the river was restored with a park-like greenway, complete with reconstructed wetlands. Trails were constructed along the greenway and, as can be seen in Figure 6.30, a boardwalk and viewing platform were included in the design to allow public access to the water's edge. The plant species for the wetlands along the river edge were selected to perform a water cleansing function as well as wildlife habitat.

Buffalo Bayou in Houston, Texas, (see Figure 5.27 on p. 105) is another example of a nearly forgotten watercourse that for years was considered an eyesore and a threat to adjacent neighborhoods due to flooding during periodic heavy rains and storms. The City of Houston, like so many urban areas, had turned its back to the water's edge, not seeing the multiple advantages of visual and

Figure 6.29 A: Bilbao waterfront promenade, Bilbao, Spain; B: Paseo de Santa Lucia walk, Monterrey, Mexico, by Enrique Albarroa, landscape architect.

Figure 6.30 Beijing 2008 Olympic Park waterfront and river restoration, Beijing, China.

physical access by including a continuous parkway and trail system along its waterway corridors. The redesign of Buffalo Bayou was originally conceived as a flood control project. The design included increasing the floodwater-holding capacity (detention) of the waterway by widening the bayou. In addition, physical obstructions were removed to enhance the water flow. The city took the opportunity of re-envisioning Buffalo Bayou as a park-like corridor. The added benefit of this approach accommodated the addition of pedestrian walks, ramps, and bridges that increased visitor access from adjacent neighborhoods. A continuous trail system was also built with pocket parks spotted along the greenway to further serve the outdoor recreation needs of an increasing urban population.

Environmental Restoration

Low impact design (LID) and other storm-water management design initiatives are covered in Chapter 5. Traditionally public works departments have constructed and managed extensive systems to gather and transport (essentially a system to get rid of) storm water or rainwater through underground pipes to a water treatment plant

or directly into rivers and wetlands. The possibility that this water could have beneficial use was not appreciated, given what was considered a cheap, almost inexhaustible resource. Today, with growing numbers of urban and regional areas experiencing water shortages, we are slowly coming to realize the benefits and opportunities of conserving storm-water runoff by basically devising ways of keeping it on site rather than disposing of it. Shown in Figure 6.31 is a project where a city utility rethought how to better manage storm water and hired a landscape architecture firm to design a series of landscape interventions to retain surface water on site. This was accomplished by the elimination of area catch basins and redesigning the street curb and gutter system. In Figure 6.31A is a newly constructed rain garden in what was a previously paved surface with area catch basins. The area was re-graded and repurposed as an outdoor garden for employee use during lunch or for holding community events. Rainwater is directed to the rain gardens that were first prepared with a series of depressions for detaining water. The detained water is allowed to percolate to the subsurface to recharge the natural underground water aquifer. The photograph in Figure 6.31B shows bioswales constructed between the sidewalk and the street. Breaks in the concrete curb were made to enable water to flow into the bio-swale or to an overflow area in the background. The water then percolates into the soil to replenish the ground water below.

Figure 6.31 *Burbank, California, utility campus: A: Rain garden; B: Bio-swale in central interior space, by Ahbé Landscape Architects.*

The Netherlands, a country with a long history of comprehensive storm-water management, has applied low impact design and best management practices throughout the country (in both urban and rural areas). The use of a modular pavement system reduces the unsightly disruption of tearing out street and sidewalk pavement for maintenance repairs of underground infrastructure such as potable water and electricity distribution lines. The modular pavement is easily replaced with little evidence of the repairs, such as the ubiquitous patchwork of pavement repairs that are visible on American roads, paved areas, and walkways.

The circulation corridor through the Delft Technical University is shown in Figure 6.32A. Three distinct traffic lanes exist side by side serving motor vehicles, bicycles, and pedestrian traffic. The surface material used for all three is either modular units or porous material allowing rainwater to penetrate to the subsoil below. The use of modular pavement in a residential neighborhood, also located in the Netherlands, is shown in Figure 6.32B. Water is allowed to penetrate the different modular surfaces rather than be carried off to be disposed off-site.

Crissy Field, a former airfield serving the historic U.S. Army Presidio,[5] is now part of the Golden Gate National Recreation Area in San Francisco, California. The scene in Figure 6.33 is of the restored bay wetlands and wildlife habitat accessible from a popular public park, both designed by Hargreaves Associates, landscape architects. The wetlands were restored using native estuarine and upland plants accessible by raised boardwalks. The location has spectacular views of the Golden Gate Bridge and the San Francisco skyline with the backdrop of the surrounding coastal mountain range. Many of the native plants were planted by organized school groups, families and other citizens in the area as part of a public education component of the project.

Figure 6.32 A: *Pedestrian and vehicle corridor, Delft Technical University, the Netherlands; B: The use of modular pavement materials in a Dutch residential neighborhood.*

Landscape architects in China have led teams consisting of other professionals and scientists designing a large number of urban river and wetland restoration projects as part of a government initiative to increase the health of these water-based landscapes and to improve the livability of the surrounding communities. Qunil National Urban Wetland Park in Harbin and the Houtan River Wetland Park in Shanghai, designed by Turenscape (Figure 6.34), garnered ASLA design awards. The urban wetland parks were created as a solution to manage storm water and serve to filter the runoff and improve the water quality and restore the biodiversity of the wetlands. The following narrative of design objectives is part of the project description by Turenscape:

Figure 6.33 Crissy Field Wetland Restoration at the Presidio in San Francisco, by Hargreaves Associates.

The initial understanding of the site was to turn the isolated wetland into a major park as well as a storm-water and wastewater remediation area that would enhance native wetland habitat. But thorny issues emerged as the result of further study. The landscape architect discovered that the seasonal change of the water table is as much as 2 meters (6.6 feet) between dry and wet seasons, which thwarts the intention to combine public [recreation] spaces with a resilient wetland landscape. In addition, such a large public space would be difficult to manage since the restored native vegetation would soon become too messy and wild to allow access and be used by the people year round.

Figure 6.34 A: Qunil National Urban Wetland Park in Harbin; B: Houtan River Wetland Park in Shanghai, both projects designed by Turenscape, China.

The design objective was to fashion a water-resilient wetland park, which functions as an integral ecological infrastructure that remediates storm-water and waste tail water from the water plant. In the process, the wastewater could rejuvenate the wetland habitat. Furthermore, the landscape architects determined that limited design interventions would best serve the project objectives and transform the wetland into an accessible public space.[6]

Environmental impact engineer was the title the oil company consortium responsible for the design and construction of the Trans-Alaskan Oil Pipeline gave to the team of landscape architects they hired. The team of landscape architects assisted in developing landscape and wildlife habitat restoration plans for the 860+mile-long (1385 km) pipeline right-of-way

Figure 6.35 Construction restoration with native vegetation, Trans-Alaskan Oil Pipeline, by Bruce Sharky, project landscape architect.

through diverse ecosystems beginning in the North at Prudhoe Bay to the southern terminus at the Port of Valdez. Figure 6.35 captures the result of the restoration activities showing the eventual dominance of native willow and other woody and perennial plant species. The efforts of the landscape architects included planning and executing a series of test plots planted with field-collected native material; collecting, storing, and later overseeing the planting of willow hardwood cutting; collecting seeds of several tree species that were provided to contract growers, then planted in selected areas; and overseeing the collection of field-collected woody species that were planted in sites disturbed during the construction of the pipeline. This was a nearly three-year project that initially began in response to federal and state environmental impact regulations, resulting in the program of restoring native vegetative cover within construction areas along the pipeline right-of-way, including gravel borrow sites, access roads, storage areas, and construction camps.

Figure 6.36 Irvine residential community, by SWA Group.

Figure 6.37 High-rise residential community, Hangzhou, China.

A lot of ground has been covered in this chapter reviewing the diverse range of project types landscape architects are responsible for designing. Among the project types not yet covered are community planning (Figures 6.36 and 6.37), the planning and design of residential neighborhoods, colleges and corporate campuses, restoration planning of open-pit mining operations, design of sports facilities, and coastal and rivers corridor restoration. And, of course, there are individuals whose professional calling is to teach and do research in an academic, university setting. Other career options include working with non-governmental organizations (NGOs), such as The Nature Conservancy and The Trust for Public Lands, in a range of capacities not necessarily associated with design but perhaps in management of resources or in administrative capacities.

Notes

1 There are low-income neighborhoods in urban areas that are not served with a food market and have been called *food deserts*.
2 The park is made up of three gardens designed by architects Huet, Ferrand, and Feugas with landscape architects Le Caisne and Raguin between 1993 and 1997.
3 Such as: Low impact design (LID), storm-water management (BMP), Leadership in Energy and Environmental Design Certification (LEED), and Sustainable Sites Initiatives (SITES).
4 POD, Project Oriented Design was a prominent Southern California landscape architecture firm in the 1970s up until the early 2000s.
5 The U.S. Army Presidio on the San Francisco Bay served as an army post for three nations (Spain, Mexico, and the United States of America). The property is now managed by the Presidio Trust for non-military uses. Many of the historic buildings are being repurposed for public use and access.
6 See www.turenscape.com/english/projects/project.php?id=4625.

Further Reading

Read more about the breadth of landscape architectural design:

Susan Heeger and Bernard Trainor, *Landprints: The Landscape Designs of Bernard Trainor*, Princeton Architectural Press, New York, 2013.

Jan Johnsen, *Heaven Is a Garden: Designing Serene Outdoor Spaces for Inspiration and Reflection*, St. Lynn's Press, Pittsburgh, PA, 2014.

Donald J. Molnar, *Anatomy of a Park: Essentials of Recreation Area Planning and Design*, 4th edn, Waveland Press, Long Grove, IL, 2015.

Peter Reed and Irene Shum, *Groundswell: Constructing the Contemporary Landscape*, The Museum of Modern Art, New York, 2005.

Gayle Souter-Brown, *Landscape and Urban Design for Health and Well-Being*, Routledge, London, 2015.

Jeff Speck, *The Walkable City: How Downtown Can Save America One Step at a Time*, North Point Press, New York, 2013.

James Van Sweden and Tom Christopher, *The Artful Garden: Creative Inspiration for Landscape Design*, Random House, New York, 2011.

Thaisa Way, *The Landscape Architecture of Richard Haag: From Modern Space to Urban Ecological Design*, University of Washington Press, Seattle, WA, 2015.

CHAPTER SEVEN

DESIGNING WITH PLANTS IN MIND

Introduction

Working with plants, living materials, gets us to the core that defines what makes landscape architects unique in the design professions. When working with living matter, one needs to not only take into consideration the intrinsic physicality of the materials but additionally take into account and project how the living materials change from season to season and throughout their life cycle. Bricks and mortar materials do not impose the same way of thinking that plants require of a designer. This is not to say that building materials are entirely static as they do age, deteriorate, and require maintenance and repair over time. However, the aging or maturation process is significantly different than plants, given that plants grow, change form, and change physically with the seasons and over the years. For instance, some trees change color during the year and they also lose their leaves for long periods of time, particularly in the late fall and winter months when the angle of sunlight is lower on the horizon than during the summer months. Trees and other plants that shed their leaves in the winter are deciduous plants. This condition of trees without leaves in the winter gives the landscape architect the design opportunity of selecting deciduous trees and shrubs to place them along the south-facing façade of buildings to reduce heat gain from direct sun in the summer and allow heat gain for the building in the winter. Landscape architects consider plant species selection to accomplish a range of applications such as create and define space. Plants are used to moderate climate, buffer strong, prevailing winds, and buffer unwanted sound or filter unattractive views.

Plants offer several different opportunities to display color in the landscape: flower, leaf, fruit, and branches. Figure 7.1 is an example of the exuberant color display that plants can show to delight viewers in the landscape. Seasonal color changes of plants, for example, Japanese maples (leaf color) or hollies (fruit color), offer another design opportunity for landscape architects. Seasonal colors of flowers and fruit that emerge at specific times of the year for each given plant species should be a consideration when selecting plant species. One can choose flower and fruit colors to complement a landscape composition, either to produce contrasting splashes of color and

Figure 7.1 Keukenhof Gardens, Lisse, the Netherlands.

visual interest or color can be used to complement a building or other structure. Plants that display seasonal color can be used to add an element of drama or visually highlight the spaces against a building or space within a grouping of buildings and along a road corridor, or at the edges of a park and greenbelt. One example is the use of the brilliant red and orange colors of Japanese maples set within a backdrop of the dark greens of conifer trees or aligned with London plane or oak tree species. The aligning or positioning of plants considering seasonal color changes of leaves and flowers can dramatically change campus and urban spaces or along parkway corridors that draw people to these spaces. They are seasonal events that people look forward to and will travel long distances to see. Consider the annual spring event of flowering of cherry blossoms in Washington, D.C. or the fall color of maple trees in Vermont and Maine. The tree-lined boulevards of Europe are visually enlivened with the drama of seasonal color changes that draw people to these places and make the color display that occurs special times of the year that residents look forward to and of course value and enjoy.

Changing Seasons

There are some parts of the world that enjoy four distinct seasons (spring, summer, autumn, and winter) while other regions may experience just two (wet and dry). The literature is replete with songs, musings, poems, and stories about or based on the seasons. The seasons—regardless of the number—punctuate the year with changes in climate, color, the arrival and departure of wildlife. The changing seasons serve as a visual timepiece noting when to plant, nurture, and harvest. The changes that vegetation makes throughout the year give physical expression to other seasonal events. As we notice, the swelling of the leaf buds of trees with the coming of spring triggers anticipation of relief from the harshness of winter. Leaf color changes in the fall signal autumn and the time of harvest. The landscapes, unlike the structures of architects and engineers, have a rhythm that infuses feelings of anticipation, relief, abundance, sadness, and joy. Consider how the lyrics in Antonio Vivaldi's *Concerto No. 1 in E Major, The Four Seasons* (1720) express the dynamics of changing seasons:

Springtime is upon us.
The birds celebrate her return with festive song,
and murmuring streams are softly caressed by the breezes.
Thunderstorms, those heralds of spring, roar, casting their dark mantle over heaven,
Then they die away to silence, and the birds take up their charming songs once more.

Plants through their growth from year to year, from seedling to fully matured plant, are markers of time advancing and in some cases, rebirth. The spaces and places created by landscape architects change physically from wide open to the sky to enclosed, from bleak and uninhabited to a verdant and exuberant density, due to the plants.

Landscape architects know about seasonal changes and the long-term transformations of plant materials and use this knowledge to create their designs. Their designs consist of plant species combinations selected to create spaces or provide experiential or sensual layers supporting the functional requirements of the spaces. While concrete, wood, and steel have their own sensual qualities and may offer the subtle reflective quality of light and other physical changes over time, the dynamic quality of these and other building materials pales in comparison to the daily and seasonal performance and display of plant materials.

Figure 7.2 contains four images representing the four seasons. The photographs are from different locations. They were selected to provide an overview of the seasonal variations a landscape architect has to work with and consider when developing a planting palette for a project. Not all sites and regions offer four distinct seasons. In the tropical regions, the seasons are described as having rainy and dry periods. The seasons one can experience in desert regions are more one-dimensional in that the landscape changes are much more subtle so that seasonal changes are only apparent to those having a practiced eye. The seasons are marked by new and old growth, muted brown-like tones during the extreme dry periods, transforming into highly varied color displays during the wetter months of the year. Also the seasons in desert and arid regions are signalled by the presence of flowers, fruit, in some cases, changes in leaf color or loss. With the loss of leaves, the prominence of a plant's branching structure emerges.

The planted and natural landscapes of spring present a visual display of new growth of leaves, often much lighter hues of green after the leaves' buds have unfurled from the bud stage. The same plants gradually darken in the case of broad-leaf and deciduous species going into the summer. Figure 7.2A shows a planting in late spring. The plant leaf colors can be described as bright green and will darken as summer advances. Deciduous species will then take on their fall color with shades of mostly yellow or simply become dry-looking and brown in more northernly regions. Further north, deciduous species display a more varied and intense color, adding red, orange, and magenta to the landscape color palette. Winter is perhaps the more varied in terms of leaf color from region to region depending on the species. Evergreen plants remain a consistent shade of green, depending on the species. Winter display may consist of seed cones remaining for much of the winter while the branches of deciduous plants will be mostly bare, thus emphasizing the branching and limb structure. This description is perhaps overly generalized, so those students with a more curious interest in plants and wishing to expand their palette will more closely study and observe the seasonal variations of plant materials in their regions. The more one understands about seasonal plant colors, the greater the potential to create

Figure 7.2 Seasonal foliage in the landscape: A: Spring; B: Summer; C: Fall; D: Winter.

spectacular plant compositions that take advantage and incorporate seasonal variations.

I remember my first experience of living in a place where seasonal color variation became more than book-learning knowledge for me. A native of coastal Southern California, I had the opportunity of working in Winnipeg, Manitoba (located in a prairie landscape), after graduation from college. We arrived in Winnipeg in the middle of winter. That was quite a jolt in many respects, such as experiencing the extreme cold and the snow-covered landscape. It wasn't until early spring on my first outing north of the city, where the landscape appeared mostly brown and gray and the snow had disappeared, that I saw the seasonal colors. We were out on a hike along a river floodplain surrounded by a gently rolling upland landscape. What struck me during that introduction to an early spring outing in a northern landscape was the enormously appealing but subtle color patterns of the native landscape. What I saw were bands of color, swaths of low-growing willows and grasses with a backdrop of taller-growing alders, both punctuated by an occasional spruce. The leaf buds of the willows, of varying heights, depending on the species, had swollen, revealing shades of yellow from a butter color to more subtle shades of the same color. The foreground contained extensive patches of grasses, many with remnants of seeds and dry flowers. The grasses varied in color from all shades of brown, sienna, and strands of burgundy. The upright, mostly gray or dark brown branches of the tall alders in the background had a soft blush of burgundy. The color was produced by the swelling leaf buds. It was on this hike that I experienced my first appreciation of the subtle nature of plant color, form, and structure revealed by a landscape waking up from winter and preparing for spring and the months ahead. The experience, I might add, was intensified when my eyes caught sight of a moose dashing through the willow thicket toward the floodplain where we were heading. I would go so far as to say that I had not realized the extent of and potential application of plants in design until this experience three or four years out from graduating with a degree in landscape architecture. It was late in coming, but I am certainly thankful it happened.

Figure 7.3 contains two photographs taken in the same general location in a public park in Hangzhou, China. The two photographs have been paired to show the color variation of similar plants from summer to late fall. While the photographs were not of the exact location, the effects of the seasonal transformations of a landscape are dramatically evident. As the plant colors change, so too does the visual composition and spatial qualities of the landscape. The landscape spaces in winter are more open while in the summer they feel more enclosed. The difference between open and enclosed is the result of bare trees and trees in leaf.

In addition to color, plants have other physical and aesthetic qualities. Each plant species has a definite physical form. Common adjectives used to describe plant forms include: pyramid, oval, upright, weeping, tall and upright, broad, spreading, and irregular. Some plants have a sculptural form while others—particularly trees—are known for the structure of their branches which provide visual interest just as their other physical qualities, such as leaf color or overall form can. For example, the ancient Gingko tree has a very sculptural, branching form, not completely evident until the leaves drop in the late fall. The Gingko leaves achieve a radiant display of yellow in contrast to the bright green of spring and summer.

A plant's texture is another design consideration in selecting plant species. Plant texture takes into consideration the size and shape of the leaves and the light and shadow patterns resulting from the changing phenomenon of sunlight. In addition to texture, plants can be described as having soft qualities or appearing stiff to the eye as well as to touch. Weeping willow is an example of a tree that is known for its soft, malleable appearance. In fact, if you were to run your hands through the leaves,

Figure 7.3 West Lake Park, Hangzhou, China. Comparing summer and fall color in the landscape. A was taken in late summer and B was taken in late fall.

they would not resist, unlike the stiffer leaves of a horse chestnut or oak. The aesthetic, physical, and seasonal attributes of plants are endless. Choosing the right plant and combination of plants is part of the art of a landscape architect.

Overview of Plant Physical Characteristics by Region

Plants that are native to particular regions are a product of their environment. Their physical characteristics allow them to adapt to the climate, soil, and other environmental conditions of the region. One way to discuss plant species variations is by their biome. Biomes are defined as the world's major communities or ecological areas classified according to the predominant vegetation and are characterized by climate, soil, and other particular environmental conditions that support organisms (in our case, plant species) that have adapted to these particular environments. For example, plants with small leaves and gray or light-green coloration are characteristic of arid regions while plants with large, green and dark green coloration are found in temperate or sub-tropical areas. We will briefly review the general differences one might anticipate in very broad terms by major regions.

- *Tropical*: The tropical regions of the Earth have the greatest diversity of plant species. This diversity is also expressed in their physical characteristics. Tropical plants are known to have large leaves with great shape variation such as broad leaves and palm-like leaf structures. Plant height varies greatly, from some of the tallest species on Earth, graduating down to smaller plants found on the forest floor. Tropical rainforests are found in a broad band close to the equator. Tropical plants are typically prolific fruit and flower producers of great variety. Tropical plants are found in regions with a highly varied annual rainfall (50–260 inches or 20–660 cm), high humidity, warm annual temperatures (70–90° F or 21–32°C), and surprisingly poor, thin soils.[1] The tropical plants produce a broad spectrum of color in the form of flowers and fruit as well as a wide range of leaf sizes and shapes. Leaf colors range across nearly the full spectrum of the rainbow. Many species have glossy leaf surfaces, and others have multiple coloration, including reds and magenta and shades of white. For landscape architects working in tropical and sub-tropical regions, the plant palette is extensive and can be overwhelming in terms of the choices possible. The possibilities of creating landscape designs are similar to an artist having nearly infinite options of color to choose from. Plant form, color, leaf size and shape, and other physical variations can be combined to create spectacular and highly nuanced landscape planting designs. Working with a tropical planting palette is not for the timid designer and it can be a daunting challenge, given the great variety of plant species found in tropical regions.
- *Temperate*: Plants in temperate regions such as North America, Europe, and Asia are found between the tropical and polar regions. As the term suggests, temperatures in these regions tend to be moderate, and while they do experience freezing or hot

temperatures, they are not extremely cold or warm for long periods of time. Annual rainfall is generally higher in temperate regions than in polar regions but not as high as in tropical areas. Plant species in the region include both deciduous and evergreen trees, shrubs, perennials, grasses, and herbs. Fall foliage colors can be brilliant and spectacularly showy, including yellow, orange, red, and burgundy-like hues. Foliage types include evergreen and deciduous, conifer, broad-leaf, and grasses. The presence of fruit and flowers ranges from showy and colorful to insignificant. Planting designs in temperate regions have the possibility of achieving multi-layered effects with an over-story or canopy of tall trees to a variety of plants filling in the under-story or mid-range heights down to ground level with woody and herbaceous plants.

- *Desert*: Deserts are regions that are arid with low annual rainfall, although with a degree of variation from 1.5 cm or less than an inch to 25 cm or 19–20 inches per year. The term arid can apply to both desert and polar regions as both have low annual rainfall. Deserts can be classified into many sub-categories from extremely hot climates (the Sahara) to cold deserts found in the Arctic and Antarctica. For the purposes of landscape architecture, the desert plants that are most commonly used are found in the less extreme arid regions such as the American Southwest and moderate deserts in South America and Africa (found along the ocean coast). Chaparral and high desert regions also belong to the arid region landscape. Plant species in this category tend toward smaller leaf size, fleshy in nature as a water conservation strategy, or thin and small to cause less water loss through evapotranspiration. The physical color of these plants (leaf and branching) falls in the range of gray and lighter hues of green. Gray contributes to a plant's ability to cut down water loss due to the process of evapotranspiration. The open branching quality of arid trees and shrubs is a prominent physical feature of desert plants and it is this quality that makes these plants selected to achieve a dramatic sculptural effect. Desert plants can also be selected for their showy seasonal flower and fruit characteristics. In some species their display of color can be stunning.

- *Arctic*: Arctic or Antarctic, these opposite polar regions both experience sustained cold, and below freezing temperatures with low annual rainfall. Soils tend to be less developed with a thin "A" soil horizon (of less than ½ to 1 inch or 1.25–2.5 cm) with gravelly or rock sub-soil. Generally the ground surface is covered in a thick mat of sphagnum moss providing insulation for the permafrost often found below the organic layer. Tree species include deciduous or conifer species. Shrubs are generally deciduous as well. Herbaceous plants are common ground cover species. This region has the lowest diversity of plant species, compared to temperate and tropical regions. For instance, the state of Alaska has 133 native woody[2] plant species with 33 reaching tree size, as compared to the state of Florida (tropical and semi-tropical) that has over 3100 native species, including over 300 native trees.[3] Seasonal color of deciduous trees tends toward yellow or brown, while the low-growing plant cover can be brilliant with orange, red, and burgundy red to purple. A friend of mine, visiting Alaska one colorful fall season, on seeing the highly diverse fall colors on display on a hillside we stopped to admire, commented that the scene reminded him of the worn, unraveling Turkish carpet in his grandmother's living room back home.

Figure 7.4 *Differences in quality of light in different regions: A: Deep shade in contrast to bright light in tropical Costa Rica; B: Filtered or dappled shade and sunlight in temperate Hangzhou, China; C: Intense bright light with minor shadows in arid New Mexico.*

Quality of Light (Sunlight and Shade) and Plants

One of the defining characteristics of plant materials from a visual and experiential perspective in various regions and climates is the interplay of sunlight with the plants. Sunlight filters through the tree canopy and shrub forms differently from region to region (see Figure 7.4). The broad-leaf, dense canopy of trees in Northeast United States and Northern Europe cast deep, dark shadows in large patterns while the more upright nature of tree cover in temperate regions creates more dispersed shadow patterns, often favoring the sculptural arrangement of limbs and branches. The characteristic shadow patterns cast by tropical plants can also emphasize the tree canopy. Where denser plantings of trees and large shrubs occur, the canopy will cover large areas of the ground underneath in deep shade. Plants in arid regions tend to be lower-growing with more open branching, casting shadows that are far less dense than in temperate and tropical regions. Plantings in arid regions tend to cast well-defined shadow patterns, revealing the structural characteristics of the plants. The descriptions of sunlight qualities and shadow patterns are generalizations so that one can expect variations and can ultimately enhance one's knowledge of a plant's aesthetic characteristics through careful observation. The designer has the highly varied palette of sunlight and shadow patterns to learn when working in various regions. This palette, when mastered as one might master color theory, will reward the landscape architect and client with a rich and multi-faceted landscape design.

Horticultural Considerations in Selecting Plants

Landscape architects must be knowledgeable of the horticultural necessities of the plants being considered. These horticultural considerations include the desirable types of soil, soil pH, and mineral requirements for plants to successfully sustain themselves. Water requirements are another consideration in the plant selection process. There are plants that prefer sandy, well-drained soils with a low water content. Should the amount of water reaching these plants be excessive—outside their tolerance range—the plants will suffer and look in grave need of care or will even die. Likewise, plants that require greater amounts of water can wither and die or become stressed and susceptible to disease when not provided adequate water.

Plant Hardiness Zones

In the United States, the US Department of Agriculture (USAD) publishes and periodically updates a plant hardiness zone map.[4] The zones are based on the average annual extreme minimum temperatures during a 30-year period. The zones are outlined in increments of 5–15-degree temperatures (in both Fahrenheit and Celsius) depicted graphically, similar to isobars that describe barometric pressure. Species of plants are rated according to their temperature tolerances. Sometimes plant hardiness zones are also referred to as tropical, sub-tropical, and arid (see Figure 7.5). However, the reference to plant hardiness is considered more precise. The plant hardiness map does not take into account microclimate variations. For example, plants

Figure 7.5 Plant hardiness zones: A: Desert; B: Temperate; C: Tropical; D: Arctic.

ranked for warmer climates may perform well in a colder zone when planted in a protected area between buildings where a heat island has formed. Likewise, a plant may not do as well as expected by its hardiness rating if placed on the north side of a tall building. The buildings in this case form a shadow, blocking heat gain from the sun, resulting in longer-lasting colder air temperatures.

Other Factors Affecting Plant Growth and Survival

In addition to hardiness zones, there are other environmental factors that can contribute to the success or failure of a plant's performance and survival. Wind, soil type, soil moisture, humidity, air and water pollution, snow and ice, and the sun angle can greatly affect the survival and performance of plants. Where plants are placed in the landscape in relation to buildings and hard surfaces, how they are planted (such as soil preparation), and their size and health at the time of planting can also influence their survival. Briefly, here are some of the other factors that can contribute to successful plant performance and survival:

1. *Temperature*: Plants grow best within a range of optimum temperatures, both cold and hot. That range may be wide for some species but narrow for others.
2. *Duration of exposure to cold*: Many plants can survive short periods of exposure to cold but may not tolerate longer periods of cold temperature. Also consider that some cold regions can be extremely dry (low humidity), such as in Alaska, or cold and wet (high humidity), such as in the Northeast US or the United Kingdom.
3. *Sunlight*: Plants need to be planted in locations where they will receive the proper amount of sunlight. Plants can be damaged by sunburn. Low angle winter sun can cause sunburn on the trunks of trees. The burns or sun scalding not only can damage the tree but also can compromise the plant's ability to survive. Precautions can be taken such as wrapping or painting the exposed trunk area with sun-protection material.
4. *Soil moisture*: The amount of water present in the soil is called soil moisture. The water is held within the soil pores and its presence is a major factor in plant growth. If the moisture content of a soil is optimum, the plants can readily absorb water held in the soil. The water dissolves various chemical nutrients in the form of salts that make up the soil solution. Soil containing the optimum range of moisture is important as a medium for supplying the nutrients necessary for growing plants and supporting the process of photosynthesis.

   Plants have different soil moisture requirements. Soil moisture requirements can vary seasonally. Plants that might otherwise be hardy in one zone might be injured if soil moisture is too low in late autumn and then they enter dormancy while suffering moisture stress. Microorganisms present in the soil require water to carry out their metabolic activities and how well they are able to function can affect plant growth and health.

5. *Air humidity*: High relative air humidity limits cold damage by reducing moisture loss from leaves, branches, and buds. Cold injury can be more severe if the humidity is low, especially for broad-leaf evergreens. Consider citrus growers who turn on overhead sprinkling systems in advance of a predicted cold snap (dramatic drop of air temperature) to protect their trees.

6. *Soil structure*: Soil conditions, such as hardpan,[5] and other soil structures can contribute to the success and health of plants. Some plants do not tolerate hardpan soil conditions and may barely thrive or in some cases not survive. Plants have their individual soil preferences. Some species do best in well-drained, sandy, and rocky soils (birch, willow, citrus) while other plants can do well in clay and more fine-grained soils (azaleas, rhododendron, and spruce). Other species perform best in soils that are acidic and contain high concentrations of organic matter. Because of the known soil preference of plants, one can "read" the underlying soil and soil conditions of a landscape by observing the plant types and species. For example, in northern climates, the presence of native birch, alder, and willow is an indicator of well-drained rocky or sandy soil. The presence of native spruce is an indicator of poorly drained organic soils with high moisture content and in some cases the presence of permafrost. While plants may be a reasonable indicator of soil conditions, soil testing is advisable before planting to specify necessary amendments or the need to import supplemental soil.

7. *Soil pH and nutrients*: Plant species do well under specific soil chemical properties. The pH is a measure of a soil's acidic or alkaline chemistry reported on a scale of 0–14. The measurement considers the concentration of hydrogen ions in a soil sample. Soil pH is measured on the scale where 7.0 is neutral, 7.1 and above are alkaline, 8.3 is too high a reading for most plants to survive. 6.9 and below are an acidic soil and anything that measures below 4.8 is too acidic for most plants to do well or survive.[6] Plants that perform best in acidic soils are referred to as acid-loving plants, for example, azaleas and rhododendrons. Some plants prefer alkaline soils, and with some species a change in the soil pH can modify their flower color (hydrangea, for example). One method of altering the soil pH is by using chemical additives such as lime (to reduce acidity). Lime raises the pH and, depending on the amount added, can reduce the acidity of a soil. Conversely, adding organic material to an alkaline soil can lower its pH. Also, modifying a soil's pH will reduce the frequency and amount of nutrients (nitrogen, phosphorus, potash and others) added to a soil and thus reduce long-term maintenance costs. Performing a soil test prior to installing the soil will include a recommendation for soil amendments depending on the plants specified.

Plant Selection Based on Climate and Other Ecological Factors

Plant species that have been selected considering their range of temperature tolerance (hardiness), their adaptability to existing

Figure 7.6 Deciduous trees planted along building windows to provide shade in summer and allow sunlight and heat gain in winter. Asunaro Building in the Woods, Reitaku University. Courtesy of Keikan Sekkei, Tokyo, Japan.

soil conditions, and annual rainfall requirements can be expected to perform and survive and thus be good choices when the landscape architect is developing a planting design. A successful planting design is one where the landscape architect thoroughly thinks through not only the aesthetic and functional requirements identified during site analysis and design investigation but also considers the environmental and horticultural conditions and requirements in developing an appropriate plant species palette. Plants that are native to the region or imported from locations with comparable climate, soil, and moisture characteristics should be expected to do well. Additional research should be conducted for non-native plants to make sure they will thrive in the new location. Consideration of the moisture requirements of plants has become increasingly important in the twenty-first century.

Growing awareness and concern about the impact of climate change and water shortages are becoming an increasing priority and in some regions a requirement[7] in planting design. Plant selection in regions experiencing water scarcity and rising annual temperatures is, by necessity, favoring the use of native species, species with a long history of adaptability to the region and plants capable of thriving with minimum or no irrigation.

Figure 7.6 presents a beneficial use of plants in the built landscape. Deciduous trees were planted along the front of the windows of a library. The deciduous trees will moderate the extremes of climate by providing shade during the summer months to block the heat from the sun, thus reducing air conditioning costs. In the winter when they drop their leaves, sunlight is allowed inside the building to increase heat gain, thus reducing building heating costs.

New Challenges in Plant Selection

Landscape architects are finding new challenges in working in non-traditional landscapes and site conditions. For instance, in developing plans for wetland restoration, landscape architects are selecting plants adapted to seasonal flooding such as runoff retention systems, including bio-swales and rain gardens. Conversely, landscape architects practicing in arid regions must develop a specialized knowledge of plants tolerant to drought conditions and the need to apply xeriscaping[8] methods to conserve water. Landscape architects working with the new challenges have come to appreciate a new plant aesthetic sensibility. With this new design aesthetic, they find that they must educate their clients to appreciate the aesthetic merits, using endemic plants from the region. A new planting design vocabulary can be particularly challenging for clients coming to an arid environment from sub-tropical and temperate areas with higher rainfall and lower temperatures. Dense, multi-layered landscape designs found in temperate regions may not be practical in the clients' new arid location. While at one time a formidable obstacle, the public has become increasingly tolerant, if not appreciative, of designed landscapes that rely on native species. Appreciating the beauty of native plants has become more the norm, particularly in regions where changing climate and other environmental conditions have forced the transformation of the public's aesthetic preferences, based in large part on understanding and accepting the desirability of sustainable approaches to landscape design.

Aesthetic Considerations

The topic of aesthetics and the art of plant selection and composition would merit volumes of its own. In fact, there are shelves in libraries covering the subject, a subject of philosophers and art historians through the ages, beginning at least with the Greeks. There are so many aspects and approaches one could take in crafting a discussion to do justice to the topic. The facets in a discussion on plant aesthetics should include at least the following few, such as visual and artistic ideals of aesthetics.

From a Western perspective, theories on aesthetics began with the opposing views of Plato and Aristotle. Plato points to the heavens and to an ideal world of forms and the notion of some out-of-the-world, godly ideal. Aristotle, on the other hand, points toward the Earth, arguing that the ideal in aesthetics is more accessible and within the grasp of human experience. The idea of an ideal suggests that human aesthetic creations are an attempt at imitation and their creations would be judged by their skill at imitating as opposed to creating something new, a concept more recent (since the Renaissance) as modern and contemporary ideas of aesthetics and art are considered.

The principles for defining what makes for a good landscape design draw from principles used in the visual arts (painting, sculpture, printing, etc.). Composition in the arts is the framework for arranging objects in two and three dimensions. A successful composition is one where the objects have been arranged in such a way that they seem united into a pleasing, balanced, and harmonious whole. What unites the elements can vary: unity can be achieved with symmetry or a grid-like organizational structure and by the repetition of elements such as color, texture, or form. An arrangement of objects that causes the eye to move through a space in a pleasing and satisfying way can unify the space and elements contained within or defining that space. The placement of objects that are balanced, not necessarily of equal form but perhaps where the fulcrum (as in a see-saw) is set, so that what may appear to be unequal weights are equalized by the fulcrum's position. Rhythm and pattern are also used to create a harmonious composition in the landscape. Think of the notes in a musical composition. The notes are ordered within a set structure (time signature) allowing for variation of speed (or duration) in which different tones as well as volume variation are played. Color and texture of the objects are also used to provide balance and create visual harmony. One should make an effort to study color theory in order to master the art of creating visually harmonious and exciting plant compositions.[9]

Planting Design: From Plans to Reality

Landscape architects, prior to the ubiquitous advent and use of the computer in the profession, did their work on drafting tables, more commonly referred to as *boards.* All work in an office was done using hand graphics, with final construction drawings prepared on Mylar film or vellum using T-square, triangles, and other drawing instruments. The drawings were drawn with ink or pencil. The euphemism: *off the board and into the ground* referred to design drawings created in the office to be later constructed on site (in the ground). The drawing in Figure 7.7 is a planting plan for a campus landscape design at the Soka University in Japan. The other images in Figure 7.7 show the resulting installed design, a beautifully conceived, multi-layered planting design that was conceived to provide a variety of visual experiences reflecting and following the seasons. This project demonstrates the unique contribution landscape architects bring to a campus, urban, or any other project type. Planting design has been discussed earlier as both an art and a science. It is an act of creative artistic expression based on knowledge and understanding of horticulture principles, environmental conditions, and natural processes.

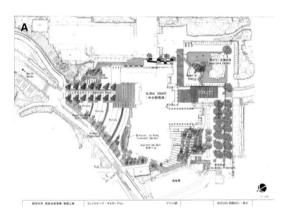

Figure 7.7 Planting design for Global Square, Soka University. Courtesy of Keikan Sekkei, Tokyo, Japan.

Notes

1 The conditions of heavy rain and high temperatures in tropical areas increase the speed of decomposition or the breakdown and decay of living matter. The increased rate of decomposition makes it possible for plants to absorb nutrients more quickly, therefore leaving the soil low in nutrient content.
2 Leslie A. Viereck and Elbert L. Little, Jr., *Alaska Trees and Shrubs*, Agriculture Handbook No. 410 (US Forest Service, 1972).
3 www.floridasnature.com/florida%20trees1.htm.
4 USDA Plant Hardiness Zone Map, available at: http://planthardiness.ars.usda.gov/PHZMWeb/.
5 Hardpan is a general term for a soil layer found beneath the surface that is both dense and impervious to water percolating through its layer, and generally impenetrable to plant roots.
6 State University of New York, Environmental Studies Series, available at: www.esf.edu/pubprog/brochure/soilph/soilph.htm.
7 Such as California and the American Southwest.
8 Xeriscaping are water-conserving principles promoted and in some cases required in some jurisdictions that eliminate the need for supplemental irrigation by primarily selecting endemic plant species. Additional principles of xeriscaping include taking care to avoid losing water to evaporation with the use of mulch in the planting beds and designing a grading plan that reduces or eliminates surface water runoff. There are landscape architects who offer specialized xeriscape professional design services.
9 H. Stuart Ortloff and Henry B. Raymore, *The Book of Landscape Design* (M. Barrows & Company, Inc., New York, 1959).

Further Reading

A few good references to further satisfy your curiosity on planting design:

Gary L. Austin, *Elements of Planting Design*, John Wiley & Sons, Inc., Hoboken, NJ, 2001.

Gertrude Jekyll, *Gertrude Jekyll: The Making of a Garden, An Anthology*, ed. Cherry Lewis, ACC Publishing Group, Suffolk, 2000.

Piet Oudolf and Noel Kingsbury, *Planting: A New Perspective*, Timber Press, Portland, OR, 2013.

Nick Robinson, *The Planting Design Handbook*, Ashgate Publishing Limited, Farnham, 2004, revised 2011.

Scott C. Scarfone, *Professional Planting Design: An Architectural and Horticultural Approach for Creating Mixed Bed Plantings*, John Wiley & Sons, Inc., Hoboken, NJ, 2007.

W. Gary Smith, *From Art to Landscape: Unleashing Creativity in Garden Design*, Timber Press, Portland, OR, 2010.

James van Sweden and Tom Christopher, *The Artful Garden: Creative Inspiration for Landscape Design*, Random House, New York, 2011.

CHAPTER EIGHT

CONCRETE, SOIL, WOOD, AND OTHER MATERIALS

Introduction

A landscape architect must be knowledgeable about a great range of materials used for hardscape and construction purposes. The design of paved areas requires a landscape architect to select materials that are durable for the intended use as well as meet aesthetic considerations including color, texture, and unit dimensions (bricks and concrete pavers). Other materials available for landscape use include wood, metal, plastic, fabric, and many others. For example, wood selection is part of the art of landscape design. The specification parameters of wood include tree species such as pine or fir; wood types such as heartwood and softwood. There are grades of wood such as select and common grades. Grade has to do with the physical aspects such as the presence of knots and other potential aesthetic and structural qualities. Further considerations in addition to wood species include the selection of an appropriate system of fasteners such as nails and screws, which is of critical importance. Screws and nails are made of steel, aluminum, and other metals. Steel fastener specifications also include stainless and hot-dipped galvanized. Wood surfaces can be finished with paint or stain or treated with preservative chemicals to combat deterioration and weathering. And wood can be selected for age as in old growth redwood.

Color and stain are also a consideration when specifying concrete. Concrete can be stained after drying or color can be added to the mix before being poured into place. Textures can be applied to the concrete surface, either in the way the concrete finishers smooth or broom-brush texture to the surface, or seed it with rock salt while the concrete is still wet to produce another range of textures, or add rock or other material for color and texture to the finished surface. There are other possibilities for the landscape architect to consider when specifying concrete pavement, including the use of porous concrete to enable surface water to infiltrate the underlying soil. It is possible to create a variety of surface patterns on concrete, including emulating the look of bricks, flagstones, and other patterns. These patterns are created by applying stamp patterns to wet concrete.

Materials used in the making of landscape projects of any function or location can vary tremendously from one region to another. The palette of materials available is enormously rich in variety and in their materiality. A landscape architect will select a variety of materials; the criteria for their selection will depend first of all on the creativity of the designer and their knowledge of the range of materials available and how they are placed, joined, fashioned, shaped, and cast, and then finally finished. Finishes can be applied to the surfaces of different types of metal and non-ferrous products such as aluminum and even plastic tubing by applying paint or baked-on color enamel and other coating materials. Steel can be treated chemically to alter the oxidation process as with the product, Cor-Ten steel. In Phoenix, Arizona, is a regional park with fountain, paving, walls, plants and other elements created using a variety of hardscape materials (see Figure 5.24 on p. 103). The materials include stacked stone for the walls, cast iron fountain and pool, concrete paving finished with a smooth texture in contrast to the large boulders placed for seating or visual effect. Water and sunlight are also part of the materials palette of this plaza. Sunlight strikes the water surface, infusing it with a glistening, lively effect. Without sunlight or artificial light, water can look gray and listless. Sunlight is what creates shadows on plant foliage and washes across a pavement surface and over boulders, furniture, and walls. The shadow and sunlight patterns intensify the three-dimensionality of the plant, the concrete forms, and the stone elements and, in the case of the boulders, they appear to be hovering over the pavement, an effect created with deep shadows on the underside of the boulders and lighter shadow washes or highlights on the top and side surfaces.

The garden pictured in Figure 8.1 is a composition with fine texture providing the underlying visual cohesion among the plants and other materials selected by the landscape architect. The process of design is much more than creating forms on paper to represent a site design. As one becomes more experienced, the landscape architect visualizes and makes mental notes of the types of materials the "drawn" lines represent. At some point, drawn circles on a preliminary plan representing trees need to be translated into specific plant species. The designer will need to specify the materials the pavement will be made of, then specify their color, texture, details of construction, and dimensionality: Roman-sized brick or common brick, for example. The decisions regarding the selection of materials of all elements of the design are considered holistically, that is, each material is considered in combination with other materials to achieve the desired visual effect and practical intent.

The Levi Strauss Plaza in San Francisco (see Figure 5.11) contains a variety of plant and hardscape materials. Lawrence Halprin, the designer, made his material selections to create a visual and experiential space based on his own experience

Figure 8.1 *Materials in combinations and selected to work together in creating a whole visual composition. Malinalco, Mexico, residence by Mario Schjetnan, landscape architect.*

during many backcountry ventures he made in the Sierra Nevada Mountains of California. The design for the plaza was informed by these experiences, not with the idea of literally transporting what he saw in the mountains to downtown San Francisco but rather with symbolic gestures. The boulders were hand-selected by Halprin from a site in the Sierra Nevada Mountains, and he specified in plans and technical details how they would be arranged in the plaza. The selection of the exposed aggregate for the concrete paving contributed to his overall design. The choices of plant materials and the forms (and material) for the fountain and seating elements were made to further the overarching feeling inspired by the backcountry walks that Halprin worked hard to achieve for visitors coming to the urban plaza.

The Great Variety of Materials Available to the Designer

We will begin a brief overview of materials employed in creating designs by landscape architects with concrete, then move on to some of the other more commonly used materials. The landscape architects of today have a great many materials to select from. Some materials can be exotic with only a short track record to determine their durability or appropriateness for intended uses. Think of the study of the exotic and emerging materials akin to the learning of new plant species. New species and new materials are constantly becoming available. Their availability requires the landscape architect to devote sufficient time to master how best and when to use them. Just as there are people in an office who specialize in plant materials, others may devote more time learning and researching building materials.

It would not be possible to fully cover the variety of materials and all their countless application options in an introductory text on the subject of landscape architecture. The hope is that the reader gains a curiosity and interest in the potential rewards when delving further into the world of landscape materials. Landscape architects find themselves on a merry-go-round of new discoveries of new materials and perhaps new ways of using old ones throughout their professional career. In this chapter we will review many of the basic materials commonly selected by landscape architects to add variety of shape and form as well as enhance the functionality of their designs. The list of materials we will cover is not meant to be exhaustive but rather provide the reader with a view through a slightly ajar window into the vast world of materials.

Concrete

There are a great variety of pastries (Figure 8.2) that come in all shapes, sizes, and number of calories. Regardless of their physical differences, they are all made from the same basic ingredients: flour, water, salt, and often eggs. Pastries that go beyond the basics can include a variety of ingredients, including cream, fruit, and other fillings. There are also a great variety of concrete recipes. Similar to pastry, the making of concrete also involves using some basic ingredients, including sand, crushed rock, Portland cement, and water. Adjusting the basic cake ingredients by adding butter, baking soda, yeast, sugar, or flavoring

Figure 8.2 *Pastries on display in Tavira, Portugal.*

will alter the texture and density of the pastry among other alterations. How moist or dry the cake, its flavor and other tasty derivations potentially available in pastry making will depend on the ingredients and their formulation (the recipe). While there are obviously many differences between pastry and concrete, the two materials share a number of similarities. Both are plastic (can be formed into any shape) when wet. They become static, a hardened form when moisture evaporates, attaining their cured state. One can alter the physical properties of the two materials by varying the proportion of the ingredients, by adding ingredients to the basic recipe, and later after the mixture dries, other materials can be applied to alter the color and texture of the surface. In the case of concrete, color stains can be applied or specific chemicals to repel stains or seal the surface.

The desired physical characteristics of concrete can be achieved, such as increasing its strength, preparing it to be resistant to salt water (dock support columns), altering its permeability (in the case of creating a paved surface that allows water to percolate to the soil below), and many other desired qualities, depending on the function and use of the concrete material in the design. Adding what are called admixtures to the concrete mix or spreading them over the surface while the concrete is still wet can alter the surface color. The surface texture can be altered by the type and quantity of rock in the concrete mix or by spreading a specified size and color of rock while the recently poured concrete is still wet. Adding salt to the wet surface will leave a pitted surface, when the salt is later washed off after the concrete has hardened. Creating a smooth, rough, or textured surface can be achieved by working the wet concrete with different finishing instruments. Placing rubber-like sheets of flexible material over the wet surface will reveal a pattern after the sheets are removed. Various rigid or flexible systems are pressed into the wet concrete to produce patterns emulating bricks, flagstones, wood grain, and other patterns. The process is referred to as stamped concrete. Another process for adding texture to a concrete surface is to alter the surface mechanically after it is dry. A mechanical hammer instrument removes concrete by repeated pounding to achieve a desired roughness. A rough surface can also be achieved using hand instruments such as a hammer and chisel or simply a hammer to chip or remove surface concrete to achieve a desired rough surface or pattern.

Concrete typically comes in three forms:

1. poured-in-place
2. pre-cast
3. modular units.

We will begin by reviewing poured-in-place concrete. It is considered the less costly and most common concrete used in landscape construction.

Poured-in-Place Concrete

There are many steps involved in constructing concrete pavement and structures. Figure 8.3 highlights some of the major steps in constructing a bus stop and shelter. Figure 8.3A shows the layout of forms that will contain the wet concrete as it is poured (Figure 8.3B) and distributed. A land surveyor, guided by the layout or staking plan prepared by the landscape architect, will locate corners and other key points to set the elevations at these points. The concrete contractor will use the information found on stakes placed by the land surveyor to construct the concrete forms. Once the forms are in place, the work crew will make ready for the delivery of the wet concrete and will guide the pouring of the concrete and manipulate the wet materials guided by the forms. Once the wet concrete has been distributed, concrete finishers prepare the final surface of the concrete as shown in Figure 8.3C. In addition to the finishing of the surface, additives (color, sealants, and decorative stones) may be applied as specified in the plans and the technical specifications prepared by the landscape architect.

Poured-in-place concrete is a manufactured material transported by special trucks from a concrete supplier or made on-site and poured wet into forms constructed by the work crews. Paving, walls, and other designed elements are generally made using poured-in-place concrete as shown in Figure 8.4. In these examples, the pavement, seating, and planters were constructed on site using poured-in-place concrete. Notice the concrete in Figure 8.4A is colored. The color was obtained by adding a color compound (admixture) to the wet concrete mix before delivery to the site. The yellow colored wall in the example in Figure 8.4C has a similar "solid" look as the other two examples; however, it was constructed in two steps. The first step consisted of building the wall using modular concrete blocks set on a poured-in-place foundation. After the wall was constructed, a slurry of Portland cement and sand with a color admixture was applied to the wall surface.

Pavement such as shown in Figure 8.5 is made with poured-in-place concrete. A color additive was added to the concrete before it was poured. The area in the center of the picture was given a textured appearance with river rock (obtained from local streams) applied while the concrete was still wet. The other surfaces were given a lightly textured appearance by spreading rock salt applied while the mixture was still wet. Later the salt was

Figure 8.3 *Steps in constructing the concrete pavement elements for a bus shelter: A: Beginning with constructing the forms; B: Pouring the concrete; C: Finishing the surface.*

Figure 8.4 *Poured-in-place concrete: A: Kerr Sculpture Garden, University of California at Los Angeles, by Cornell, Bridgers & Troller, landscape architects; B: Plaza Salvador Dalí, Madrid, Spain; C: Concrete block wall with poured-in-place concrete fountain, by Steve Martino, landscape architect.*

washed off after it had dissolved and after making an impression in the wet concrete. Other methods are commonly used to add texture to concrete surfaces, such as brushing and raking the wet surface after it has been pre-finished. Geometric and non-geometric patterns can be added with stamp-like tools to give the appearance of brick, rock, and other imprinted patterns. Other patterns and texture can be added, limited only by one's imagination. The effect of leaves embedded in the concrete surface is accomplished by lightly pressing dry leaves onto the wet surface. The leaves are later washed away, to reveal an attractive leaf pattern.

Figure 8.5 *Variety of color and texture in poured-in-place concrete paving, by Christine Ten Eyck, landscape architect.*

As the reader can see, there are many ways to transform the look of concrete by adding color, stones and other materials, as well as adding texture to the surface. Another method for adding texture is accomplished after the concrete is dry and cured. The surface texture shown in Figure 8.6 was achieved by using hand tools such as a chisel and hammer or a mechanical hammering tool to create a non-slip texture. One final method of creating

Figure 8.6 Hand-tooled texture on poured-in-place concrete steps to prevent slipping and for aesthetic interest. Summer Palace, Beijing, China.

a surface texture is by sandblasting. This method removes mostly the Portland cement on the surface, revealing the rock contained in the concrete mix.

Pre-Cast and Modular Units

Concrete can also be found as a manufactured product such as pre-cast or modular units made off-site in a factory. Modular concrete units, such as shown in Figure 8.7, are commonly used for paving as well as walls and other structures. Concrete block is one example of a pre-manufactured, modular material. Modular concrete units were installed for the tread surfaces of the terrace-like steps at the San Antonio Botanical Garden. The units selected have a tan color, one of many colors the designer could choose from a manufacturer's catalogue. There were most likely other unit dimensions and shape options as well. The step risers were made of poured-in-place concrete although they could have been constructed using a pre-cast manufactured product.

The walls and paving shown in Figure 8.8 are made from pre-cast and modular concrete material. The walls were constructed by first using poured-in-place concrete for the structural footing and walls. Or they could have been built by a second method of using poured-in-place concrete for the footing and concrete blocks for the wall. The

Figure 8.7 Modular concrete units for tread with poured-in-place concrete as riser, San Antonio Botanical Garden, Texas, by Emilio Ambasz, architect.

Figure 8.8 *Pre-cast modular concrete units, Telefónica office park, Madrid, Spain.*

Figure 8.8 *Pre-cast modular concrete units, Telefónica office park, Madrid, Spain.*

Figure 8.9 *Construction detail of a concrete wall faced with quarried stone, Manzanares River Park, Madrid, Spain, by West 8.*

walls were then faced with pre-cast concrete units or quarried rock. See Figure 8.9 for details of attaching granite rock facing on a wall. The pavement surface is made from two sizes of modular concrete units: a smaller square unit at the base of the seat bench and a larger square unit for the walking surface.

Stone

Stone is a common material found in nature. Stone is quarried from many geologic origins including igneous, metamorphic, or sedimentary. The choice of geologic formation is based on use as well as achieving some aesthetic intention. Stone comes in many different forms as shown in Figure 8.10. It can be a processed product such as crushed rock or rock quarried with specific dimensions cut into a modular form (such as for paving) or cut in a variety of predetermined shapes for walls, outdoor furniture, or a variety of designed

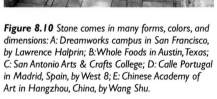

Figure 8.10 Stone comes in many forms, colors, and dimensions: A: Dreamworks campus in San Francisco, by Lawrence Halprin; B: Whole Foods in Austin, Texas; C: San Antonio Arts & Crafts College; D: Calle Portugal in Madrid, Spain, by West 8; E: Chinese Academy of Art in Hangzhou, China, by Wang Shu.

structures such as signs, fountains, or architectural elements. And of course stone and boulders can be selected, as they are found in situ in nature, then transported to the construction site, as was the case for the Levi Strauss Plaza shown in Figure 5.11. Stones excavated from rivers or quarried from geologic strata are further processed and separated by size, perhaps washed clean for use in exposed aggregate concrete mixes, or placed directly loose on the ground as a mulch or decorative surface.

Examples of the various applications of stone are shown in Figure 8.10 (A–E). The stone shown in Figure 8.10A consists of two different materials, including natural boulders used for informal seating and for definition of a small employee seating area. A processed product in the form of crushed rock is used as a walking surface in the seating area. Poured-in-place concrete paving provides access to the area. The outdoor eating area of the Whole Foods store in Austin, Texas, shown in Figure 8.10B consists of both quarried flagstone and natural stone of varying sizes to create the flowing stream feature. Quarried limestone was used to face the low seating wall and flagstone pieces set in mortar[1] over a concrete sub-base provide the walking and seating surfaces. Figure 8.10C demonstrates the use of quarried limestone as facing materials for the low garden walls, pavement, and the classroom building. Quarried rock processed into modular sizes was installed on a sand base to create the black and white pattern of the paved plaza shown in Figure 8.10D. The seating walls were made with poured-in-place concrete. Figure 8.10E is an entrance walk and garden to a conference facility at the Chinese Academy of Art, by Wang Shu.[2] A variety of stone materials were used to add interest, including a boulder found in nature, crushed rock, and broken clay tile for the central walking surface. A small vessel formed from rock was placed opposite the boulder.

The two examples in Figure 8.11 were paired together to show the contrasting range of visual effects one is able to achieve by selecting stone as a surface material. The walk and stairs shown in Figure 8.11A were constructed with river-washed stones arranged with a flower motif and set in mortar to secure the stones. Larger quarried rock pieces form a border for the washed stone pattern. The width of the walk was extended with a similar quarried rock as well as in constructing the stairway. Quarried igneous rock was used in the construction of the plaza shown in Figure 8.11B. The modular rock units were secured with mortar with an added mortar joint between the units. The

Figure 8.11 A: Stone walk and stairs at the Summer Palace, Beijing, China; B: Broken fragments of flagstone and modular stone pavers, plaza in front of the Church of Santo Domingo, Zacatecas, Mexico.

broken rock portion of the paved surface was given a wider spacing with smaller broken rock pieces used to infill the joint spaces. Since occasional traffic from motorized vehicles was anticipated, the plaza surfaces were constructed over a concrete sub-base at least 4 to 6 inches (10–15 cm) thick with compacted fill underneath for structural support.

Stone and rock materials support a wide variety of applications and potential patterns from the exuberant (see Figure 8.12A) to modular and symmetrical patterns (see Figure 8.12B). Both examples used quarried stone and in the case of the stone used in Figure 8.12A, it was set in a sand base. A great many of the public sidewalks and public spaces in Portugal—and to some degree in Brazil—use a similar stone and construction method. One of the benefits of stone set in sand is that it allows portions of the pavement to be removed in order to repair underground utilities and other maintenance operations. After the underground work is completed, the stone is replaced on a new sand base with sand swept in to fill the cracks, thus locking the stone in place. The stone in the Madrid, Spain, example was set on a concrete base and filled in with mortar. A solid base was necessary as trucks and other heavy equipment are driven into the space to set up many public events.

Two more examples to demonstrate stone's versatility are shown in Figure 8.13. The two examples have been paired to show the contrast in size of stone that can be specified. The limestone stone in Figure 8.13A was quarried from a local source and used in the construction of a contemporary visitor center. The same stone was used to match the much older Spanish Colonial mission complex, a decision made by the US National Park Service to provide visual cohesion between the architecture of two time periods. Though the architectural styles of the mission and visitor center are very different, a successful visual cohesion was created. A crushed limestone-like material was used in the construction of the linear pathway and several gathering areas in the Madrid park shown in Figure 8.13B. The rock is manufactured mechanically with rock crushing equipment.

Figure 8.12 A: Dom Pedro IV Plaza, Lisbon, Portugal; B: Plaza Mayor, Madrid, Spain.

Figure 8.13 A: Quarried local limestone used for paving and facing of National Park Service visitors center, Mission San Jose, San Antonio, Texas; B: Crushed rock walkway, Parque Lineal del Manzanares, Madrid, Spain, by West 8.

Figure 8.14 A: Stone and concrete wall, Taliesin West, Scottsdale, Arizona, by Frank Lloyd Wright, architect; B: Gabion wall, Phoenix Waterworks Park, by Christine Ten Eyck.

The material produced has sharp edges, facilitating compaction to 95 percent density that can support occasional vehicle maintenance traffic but, more importantly, allows surface water to percolate to the soil below. The crushed rock also enhances the experience of pedestrians as their footsteps produce a soft crunching noise. The crushed rock produces a more resilient surface than concrete, affording greater comfort for pedestrians.

Two walls made with rock with very different appearance are shown in Figure 8.14. The wall in Figure 8.14A was constructed first by building a wooden form. Native rocks of different shapes and sizes gathered from the surrounding landscape were placed in the form as a wet concrete mix was being poured into the form. Wood strips were nailed inside the form so that after the concrete had set, the forms were pulled away from the concrete. The wood strips left an impression in the face of the exposed wall surface. The garden walls, much of the pavement, and the building architecture used a similar system, furthering the architect's desire to blend the structures in with the natural landscape. The wall in Figure 8.14B used a gabion wall system. A gabion is modular system, essentially wire baskets made from welded wire mesh. The baskets are filled with loose stones and later secured in place by a lid on the top. The lid is secured shut with wire after the baskets are filled. The baskets are generally constructed of a consistent dimension for a specific project. The stone-filled baskets are then stacked like bales of hay or bags of sand to construct the wall. The baskets remain held in place by gravity. The stone used in making the wall pictured came from a quarry, was crushed to the desired size, then transported, and placed in the wire baskets at the project site.

Brick: Another Type of Manufactured Modular Material

Bricks have been used in building construction in regions around the world for many thousands of years. Early cultures produced bricks using clay soil, sometimes mixed with sand and straw, then left in the sun to dry. The bricks from this method are referred to as adobe and, while suitable for wall construction, the material was susceptible to erosion if left unprotected. Covering the surface with a protective slurry material reduced the destructive erosion from rain. The slurry could easily be reapplied as weathering occurred. Bricks used in masonry construction today are fire-hardened in kilns and are not susceptible to erosion. Fired bricks are one of the longest-lasting, most durable, and strongest materials used for landscape and architectural purposes. Bricks are produced in numerous sizes, shapes, and colors. The color is a result of the type of clay and other ingredients used, as well as the method and duration of the firing. Brick units are individually laid in courses (layers) and patterns. Mortar is used to bind the bricks together. Generic brick is made from clay as opposed to other modular unit products that may look similar to clay brick but are usually made from concrete.

The walk shown in Figure 8.15 uses two materials: poured-in-place concrete and brick. The concrete has no color additive but does have a light exposed aggregate surface. The brick pattern was applied after the concrete had been poured and hardened. Pre-cast light-colored concrete squares were also laid at the same time as the brick. The brick and concrete units were laid over a concrete slab, then mortared in place.

Brick is an amazingly flexible material in terms of patterns that can be created. The patterns can be "large-grained" with bold, repeated

Figure 8.15 Concrete walk with brick detailing. University of California at Los Angeles, by Ralph Cornell, landscape architect.

Figure 8.16 Brick-surfaced public courtyard and seating area on the Viaduct, in Paris, France.

forms as shown in Figure 8.15 or they can be "fine-grained" producing a textural quality such as shown in Figure 8.16 on the Viaduct[3] in Paris. The pattern of brick in Figure 8.16 acts as background allowing the water rills and tree wells that were installed to be more prominent. The visual effect is created as if the shapes for the rills and tree wells were cut out of the brick pavement surface. The shade cast from the tree canopy creates added visual interest to the pavement surface. The deep shade pattern, as seen from a walkway above the seating area, suggests a cooler place to get away from the heat of the day.

The worker in Figure 8.17 is installing modular concrete units on a bed of sand. Prior to placing a layer of sand, a crushed rock base was first placed, then compacted to 90–95 percent density. The compacted rock serves as the structural base to support vehicle traffic. The sand allows the modular units to be made level. After they are set in place, loose sand is swept between the spaces to secure the bricks in place.

Metal

The world of materials can be bewildering, and, for the uninitiated, sometimes daunting.

Figure 8.17 Installing modular concrete units, Amsterdam, the Netherlands.

Take something as common as a nail. Nails not only come in different sizes and shapes. They are also made of different materials, such as steel, stainless steel, aluminum, and for specialized applications are coated, such as galvanized nails. And then there are nails that you apply by pounding in by hand with a hammer or with a power stapler (the nails of a staple are akin to staples). In the construction documents the landscape architect specifies the choice of nails the contractor is to use. The choice is not simple and would depend on the application. In this section we will look at several metal materials and how they are used in landscape architecture.

Steel is a common material used in the construction of outdoor furniture, railings, walkway and decking surfaces, fences, signage, outdoor building structures, such as pergolas, shade structures, and enclosed structures associated with outdoor uses. Steel materials can be composed of a variety of ingredients depending on the intended application. Steel is a manufactured material created through a variety of fabrication processes. When the designer is considering the use of steel for either fastening—such as nails and bolts—or in the fabrication of a designed element—such as a bench, railing, or outdoor structure—the type of steel must be considered, followed by a technical specification. The primary ingredient of steel is iron. Iron is a metal produced from quarried iron ore[4] and in a furnace in combination with coke and other materials. It is then processed into other materials, including these common products: steel (rolled and cast), wrought iron, and stainless steel. These materials can then be further processed into a rolled form for later fabrication into a great variety of products, cast with the use of a mold into modular units, and welded together to make girders and other structural steel products. A reinforcing bar is a product of steel used primarily to increase the structural properties in the construction of concrete walls, footings, and pavement. Part of the responsibility of the designer when specifying steel or any metal product is to indicate the type of steel and other desired pertinent physical properties required, depending on the application. For instance, a steel bench could be made from wrought or cast iron, stainless steel, or fabricated from rolled steel. Detailing must further specify the product dimensions, the surface treatment (galvanized, acid, baked enamel or other product), and method of assembly (fasteners or welded) described in the technical specification requirements. Figure 8.18 is a steel shade structure constructed from a product called corten steel or under the trademark: Cor-Ten. Cor-Ten is a steel alloy formulated to eliminate the need for painting or surface treatment. When installed, it is allowed to weather (corrode) to form a rust-like, stable finish. Other forms of steel products, if left untreated without a protective coating (such as paint and galvanized

Figure 8.18 *Steel shade structure, Phoenix Botanical Garden, by Steve Martino, landscape architect.*

Figure 8.19 *Reinforcing bar used to create a see-through wall or fence at a residence in Scottsdale, Arizona, by Steve Martino, landscape architect.*

Figure 8.20 *Woven sheet metal wall, Scottsdale, Arizona, by Steve Martino, landscape architect.*

treatment) will corrode or rust. The corrosion process, if left uncorrected, may result in structural failure. In Figure 8.19 the landscape architect has designed a see-through fence or physical barrier with the clever use of a common steel material: the reinforcing bar. This fence detail is an example of the range of innovations available to landscape architects when selecting and designing with different materials.

Sheet metal (ferrous or aluminum) is another form of steel that comes in rolls for later use in fabricating landscape features, such as the fence shown in Figure 8.20. The steel used is an alloy developed to resist rusting or corrosion. The fence was constructed on the site using rolls of the material woven between upright reinforcing bars anchored in a concrete foundation.

Aluminum is another common metal used in the landscape. Figure 8.21 presents an area barrier that was designed to have a dual purpose: as a continuous bench and a crowd barrier. The protective railing shown in Figure 8.22 was fabricated from aluminum. The pieces were arranged into a cat-tail motif, and welded in a shop into panel modules prior to installation on site.

Wood is one of the most often used materials in the construction of features designed by landscape architects. The world of wood can be as confusing to students as metal can be. The specifications and options for wood can be extensive. One needs to specify the tree species of the wood source (pine, fir, redwood, teak, etc.) as well as how the wood was cured (dried after being milled from the trunk), the location of the wood from within the trunk (heart or an outer layer), and whether or not it has been treated, such as pressure treated to resist rotting. One also must specify if the wood is to be free of knots, and how it is positioned into place, whether the "curl" of the wood grains is facing up or down.

Figure 8.21 *Aluminum bench–railing combination, 2008 Summer Olympics, Beijing, China.*

Figure 8.22 Metal railing, Lake Austin, Texas, by TBG Partnership.

Depending on the application, further specifications might be needed to ensure the correct wood product is used, fabricated correctly, fastened with the appropriate fasteners (for instance, iron, brass, or stainless steel bolts or nails), and finally finished with the correct paint, stain, or other surface treatment. To mention in passing, the choice of finishing products also requires careful consideration. Choosing the correct type of paint or stain is the responsibility of the landscape architect.

Wood is an adaptable material for a great many uses in the landscape. Wood is used in the fabrication of outdoor furniture. The two different benches shown in Figure 8.23 were made from different wood materials, surface treatment, and fabrication details. Wood is also used in the construction of fences and railings (Figure 8.24), and decks (Figures 8.25A and 8.25B).

Figure 8.23 A: Wooden bench, Telefónica office campus, Madrid, Spain; B: New York City High Line wood benches, by James Corner, landscape architect.

Figure 8.24 A: Wood boardwalk with wood railing, wildlife visitor center, Louisiana; B: Boardwalk providing access across marsh, Marin County, California.

Figure 8.25 A: Wooden pedestrian deck, Zud Park, Rotterdam, the Netherlands; B: Wooden stage, and covered structure, Discovery Green, Houston, Texas, by Hargreaves and Associates.

Examples of Material Selection to Create a Variety of Results

Two examples of outdoor amphitheater seating are shown in Figure 8.26. Both amphitheaters were constructed with quarried stone. The seating in Figure 8.26A was constructed with a highly finished stone while for the seating in Figure 8.26B the material was purposefully selected to give a rougher appearance, reflecting a more natural setting.

Wood can be selected in its more-or-less natural form. The information kiosk shown in Figure 8.27 was constructed using tree logs for the support columns. The roof and information panels were made from more processed wood materials as well as river-washed stone for the column bases of the structure.

Figure 8.26 Amphitheaters: A: Poured-in-place concrete, Paseo de Santa Lucia, Monterrey, Mexico, by Enrique Albarroa; B: Quarried rock, Stern Grove Amphitheater using quarried stone, San Francisco, California, by Lawrence Halprin, landscape architect.

Figure 8.27 Information kiosk, Denali National Park, Alaska.

Figure 8.28 *Three benches designed for public outdoor use areas. A is a manufactured wood and aluminum product; B are benches made of quarried limestone stone; C is custom-made with quarried stone base, pre-cast concrete pavement detail, and wood seat.*

Figure 8.28 provides a comparison of three benches constructed from three different materials. Not only are the designs different but so are the materials used. To some degree, the design or shape of the benches is a reflection of the physical attributes of the materials themselves.

The bridge and adjacent elements shown in Figure 8.29 are an example of the design potential of using a variety of materials to create an attractive, functional design. The decking and handrail were fabricated from wood with steel guardrail uprights. The railing abuts a masonry wall faced with native stone. A gravel path made from crushed stone leads to the decking of the wood bridge. The detailing of the stone wall and railing visually blend within the forest context. This excellent example of designing with a light hand is an attempt to be compatible with the forested context.

Figure 8.29 Bridge leading through a fern and mixed hardwood forest.

Fountains and Pools

Fountains and other water features are also designed by landscape architects They can be made from a wide variety of materials in combination with a variety of equipment, such as pumps, nozzles, or lighting systems. As you will see in the following figures, material selection can produce many different shapes and ways of displaying water. The fountain in Figure 8.30A is a traditional fountain design of a Romanesque or Mediterranean style. The design is similar to fountains found in Spanish or Latin American courtyards and public spaces. The body of water with the central water feature in Figure 8.30B might be more difficult to place stylistically but is reminiscent of the romanticized water features that have elements taken from nature.

In contrast to these two water features that are found in contemporary public spaces, we turn to seventeenth-century France and the beyond exuberant display of water found at Parc de Sceaux designed by André Le Nôtre in Figure 8.31A. Nearly still water can also produce dynamic visual effects when the fountain is positioned to take advantage of the movement of sun during the day (Figure 8.31B). The materials used to build the fountain and the degree of roughness of their surface can reflect sunlight through the lens of the water (moving or still), creating a vibrancy normally associated with splashing water.

Figure 8.30 A: Traditional courtyard fountain, Getty Villa in Los Angeles, by Emmett Wemple, landscape architect; B: Contemporary fountain and lake by Lawrence Halprin on the Dreamworks campus at the Presidio in San Francisco, California.

Figure 8.31 A: *Parc de Sceaux, Paris, by André Le Nôtre;*
B: *Xintiandi, Shanghai, China.*

Water assumes the form of the vessel that contains it. The water then can be brought to life by moving the water as in a stream or canal or by the water falling by gravity such as over rocks or down a constructed wall. Sunlight or artificial light is needed to increase the intensity of the lively quality of the moving water. Water can be caused to defy gravity with a force supplied by mechanical pumps through a nozzle or series of nozzles. A water stream is directed by mechanical means into the air, such as shown in the two images in Figure 8.31: Parc de Sceaux in Paris and Xintiandi in Shanghai or the fountains at the Santa Monica City Hall and Los Angeles' Grand Park in Figure 8.32. Designed bodies of water can be still, quiet, and calm. The water comes to life with sunlight and the shadows cast by clouds or adjacent trees and structures as shown in the two examples in Figures 8.33A and 8.33B.

Figure 8.32 A: *Santa Monica City Hall fountain, by James Corner, landscape architect; B: Grand Park in Los Angeles, California, by Clementi and Ríos, landscape architects.*

Figure 8.33 A: Golden Street, Shanghai, China, by SWA landscape architects; B: Paseo de Santa Lucia River Walk, Monterrey, Mexico, by Enrique Albarroa, landscape architect.

Wind can cause a still sheet of water to shimmer as it produces ripples which in turn act as prisms bending and contorting the sunlight that is reflected by the water.

Soil

Soil is a living entity. It is living in the sense that it is full of life: billions of microorganisms. These organisms are beneficial to the lives of plants and other living creatures that are dependent on soil. The presence of these microorganisms is central to the process of soil nutrient creation and air and water transfer to other organisms including plants. Soils are the resulting product of geologic, climatic, hydrologic, and biological processes. Soils are created in the process of mountain building and their erosion from wind and temperature fluctuations, water movement, such as streams and surface runoff, and the grinding action of advancing and retreating glaciers. Soil creation is the result of erosive action, deposition, and chemical and biological processes. Plants are contributors to soil creation in several ways. The decomposition process of leaves, branches, and whole trees contributes to the build-up of soil. Various fauna such as worms, bacteria, various microbes, and other life-forms further the breakdown of large soil particles into finer and often nutritionally enhanced chemical nutrients, including nitrogen and other elements important to plant life.

And there are many different types of soils: both found naturally and formulated by landscape architects for specific purposes. The soil needs of plants installed in a designed landscape vary greatly, depending on a range of considerations, including climate, rainfall, location of the planting beds, and the uses that could affect plant performance such as playfields for active sports.

Whenever feasible, landscape architects will include the stockpiling of the valuable surface soils occurring on a project site at the outset of earth-moving operations. Provisions for setting aside these soils are made in a site grading plan and the earthworks section of the technical specifications. The stockpiled soil is used later during construction for various landscape purposes, such as the preparation of planting beds and lawn areas. In situations where soils suitable for later landscape use are not available, the landscape architect will prepare a technical specification, setting forth the composition of materials (sand, silt, clay, and organic materials) to create appropriate manufactured soils for specific uses. Soil amendments such as lime, fertilizer, organics, and sand are often specified and included in the soil technical specifications. Often times a landscape contractor will purchase or secure soil from another site. The landscape architect will have the final say whether to accept or reject the contractor-furnished soils. The basis of the evaluation will include soil composition, testing, and even approval of the source location. Soils brought from bogs would probably be rejected for a variety of technical reasons, for instance, the material had not been excavated, dried, and properly stored a year in advance of use on a project. Soils that contain sticks, branches and stones of a certain size (that are too large) would be rejected as well as soils containing pieces of concrete, metal, and other potentially harmful materials. The science of soil has a long history involving much research. To the uninitiated, soil is soil. However, it is the responsibility of the landscape architect to ensure the appropriate soil is provided for each landscape application. The same is true for general fill material in site preparation. For instance, gravels used in structural fill for pavements, roads, and structural backfill for walls must meet the standards set in the technical specifications for constructed backfill. Technical specifications for each fill type are included and are a part of the contract document package prepared by the landscape architect and, in some cases, the civil engineer.

Soil Stewardship

Soils can suffer degradation of their plant and microorganism support properties through intense and continuous cultivation or animal overgrazing. Soils can be further degraded with inappropriate water management, contaminated by the impact of poorly managed mineral extraction and the resulting runoff of toxic chemicals. Previously misused and degraded soils can be improved and built up towards their previous healthy condition through the application of systematically employed management techniques. An example of a once-depleted soil is shown in Figure 8.34. This is an example of agriculture land under managed cultivation. The land was once healthy oak-grassland community and was biologically diverse until the 1930s. The Portuguese government decreed that the thin, rocky soils of the Alentejo Province were to be cleared of their oak and grassland cover, then prepared for growing wheat. Predictably and unfortunately, this government policy did not achieve the desired results of production. After a few years of unsuccessful harvests, the program was dropped, leaving vast areas of depleted and mostly denuded land. The other impact from the disastrous government policy was extensive erosion intensified by the lack of soil-holding grasses. Recently the Portuguese government has established a policy with partial subsidies for interested farmers and landowners to rebuild the soil and re-establish native plant communities. Notice the furrows in Figure 8.34, showing an area prepared for planting of crops. Other areas with oak tree and native grass cover are systematically managed as part of a national effort to rebuild native soils and re-establish native plant species. Soils are similar to water and air resources. They must be cared for and not used with little regard to the potential and devastating impacts that human actions might cause. While depletion and degradation of a region's soils may be evident, reversing the process towards a more healthy and sustainable result is possible. This can be achieved through an enlightened and responsible citizenry and government in partnership, implementing a land and soil stewardship program.

Figure 8.34 *Farm in the Alentejo Province of Central Portugal.*

Having Fun with Materials

One of the messages of this chapter is that materials are a kaleidoscope of possibilities: possible choices and possible design directions. It is a subject that should be seen as an opportunity to challenge and reward the landscape architect throughout one's professional career. While the selection and specification process of materials may seem like work—and it is—it also can produce some fun results. In Figure 8.35 you can see two examples of the playful use of two different materials. Concrete and iron may not seem to have attributes that can add a stroke of

Figure 8.35 A: *Man emerging from stone wall, Santa Barbara, California; B: Bridge railing made of cast and wrought iron, Amsterdam, the Netherlands.*

Figure 8.36 *Rubber garden gloves found in a private garden in Amsterdam, the Netherlands.*

humor or just plain fun to a design. Of course, the materials in and of themselves are not necessarily imbued with fun qualities but they are of sufficient flexibility that they can be formed and molded into design moments that not only produce a fun or humorous touch to a landscape feature but bring attention to the feature that might be overlooked otherwise. Design is a potential vehicle for a landscape architect who cannot help envisioning the potential joy someone might experience by adding a humorous touch in the landscape. Maybe humor might not seem appropriate but certainly there is nothing wrong by making sure the human touch or presence is experienced. One never knows what might pop into one's mind while in the midst of the design process. Be ready to respond when it does happen with the knowledge and understanding of how to select and use the range of materials possible to fully realize the unexpected stroke of inspiration.

Figure 8.36 captures what might be visual communication between neighbors sharing a common garden wall in a dense residential neighborhood in Amsterdam. The intent of the one neighbor who went to the trouble of carefully placing some rubber gloves on the garden wall can have several explanations. Perhaps it was simply an attempt at a bit of neighborly friendliness as if waving "hello." There are other explanations that for now we will leave up to the reader to have a bit of fun with in coming up with an interpretation.

Notes

1 Mortar consists of Portland cement mixed with water and, in some cases, sand. It was used in this example to bond slabs of flagstone to the concrete sub-base. Mortar is also used as the bonding materials in constructing brick and stone walls and pavement.
2 2012 recipient of the Pritzker Architecture Prize.
3 Raised linear park built on top of an abandoned railroad viaduct in Paris, France.
4 Steel is also made from recycled scrap steel.

Further Reading

Readings to expand your appreciation of landscape materials and design detailing:

Robert Holden and Jamie Liversedge, *Construction for Landscape Architecture*, Laurence King Publishers, London, 2011.

Niall Kirkwood, *The Art of Landscape Detail: Fundamentals, Practices, and Case Studies*, John Wiley & Sons, Inc., Hoboken, NJ, 1999.

Virginia McLeod, *Detail in Contemporary Landscape Architecture*, Laurence King Publishers, London, 2012.

David Sauter, *Landscape Construction*, 3rd edn, Delmar-Cenagage, Clifton Park, NY, 2011.

CHAPTER NINE

DESIGN REALIZATION

Introduction

The technical aspects of landscape architecture are commonly referred to as *site engineering* or *landscape technology*. In this book the term *design realization* will be used. Design realization is generally concerned with site grading and drainage; road and trail design; landscape planting; and structural aspects of pavement, walls, decks, and special features such as fountains. Design realization can extend to the more general realm of the preparation of the technical drawings and details that translate design drawings of Schematic and Design Development Phases (the illustrative plan, perspective three-dimensional drawings, and sections) into the types of drawings a contractor would use to construct the project. In this chapter we will review the subjects and the technical aspects that a landscape architect would have all or some responsibility for preparing the drawings used to guide construction.

A design is a proposal usually communicated with drawings and models of what the landscape architect imagines for a project when considering client program needs (functions or activities), government design and planning requirements, and the physical characteristics of the project site. The design translates the wants, needs, and desires of a client or users into a design, by considering the physical site and its topography, the project program, government requirements, climate, and host of other considerations. The design proposal consists of a range of drawings, including plans, perspectives, sections, and diagrams that together communicate to the client and users the landscape architect's design proposal. In the case of a government client, the drawings prepared by a landscape architect are also used in the approval process. The approval process may extend to additional stakeholders such as government agencies having specific authority over the type of project or the specific project site requiring their administrative or legal approval.[1] Once the client approves the initial design proposal (schematic design), the subsequent steps follow to further develop the initial drawings into a second and third iteration of drawings that advance and develop the design into further detail. The final step (construction documentation) includes preparing a set of detailed drawings including: grading, layout, demolition, and planting plans, and construction details, together with supporting written technical specifications that will be used by the contractor to build the project.

Contractors develop their bids to construct the project using the package of drawings and specifications together with a construction contract. Once the client, in consultation with the landscape architect, selects a contractor, a construction contract is signed and work can begin.

The type of drawings required will depend on the design project elements:

- If plants are to be planted together with an irrigation system to be installed, then planting and irrigation plans with supporting technical details will need to be prepared.
- If the existing topography is to be modified, then a grading plan with supporting details and sections will need to be prepared.
- If walls, paving, fountains, bridges, and other structures and physical elements are to be built, then detailed site layout plans, sections, and structural details will need to be prepared.
- If lighting, site furniture (benches, tables, and such items as bicycle racks) are to be installed, then layout plans, electrical and water service plans with supporting details will need to be prepared.
- If infrastructure, including storm drains or low impact design features is needed, then a piping plan, service connection layouts, and technical sections with supporting details will need to be prepared.

Below is a list of the more common plans/drawings included in a construction drawing package for a residence or small commercial project. A small landscape project has a limited scope of work and level of complexity. Large, more complex projects having specialized design features such as a fountain or pool, specialized equipment such as children's play structures and play environment, skateboard facility, or low impact design features would require additional plan drawings, sections, details, and equipment schedules. For example, the construction drawing set for a zoo design could easily have 200–300 or more sheets of drawings in order to adequately cover the scope and complexity of this specialized project type. The redesign of urban streets as part of an area re-vitalization project could easily require 100 or more sheets of drawings. A team of consultants would contribute to the preparation of these drawings, including civil and electrical, and geotechnical engineering with structural recommendations, architects, traffic engineers, and others, depending on the scope of work. A topographic survey prepared by a land surveyor may also be included, showing all the existing site conditions, topography, and structures. This same information—in a modified form—will be the basis of the proposed site grading and demolition plans. A typical construction drawing package would include the following:

- A cover sheet that would include: name of project, client, list of consultants, and sometimes a list of sheet titles (sheet index) and their page reference number. A project location map may also be included.
- Site reference plan and general notes, abbreviations.
- Plant protection and removal plan.
- Site demolition plan.

- Hardscape: layout of paved surfaces, walks, roads, and parking (Figure 9.1).
- Site layout plan.
- Site grading and drainage plan (Figure 9.2).
- Tree, shrub, and groundcover planting plan with plant list.
- Site lighting plan.
- Planting details.
- Irrigation plan with equipment list and details.
- Site furnishings plan with equipment list and details.
- Site details: including construction details and technical sections/ elevations.

Each sheet is numbered, following a numbering convention where all drawings related to landscape, for instance, begin with the prefix letter "L," such as L-1, L-2, etc. and A-1, A-2 for architecture. The convention is that each sheet has a page number and the number appears in the lower right-hand corner of the sheet along with a title block that runs along the right side of the page or along the bottom. The title block appears on all sheets and includes as a minimum: project name, location, client; sheet subject (such as grading plan);

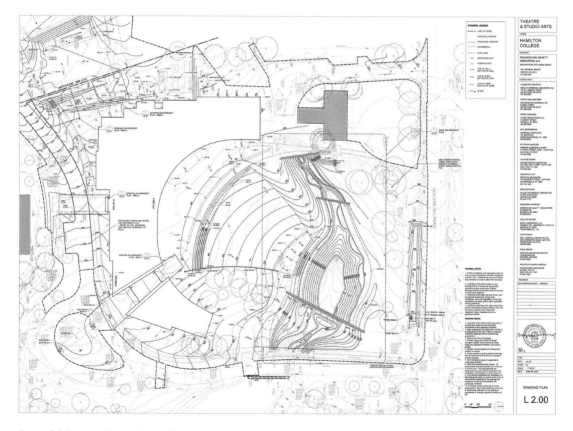

Figure 9.1 Paving and materials plan. Courtesy of Reed-Hilderbrand Landscape Architects.

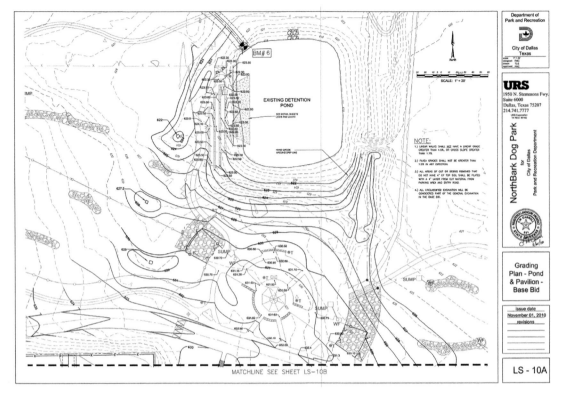

Figure 9.2 *Grading plan for Northbark Dog Park. Courtesy of Parks and Recreation Department of Dallas, Texas.*

consultant (prime consultant and the sub-consultants responsible for their appropriate sheet); date and list of revisions with dates; author and project manager; and a stamp where professional licensure is required. All plan drawings must have a scale and a north arrow, while a north arrow may not be necessary for individual details and section drawings. Where drawings are not drawn to scale, it must be so noted.[2]

Drawings and details show where (location) the designed elements are situated on the project site, the materials of construction (concrete, wood, stone, metal, finishes (paint, stain, coatings)), and details showing how the materials are to be installed, fastened or joined to one another. The landscape architect together with consultants on the team prepare the necessary drawings that basically show what, where, and how the materials are to be installed as well as the type and quality of materials. Complementary to the drawings the team members will prepare technical specifications for their respective area of design responsibility. The technical specifications explain the standards of quality expected of all materials and workmanship. For instance, what type of wood, the grade of each type, and the physical attributes that will be acceptable. In the case of soil, the technical specifications would define—if there is more than one type or grade of soil—the percentage content of organic material, sand, clay, silt, and any additives, the pH limits, and would specify such requirements as the absence of stones, rocks, twigs and other plant parts, and deleterious materials such as metal parts or rubbish.

Professional Responsibility: Protecting the Health, Safety, and Welfare of the Public

The Americans with Disabilities Act (ADA), administered by the U.S. Department of Justice, promulgates design standards, providing for enforceable accessibility and barrier removal standards in public places and facilities.[3] The published standards for accessible design apply to new construction and for older facilities undergoing updating and alterations. The design accessibility and barrier removal standards apply at the federal level with states and local governments having adopted similar standards. For example, access to public buildings or outdoor spaces must allow for wheelchair or other ambulatory considerations of the public. In order to comply, new designs must provide access ramps to enter the building or outdoor spaces. The ramps must conform to design standards of ramp length, width, and maximum slope. Where handrails are provided, they must conform to specific design standards. The general idea of the accessibility of design standards is to provide equal access to all populations. A facility that was designed providing wheelchair access other than at the front or main entrance may conform to the letter of the law; however, a building with a back or service access would be considered an insensitive design, creating a psychological barrier. Landscape architects must adhere to accessibility design standards for all design elements and project types, including parks, plazas, pedestrian circulation, children's play areas, and all outdoor use areas and facilities. At the outset of a design project, a landscape architect must carry out *due diligence*[4] to research all applicable laws and design standards to ensure their designs will conform.

Landscape architects are expected to be familiar with and understand the pertinent laws and government requirements in carrying out their work. They are expected to know, for instance, the zoning laws, design standards, and other regulations including the following areas:

1. FEMA flood plain elevation criteria, including 100-year flood requirements.
2. Wetland protection requirements, including the design review process necessary to determine whether conformity has been achieved and approved.
3. Vehicular circulation design standards, including turning radii, roadway lane width, line-of-sight design standards, parking lot design, and other design metrics associated with the vehicular circulation systems.
4. Municipal zoning, including green laws (landscape requirements), building setbacks, parking lot provisions, and signage design standards.
5. Storm-water management design standards, including Best Management Practices (BMP) and Low Impact Design (LID).

6. Specialized requirements, such as design for reduced water consumption (particularly in arid regions), snow removal and storage design standards (in cold weather regions), irrigation system design requirements, regulations guiding use of invasive plant species, and construction-related restoration requirements.
7. Surface soil erosion and dust control impacting adjoining properties and public roads.

Design Considerations

Matching Program Elements with Suitable Topographic Slopes

Earlier in the design process chapter, Chapter 3, *program analysis* was discussed. The process begins with meeting with the client to identify the project program: the activities and facilities to be incorporated in what will ultimately be the design. For example, if the project is a neighborhood park, the landscape architect would meet with the client (the professional staff of the parks department) to identify what types of facilities and activities are desired. Will the park serve as a passive or active facility?, should it have a children's play area and for what age groups?, should there be a group picnic area or playfield for active sports?, and should other functional elements and facilities be incorporated in the proposed park plan? Programming under a professional contract scope of work may also include such activities as wetland protection and storm-water management, both important aspects of site development that the landscape architect may have the responsibility to consider and incorporate into a design solution.

Once a program is identified, a diagram showing the desired physical relations between the design elements would then be prepared. This diagram is also referred to as a program coordination diagram, that groups program activities that are preferably adjacent or in close proximity and that might share certain functional elements such as parking or outdoor common areas. A circulation diagram would be superimposed, showing access, vehicular traffic flow and sequence, and pedestrian circulation requirements. Based on these other diagrams the landscape architect would prepare one or more preliminary schematic design proposals.

One approach to deciding the best location to place each program use area is to match each program with the most suitable percentage of slope category prepared during the slope analysis. The slope recommendations should cover most situations; however, special circumstances may require adjustments. The exception is where maximum slope standards must be adhered to, as in the case of 8 percent for ADA accessible ramps and where government codes dictate specific maximum–minimum slope standards. Creating a slope analysis of the project site is useful to help determine the optimum locations for the various program elements. The slope analysis map might be constructed identifying four or five classes of slope. For instance, areas that are 0–5 percent, 6–10 percent, 11–20 percent, and areas over 21 percent. After completing the slope map for a project site, the landscape architect would then match the slope preferences of each program activity (parking lot, building structures, outdoor use areas, etc.) to the slope analysis map created for the site. At least one preliminary site bubble diagram would be created, eventually leading to the preparation of a preliminary site design plan.

Grading and Drainage

It is interesting how compartmentalized the various topics in a landscape architecture curriculum are presented. Design, plant materials, site grading, history and theory, and other topics are offered as separate courses. The integration of the different subjects generally comes about after graduation and during the apprenticeship phase of professional development. This process of integration—making whole—should occur much earlier than it does, and in some curricula this happens. The accomplished landscape architect thinks about and considers all the elements that are part of a landscape design nearly simultaneously. As the seasoned designer develops a design, the physical manifestation of the design, including grading, planting, materials, and details, are simultaneously in mind, whether drawing by hand or working with a computer. Landforms and all the various terrain features that are the underpinnings of a design are visualized, at least in one's mind, as a design develops and unfolds in schematic and later phases in the design process. The landscape architect is thinking about elevation—not necessarily in terms of specific numbers but the relative elevation differences—when designing an outdoor space, considering the alignment of a walkway or trail, or how a walkway connects to an entry plaza.

Once a design has been resolved, the relative ups and downs of the designed landscape are translated into contours, spot elevations, and sections. The building blocks for achieving competency in designing (solving)[5] grading plans for a project begin with being able to read topographic maps, including understanding scale and understanding various frames of survey reference such as datum terms of elevation and grids. After learning how to read a topographic map, one needs to learn the principles of working with contours, spot elevations, and slopes to arrive at grading solutions. The activity of landscape site grading design requires the knowledge and skills that include the following competency areas:

1. Be capable of integrating landscape site grading as one develops a site design plan and recognizing that site grading provides the underpinnings and three-dimensional framework of a landscape design. Thinking about landform and elevation is equally important to thinking about creation of forms, spaces, and the circulation system linking spaces.
2. Be familiar with drafting (drawing representation) conventions and use of architectural and engineering scales.
3. Be able to read topographic maps and be able to identify landform features such as hills, valleys, and steep and not so steep terrain, and drainage patterns. Be able to determine elevations of any point or feature from a topographic map.

4. Be able to visualize three-dimensional landscape from contours from a published topographic map, such as produced by the U.S. Geological Survey, or one prepared by a professional land surveyor.

5. Be able to create a land surface, path, or hardscape feature such as an entry plaza that has a prescribed or intentional slope.

6. Be able to manipulate (change or modify) contours in order to create desired landforms and sloping surfaces. Also, one must be able to manipulate contours so as to direct the flow of surface water in a desired direction such as away from a building entrance.

7. Be able to assign spot elevations in plan and on sections.

8. Be able to calculate the volume of earth moved within a project site and determine the volume of earth or other soil or rock material that needs to be transported to or off the project site.

9. Be able to prepare (draw) grading plans following graphic conventions so that contractors know what to build. The grading plans must be of sufficient detail so contractors can prepare with confidence a cost estimate for doing the required work as depicted in the drawings and other contract documents.

10. Be knowledgeable and understand the pertinent design standards and legal requirements associated with grading. This knowledge base may include functional design requirement of minimum and maximum slopes for various program elements (recreation fields, parking and circulation, and handicap access—standards for persons with ambulatory and other physical disabilities).

11. Be able to prepare grading plans that meet standards of care related to meeting public health, safety, and welfare design standards. That is, to produce grading plans that limit and reduce the chance of public harm, such as physical injury.

12. Be able to develop grading designs that fall within project budget constraints while meeting the client's program and functional requirements.

The preparation of site construction plans involves the collaboration of many disciplines. The typical team of consultants might include a landscape architect, a civil engineer, a land surveyor, an architect, a geotechnical engineer, and structural and electrical engineers. Professional land surveyors prepare the site survey and what serves as the base drawing for much of the site grading work required.

A landscape architect, civil engineer, or both in collaboration, typically prepare site-grading plans. How the two collaborate will vary by project. It is common for the landscape architect to prepare a preliminary site-grading plan during the schematic and design development phases of a project. These plans lay the foundation of the landscape grading, including the earth forms, slopes, and critical elevations of hardscape areas and structures. The civil engineer may then take over in the design of storm-water systems, principally sizing catch basins and below ground piping systems determined by runoff and infiltration calculations and the sizing of drainage channels. The civil engineer may also prepare the final site grading design of roads and parking lots. Assignment of responsibilities is established during the negotiation of the professional services contract and may also be dictated by local or state laws that specify the assignment of responsibilities for "stamping"[6] construction document drawings.

Notes

1 For example, a residential subdivision would require design review and approvals from several departments of a city where the project is located, and if the project contains wetlands design review, an approval would extend to other government authorities such as state and federal environmental quality or flood water management.
2 A good reference for drawing requirements and conventions is Design Workshop, *Landscape Architecture Documentation Standards: Principles, Guidelines and Best Practices* (John Wiley & Sons, Inc., New York, 2015).
3 Americans with Disability Act, U.S. Department of Justice, Civil Rights Division, *Information and Technical Assistance on the Americans with Disability Act,* see www.ada.gov.
4 Carrying out one's professional responsibility in conducting reasonable research of applicable laws, design standards, and other governmental requirements that apply in protecting public health, safety, and welfare so as to avoid harm to persons or property.
5 The word "solving" is commonly used to describe what a student does when given a grading assignment. Solving suggests the use of mathematics and formulas and therefore may reveal why students find it convenient to separate grading from studio design. The use of numbers and the employment of numerical calculations while implicit to solving grading and drainage problems are not implied in solving or creating design solutions.
6 *Stamping* is a term referring to a professional landscape architect physically imprinting his or her licensure number and signature on a construction drawing. The stamp is an indication of professional responsibility where governmental jurisdictions (usually at the state or federal level) require professional licensure and the disciplines required to prepare various construction documents. By stamping or signing a technical plan, the individual or firm represented by the stamp is responsible for the accuracy and completeness of the drawings in protecting the health, safety, and welfare of the public under the governing laws and design standards.

Further Reading

Furthering your understanding of the knowledge and skills in realizing landscape design:

Charles Harris and Nicholas Dines, *Time-Saver Standards for Landscape Architecture*, 2nd edn, McGraw-Hill Professional, New York, 1997.

Daniel Roehr and Elizabeth Fassman-Beck, *Living Roofs in Integrated Urban Water Systems,* Routledge, London, 2015.

Bruce G. Sharky, *Landscape Site Grading Principles: Grading with Design in Mind*, John Wiley & Sons, Inc., Hoboken, NJ, 2014.

Steven Strom, Kurt Nathan, and Jake Woland, *Site Engineering for Landscape Architects*, 6th edn, John Wiley & Sons, Inc., Hoboken, NJ, 2013.

Astrid Zimmermann, *Constructing Landscape*, 2nd edn, Birkhauser, Berlin, 2011.

CHAPTER TEN

GREEN INFRASTRUCTURE AND SUSTAINABLE DESIGN

Introduction

What is constructed on or taken from the land will most certainly have an impact on ecological systems. What is extracted out of the Earth and harvested in the landscape will have ecological impacts. What is consumed for energy will have impacts and affect the balances on the air, water, and land. All construction, extraction, harvesting, and consumption of the Earth's resources will affect the health, safety, and welfare of the world's flora and fauna, including humans. These human activities have affected and will continue to affect the quality of the Earth's resources, reduce biodiversity, increase the frequency and strength of natural disasters (hurricanes, floods, air pollution), and greatly alter (deteriorate) the quality of lives of future generations unless we reduce if not eliminate our detrimental exploitation of nature.

Sustainable Design: Myth or Achievable Goal?

There is a long history of human abuse of the Earth and its landscape. Oil exploration and development in the Gulf of Mexico and the resulting losses of tremendous areas of coastal wetland are one example of human activity that has resulted in an extreme deterioration of a once healthy coastal environment. The global extent of burning fossil fuels has caused an accelerated rise in global warming, resulting in sea-level rise with the potential of extensive flooding of the urban development that is located along the world's coastlines. History, first-hand experience, and science should be enough to influence the making of better or more enlightened decisions with respect to economic development, urban growth, and other human activities that require the utilization of natural resources and land development. In many cases, we continue to make the same decisions (planting Eucalyptus in the hope of some short-term economic gain) where the potential for environmental impact is predictable and measurable. In this chapter we will explore the meaning and the ambition of the term

Figure 10.1 *Traditional approach to disposing of surface rainwater by grading paved surfaces to drain toward an area catch basin.*

sustainable design. Sustainable design implies making design decisions that could result in less impact on environmental resources (land, water, and air). The aim of the term is not to reduce the quality and extent of environmental resources to the eventual detriment of future generations. Well-researched and reasoned decisions related to design in the environment should maintain or improve air and water quality, preserve or enhance biodiversity, and reduce if not eliminate any adverse environmental impacts such as soil erosion or flooding. Design based on informed thinking can improve the quality of life of the places where people live, work, and recreate. More simply put, I am reminded of the phrase: *Think globally, act locally* from the Whole Earth movement of the 1970s.

We do not need to be frozen in a state of inaction when we realize the enormity and complexity of the threats from global-scale environmental impacts such as the burning of coal and other fossil fuels. Through the implementation of thoughtful and broadly considered landscape designs that reduce energy demands, positive incremental improvements can make a significant difference. Collectively, incremental improvements can add up to substantial gains. Figure 10.1 shows the traditional approach to storm-water management. A tweak to the design of this way of managing unwanted surface runoff water is an example of how making incremental improvements can lead to solving a larger problem. The surface water could be diverted to the adjacent grassy area and allowed to percolate into the underground aquifer instead of being carried away by an underground storm-water infrastructure system. This "new" approach reduces overall water consumption by reducing the need for irrigation and eliminates the costly construction of an underground storm-water disposal system. Design innovations like this and others are now part of the increasing implementation of green infrastructure: using lessons learned from nature to solve traditional infrastructure needs.

Nature, a Model for Infrastructure

Thinking of nature and natural systems as infrastructure is a concept deeply rooted in historical precedence. Humans, certainly by the time they had evolved from hunter–gatherers to settle and create agricultural communities, worked with nature in establishing their fields and developing the means to irrigate and gather and store water. The systems of gathering and distributing water to irrigate fields cleverly harnessed the natural processes of annual flooding and surface water drainage patterns. Later, the flowing water of rivers and streams was used to power grain-milling apparatus, basically employing gravity flow to power the mill. Rivers and streams were later tapped as a source of energy to power factory equipment in the industrial age. Beginning in the 1970s with the environmental movement and renewed interest in reversing the ills caused by rapid industrialization in the twentieth century, sustainability and creating healthy, livable communities gained support. The idea of design with nature[1] was understood as a workable means to making better decisions. Natural systems can be incorporated into effective and sustainable strategies to significantly protect communities from flooding, moderate unwanted heat gain, and help to improve air and water quality. When nature is harnessed and incorporated into the design of infrastructural systems, it is called "green infrastructure."[2] Green infrastructure can be applied at all scales of the built environment and is closely associated with storm-water management, although it is being applied to a growing range of applications toward improving biodiversity, creating natural barriers or recovery systems from natural disasters, and improving the quality of life for urban dwellers.

Through the process of design, landscape architects incorporate site design and development practices that will allow healthy, naturally functioning ecosystems to continue. Incorporating the idea of design that maintains the healthy functioning of the ecosystems applies whether the project site is a large neighborhood, a commercial center, a park or sports facility, or an individual residence. By considering the implementation of sustainable design strategies. development on the land can avoid, mitigate, and possibly reverse detrimental environmental impacts and at the same time advance the quality of life and enhance economic values. By example, the environmental impact—specifically of hydrologic systems—of the construction of new roadways in the city of Houston, Texas, and other cities in North America has been substantially reduced by applying low impact design measures in the design of the roads. Implementing low impact development (LID) has been shown to reduce the total cost of construction substantially versus the cost of constructing traditional roadway designs. Long-term maintenance costs of the roadways designed with low impact development guidelines have been substantially reduced by 25–40 percent. This is a conservative range of savings as compared to the range reported by the Environment Protection Agency. Less easily quantifiable is the added value realized in terms of aesthetics with increased landscaping. An increase in property values of the adjoining neighborhoods is also a result of LID design guidelines.

Plants in Combination with Grading and the Environment

While plants have been a constant presence in human history, new ways of appreciating their impact on our lives are revealed as their extent and diversity are diminished with our desire for progress and capacity for consumption. Natural and planted trees and associated plant cover help regulate local climate and reduce the energy costs of buildings by providing shade and reducing the action of wind. Through evaporation, transpiration, and the uptake and storage of carbon, plants moderate the climate and improve air and water quality. Natural plant communities, such as wetlands, reduce the impact of storms and function as valuable animal habitat. Similarly, planting of vegetation in urban areas serves as animal habitat, reduces heat gain, and revitalizes disused or derelict sites. Plants host myriad pollinator species associated with their flowers and play a central role in the growth of a multitude of plants and crops. Plants are a source of delight and sense of well-being for humans. The presence of plants either as a natural or constructed landscape is a contributory factor to property values and to the overall quality of life and health of communities. The physical and visual presence of plants is now known to improve and speed up the healing process of patients recovering in hospitals.[3]

Managing Storm Water

The term *green infrastructure* discussed earlier refers to systems and practices designed by landscape architects and other professionals such as civil engineers that mimic natural processes. One example is the design for handling storm water so as to retain surface water in rain gardens or retention ponds, allowing time for the water to infiltrate the soil and to return the water to the atmosphere either through evaporation or by plants. The designed retention systems hold storm water on the site where it can later be used for irrigation and other purposes (fire control, for example).

Green infrastructure systems are appropriate for a wide range of landscape project types in place of, or in addition to, the traditional storm-water management infrastructure. A landscape architect can employ any one or a combination of the following elements from the green infrastructure tool kit in designing a storm-water management plan:

- *Bio-swales* are vegetated, shallow, slightly sloping, landscaped depressions designed to capture and to treat storm-water runoff as it moves through a select palette of plants across the topography and downstream (see Figure 10.2). Bio-swales are typically sized to accommodate the volume of the water from a prescribed storm event. The initial runoff collected is also known as the "first flush." The swales are designed to allow sediment and pollutants to settle out prior to recharging the ground water. The plant species used, in addition to achieving some other functional or aesthetic goals, are selected to absorb targeted pollutants and hold loose sediment in place.
- *Rain gardens* are designed to capture, temporarily hold, and allow storm water to infiltrate the soils of a property. They are created with plants in combination with a depressed ground form designed to be an attractive addition to a property, in addition to managing storm water, often in combination with other storm-water management systems (Figure 10.3). Detained water has time to percolate into the soil and to provide moisture for the rain garden plants. In some cases the rain garden itself is designed to slope—in the way that a swale slopes—carrying excess water farther downstream to a larger-capacity retention area.

Figure 10.2 Bio-swale along a city street, City of Burbank, California, Department of Water and Power, by Ahbé Landscape Architects.

Figure 10.3 A: Rain garden, Burbank, CA, by Ahbé Landscape Architects; B: Concrete pavers imbedded in lawn area allow for some foot traffic and surface water runoff to infiltrate soil, Sichuan Agricultural University, Chengdu, China.

- *Retention and detention ponds* are constructed ponds or depressions designed to hold or slow down storm water collected before the water moves downstream within a site or later off-site to a water body such as a stream or wetlands. The intent of creating these ponds is to reduce flooding on a property and to allow sediment and pollutants to settle out or be absorb by plants. A retention pond is designed to allow excess storm water to move further downstream when the pond is connected to a constructed drainage swale or where the topography slopes toward a potential watercourse (Figure 10.4). The purpose of a detention pond is to slow down and temporarily hold water before it moves downstream while a retention pond is designed to retain a certain percentage of the storm water. These ponds can be a single body of water or a series of ponds connected by a swale. The first or upstream pond serves the purpose of slowing the water flow, allowing solids (sediment and even trash) to settle out. The subsequent ponds in the chain serve to act as cleaners to remove undesirable chemicals (pesticides and fertilizer products, for instance) so that the water exiting the designed system and before it enters a stream or wetlands is of higher quality than the water entering the system.

  Water detention ponds in combination with swales serve to slow down storm water and store it for later use. The combination can be graded and planted so that it is also a site amenity, adding visual interest, providing recreation opportunities, and increasing biodiversity. Detention ponds with swales are also designed to serve their intended purpose but appear more integrated into a larger landscape as in the examples in Figure 10.5. A wide drainage swale was created in two parks, allowing for the detention of extreme storm water during heavy rains. Both were designed with a minimum slope to slow the movement of the water so that it can penetrate the soil and eventually dry out. When dry, the feature allows for informal park uses. A trail of boulders, seen in Figure 10.5A, provides passage across the swale during

Figure 10.4 A: The retention pond is situated in a residential neighborhood in Delft, the Netherlands, and was designed as a part of a park-like greenway system with trails and passive recreation elements; B: The retention pond was designed to create a more natural-like setting in Zud Park in Rotterdam, the Netherlands.

Figure 10.5 A: Boulder trail crossing a drainage swale in Zud (South) Park, City of Rotterdam, the Netherlands; B: Limestone plinths used for trail crossing of a bio-swale in Manzanares Park, Madrid, by West 8 landscape architects.

low-water events while providing a connection to a paved walking trail on the higher ground. A narrower and deeper swale could have been constructed, providing for a similar flood capacity, but that would limit the use of the area for recreation. The narrower swale would create a physical and visual barrier that would unnecessarily divide the park. Another trail crossing design to continue a park trail through a drainage bio-swale is shown in Figure 10.5B.

- *Constructed wetlands* are designed with three main purposes. They are artificial wetlands created as new habitat for native and migratory wildlife, wetlands constructed to manage wastewater either as the primary treatment before water flows downstream or as the final stage of treatment termed polishing. Constructed wetlands are also created as part of a larger strategy for a community to manage storm water and for storm protection.

- *Permeable modular and pervious paving surfaces* for roads, parking lots, and just about any paved surface can be designed to allow surface water to infiltrate the soil below (Figure 10.6). Modular units are made in a factory. They are installed by placing the units on a bed of sand. The sand base, in turn, is constructed with a compacted crushed rock base. Rain and surface water seeps into the space between the units, passing through the layers of sand and rock to the soil below. Pervious paving is similar to traditional concrete and asphalt but manufactured in a plant with material additives that leave void spaces after the concrete sets or the asphalt hardens. Rain and surface water can flow through the pavement to infiltrate the soil below.

- *Rock reed or plant filters* are a sub-surface cavity constructed beneath the soil surface and filled with organic materials (plant materials such as branches and graded rock material). They are located in areas where soils are not suitable for absorption fields or will not allow water to percolate to the aquifer below (Figure 10.7).

- *Green roofs* are an old idea[4] and technology applied to mitigate against cold weather in the form of roofs covered in sod (grass) to insulate a building in cold climes (Figure 10.8). Green or landscaped roofs are used to mitigate contemporary undesirable urban environmental conditions such as to reduce the heat island effect caused by the large percentage of pavement in urban cities, as means of collecting and cleaning rainwater for use on site, and by providing an added layer of roofing insulation to moderate the internal climate control of a building. A roof garden enhances the aesthetic and economic value of a building and at the same time is a place for the enjoyment of a building's inhabitants just as any outdoor garden would be. The installation of a green roof is suitable for an old or new residence, commercial or industrial building, or any structure with a roof. The design of a garden roof requires specialized knowledge of materials and infrastructure support (leak-resistant membrane materials, light-weight soil design, and a drainage system, for instance). There are a growing number of

Figure 10.6 Permeable surfacing for the campus courtyard consisting of concrete modular units set in sand for walks and compacted crushed granite under picnic table, by Ahbé Landscape Architects.

Figure 10.7 Rock reed filter at Bluebonnet Swamp parking lot, Baton Rouge, LA, by Ted Jack, PLA.

Figure 10.8 Library with sod roof, Technical University of Delft, the Netherlands.

landscape architects who have developed green roof design into an area of specialized practice.

- *Low impact development* (LID) is an approach to managing storm water applied to new land development or the redevelopment of old urbanized areas. The approach values storm water as a resource to be used on-site rather than as a waste product that needs to be removed as quickly as possible (Figure 10.9).

LID applies a diverse range of designed topographic, landscape, and infrastructure features that mimic how natural landscape systems manage storm water, keeping the water as close to its source as possible. LID employs principles such as preserving and reconstructing natural landscape features (such as wetlands), minimizing the application of impervious paving surfaces, gathering and storing surface water, and other design devices. The aim of LID design is to create functional and appealing ways of handling storm water that treat the water as a resource rather than a waste product to be removed. There are many systems designed by landscape architects that have been used to adhere to these principles, such as building bio-retention ponds, constructed wetlands, rain gardens, vegetated rooftops, introducing cisterns for water storage, and permeable pavements. By implementing LID principles and practices, water can be managed in a way that reduces the potential for flooding and promotes the natural movement of water within a project site toward an adjacent ecosystems or watershed. Applied on a broad scale, LID can maintain or restore a watershed's hydrologic and ecological functions that have been altered by previous land development that employed storm-water disposal infrastructure. LID is appropriate and effective for new development or to retrofit an existing development for a range of land uses from high-density, ultra-urban settings to low-density development. A well-planned development employing LID principles adds economic value to a project, increases the quality of life

Figure 10.9 *Storm water directed from street and sidewalk to depressed planting area designed to detain water and allow time to penetrate into soil. LID design has added benefit to supplement irrigation of landscape.*

Figure 10.10 *Comprehensive low impact storm-water management design for a condominium complex in Amersfoort, the Netherlands.*

of its inhabitants, and reduces if not eliminates harmful impacts on the natural environment.

The high-density condominium complex located in the Netherlands shown in Figure 10.10 contains a garden designed using LID principles. This particular design serves several complementary and important purposes when implementing a water retention strategy. The gardens are primarily planted with seasonal flowers, herbs, and vegetables. The canal in Figure 10.10 adds interest as only a water feature can in a dense urban setting. The gardens are essentially a large basin or vessel that has been designed with a capacity for detaining water during heavy storms. Eventually the water is absorbed in the soil and a portion evaporates. Some of the water stored in the concrete canal is used to supplement irrigation of adjacent planting.

The Role of Plants in a Sustainable Landscape

It is their interest in nature and perhaps the opportunity of working with plants that draw people into the profession of landscape architecture. Many of the past's well-known landscape architects considered themselves plants-men and as such knew a great deal about both the aesthetic possibilities of plants as well as their horticultural requirements. Plants also were appreciated for their functional possibilities as well. Plants can provide shade from direct sun and for their cooling effect on a space. Plants are used to create the physical structure to define and create outdoor spaces. Plants can be used to moderate climate (particularly air temperature) of both the exterior spaces and the interior spaces of buildings, thus reducing energy consumption and utility costs. Plants are also used to screen or buffer views, sound, and wind. Plants can be placed with the goal of screening out or making undesirable views less obtrusive. For instance, blocking the view of your neighbor's windows into your outdoor entertainment space. Selecting particular plants having a density of leaves and favorable leaf shape can buffer the impact of unwanted noise from a known source such as a highway or diminish the intensity of prevailing winds. There are myriad design opportunities for using plants for aesthetic, functional, and cultural reasons. Plants are a flexible material that, in addition to serving some design purpose, will add layers of sensory-related value with their physical changes throughout the seasons and over the years. They instill a sense of permanence and belonging to the spaces created by landscape architects. The term *sense of place* comes to mind, meaning the physical and ephemeral qualities of a designed space having similarities and providing visual continuity to their context or endemic surrounding.

Plants as Modifiers of Climate

Vegetation can be an effective means to lower building energy consumption. Selecting the right plant and placing it in the strategically correct location can reduce energy consumption and costs associated with building heating and cooling control. The presence of plants can reduce urban heat island effects if trees are installed to shade paved areas, or the installation of green roofs, or vegetated structures (such as trellises) to cover non-vegetated surfaces, such as walkways, roofs, or parking lots. With the planting of appropriate species of deciduous trees and shrubs and placing these materials strategically along the south-facing side (or sides exposed to sunlight) of a building, the plants can reduce heat gain inside the building in the summer months and allow heat gain to enter the building during winter months.[5]

During the height of the summer sunshine (and heat!), it is helpful to discuss ways to reduce the harmful effects of sun glare and heat zones. Too much light—and the wrong kind of sunlight—can create glare, which can affect our ability to see clearly. The glare from sunlight can also be a source of discomfort, in terms of heightened sense of heat as well as its effect on our eyes. Artificial light can be another source of glare, particularly from a high intensity light source. One can combat sunlight glare with sunglasses or by wearing a wide-brimmed hat. By planting trees within an urban plaza or any location with extensive paved surfaces, the effects of glare can be reduced. In addition to the planting of trees, a landscape architect might design a trellis or some type of overhead shade structure together with climbing vines where an architectural solution is warranted. Heat islands within urban districts can be the cause of unnecessary discomfort (excessive heat) where a significant surface area in the streets and spaces between buildings are paved with concrete and asphalt. The build-up of heat islands in urban areas can increase summertime peak energy demand, air conditioning costs, air pollution and greenhouse gas emissions, heat-related illness and even mortality. Reducing the urban heat island effect can be achieved through the use of green roofs and the strategic planting of shade trees. With the incorporation of significant areas planted with trees to provide shade, heat gain is reduced, thus reducing the physical discomfort of excessive heat as well as producing a positive psychological effect one experiences walking or resting in the shade under tree cover. Further reductions in heat and glare can be made by the installation of earth-colored paved surfaces in urban areas, which will mediate reflective sunlight and absorb less heat.

Vegetation Provides Valuable Habitat

Habitat is the place where animals normally can be found and the environmental conditions exist to support their survival and life cycles. Plants have specific requirements to successfully take hold and maintain their existence. The primary requirements are soil, climate, moisture, sun and shade, altitude, and longitude. Animals can also be contributory factors to the presence and maintenance of plants. Consider the honeybee and its symbiotic relation with flowering and fruit-bearing plants. A whole host of animals have a semiotic relation to specific plants, from the microscopic fauna in the soil through the animal kingdom phyla to the larger vertebrates and mammals. Likewise, animals have their habitat requirements and preferences for choosing and circulating throughout the seasons. Plant habitat is a source of food, shelter, and procreation for animals. Animals will migrate to meet requirements that each habitat provides in their life-cycle. Animals, specifically birds and whales, will migrate thousands of miles throughout the year as the seasons progress.

In urban areas animal habitat can be of two types: natural habitat set aside and protected or created habitats reconstructed to simulate the physical characteristics to support specific animals. Habitat conservation or creation can be established as a goal in planning new development or retrofitting older development. In addition to setting aside or creating open space and habitat, green corridors are often necessary for connecting smaller patches of habitat and open space. The establishment of wildlife corridors is an effective strategy to increase the effectiveness of smaller slivers of interconnected habitat in lieu of setting aside large expanses of natural areas. Habitat creation in urban areas can take many forms. Small patches of landscape such as parkway plantings can serve a valuable animal habitat function with an informed selection of plant species. And of course habitat creation to attract specific animal species is increasingly popular as urban dwellers seek to attract birds, butterflies, and other colorful and interesting animal visitors within sight of where they live and work.

Food, water, and shelter are the prime components necessary in creating habitat for animals. The more knowledge the designer has about the animal species they wish to attract and support, the greater the potential success. Landscape architects will often research the habitat preferences of the wildlife they wish to attract. They will create planting plans using selected plant species to attract and support desired wildlife. The designs of specific spaces for butterfly or hummingbird gardens are an example of targeted habitat creation. Where other animals are desired, the landscape architect will create, for example, water features (rain garden or pond) and allow dead trees and large limbs to remain as part of a larger design strategy of creating a viable and robust habitat for wildlife.

Plants Increase Economic Value

Generally, individuals will base their choice of a particular neighborhood to live or a particular house to purchase among several that are similar in style or with comparable spatial features, based on the quality and extent of the plant material present. Well-landscaped neighborhoods and homes tend to sell more quickly and at a higher price than similarly laid out neighborhoods and building architecture but without a well-designed landscape. Of course, amenities such as the presence of parks and access to public services, good schools, and transportation will also influence a purchase decision. The extra dollar of cost in adding plants will have a greater increase in economic value to a project than does the increase in project costs by adding architectural elements. The curb appeal of a well-designed landscape directly increases the market value of real estate.

Plants Fix Things

If used correctly and informed by solid research and experience, plants can be used by landscape architects to perform remedial functions in the landscape. Plants, as you will see in a moment, are not just used to make things pretty. Vegetation in the landscape performs a variety of functions that include:

1. *Improve water quality*: Plants associated with specific environments naturally perform a water cleansing function. They do this by filtering out specific chemicals that enter their environment from surface water runoff. Plants have the capacity of creating a chemical bond that either converts the chemicals or sequesters them in their roots, stems, or other physical components. The plants found in wetlands, for instance, efficiently remove heavy metals such as mercury and arsenic from the environment. They also increase dissolved oxygen in the wetlands and other water bodies such as lakes and ponds. Plants are selected to perform a similar water quality improvement function for constructed wetlands or detention ponds. There are examples where municipality public works departments have constructed wetlands as part of their wastewater management infrastructure. Water that has been treated is given a final cleansing after it is discharged into the wetland. In some instances untreated effluent is discharged directly into the created wetlands and processed (removal of undesirable compounds) as it moves downstream eventually considered as acceptably treated water.

2. *Plants purify the air*: Trees and other vegetation contribute to improving air quality by intercepting airborne particles (dust and soot) and absorbing carbon monoxide, sulfur dioxides, and nitrogen dioxide. Through the process of photosynthesis, plants remove these pollutants through respiration then release oxygen and other elements back into the atmosphere.

3. *Reduce soil erosion and slope failure*: The soil-holding capability of the root system of many plant species serves to reduce soil erosion in nature. Grasses, willow, and alder are examples of species that reduce erosion as surface water flows down the surface of a slope. Vegetation with a vigorous root system will also reduce slope failure, establishing a strong organic mat that protects the slope from either the mechanical damage of rain or the flow of surface water.

4. *Wetlands are habitats for wildlife and reduce harmful impacts from seasonal phenomena*: Wetlands occur at the edge of aquatic or terrestrial systems. A variety of wetland types occur throughout the world and include bogs and swamps, tidal marshes, prairie potholes, sea grass beds, and seasonally wet forest wetlands. They are one of the most diverse ecosystems of flora and fauna. They perform vital functions, in addition to supporting an abundance of wildlife. They improve water quality, reduce the impact of winter storm surges, and contribute economically to a region in the commercial harvesting of fish and shellfish. The reconstruction of wetlands lost to human activities (such as urban and industrial development) is often an integral part of a larger strategy to reduce the impact from winter storms and impacts from other natural phenomena. Wetlands intercept storm-water runoff to reduce flood damage, and support the re-establishment of wildlife and commercial fisheries as part of biodiversity protection efforts.[6]

Wetlands also contribute to maintaining good water quality, given their ability to capture sediment and filter pollutants. Wetlands contribute to the quality of life of a region serving a variety of recreation activities (urban fishing, boating, hiking, and birding), locations for outdoor education programs on ecology and natural history, and provide a place of beauty for people to appreciate and enjoy, as well as gain a sense of well-being by having access to nature.

For the curious, the process and mechanisms by which vegetation improves water quality, reduces erosion, and serves to ameliorate the other undesirable impacts discussed above are easily researched. The benefits in following your curiosity may be the basis of establishing a professional services specialty such as wetland restoration consultant. Knowledge gained from your research may also serve as one of the sources of design inspiration for projects you are working on. In the process of finding a way to repair a lost or dysfunctional landscape, a designer may be inspired in creating a new one with added benefits not considered at the outset of the design process. The term "added value design" comes to mind, a process that can lead to enhancement and innovation as well as increased economic value. The perceived emotional and/or functional benefits of a landscape architect's design services can be a major factor that influences user or client satisfaction of a project or development. The work by the hand of a landscape architect can also instill pride of place for inhabitants benefiting from the creation of the designer.

Plants and Their Relevance to Sustainability

One can approach the subject of plants from many directions. There is the subject of their aesthetic attributes with their great variety of form, color, texture, structure, and their physical changes over the course of a year and their lifetime. With this knowledge, one can then select and arrange plants in a composition of aesthetic value that creates comfortable spaces to accommodate human activities. Then there is the horticultural knowledge of plants and their needs and preferences in terms of soil, moisture, sunlight and shade, climate, and preferred longitude and altitude on Earth. The use or utility of plants is another consideration. Plants are habitat for animals, birds, and insects as well as a source of food. Plants are associated in a web of functions with bacteria, fungi, mushrooms, and the like. Knowledge of a plant's reproduction cycles and needs must also be considered to further ensure well-informed plant species choices are made. In this chapter the focus on plants was on their utility in terms of one or a combination of components that can be employed to improve and moderate the environment, contribute to water, air, and land quality, and mediate the environment to improve the livability, health, and safety of humans.

Notes

1 A term popularized with the publication in 1970 of *Design with Nature* by Ian McHarg (25th Anniversary Edition, John Wiley & Sons, Inc., Hoboken, NJ, 1995).
2 Craig E. Colten in *An Unnatural Metropolis: Wresting New Orleans from Nature* (LSU Press, Baton Rouge, LA, 2006) discusses alternative means of mitigating flooding in Coastal Louisiana using no-structural or green infra-structural approaches in lieu of levees, canals, and water pumping systems.
3 For additional information regarding the therapeutic benefits of plants in general and gardens, see Clare Cooper Marcus and Naomi A. Sachs, *Therapeutic Landscapes: An Evidenced-Based Approach to Designing Healing Gardens and Restorative Outdoor Spaces* (John Wiley & Sons, Inc., Hoboken, NJ, 2014).
4 Think of the sodded roofs of log cabin structures of Arctic regions and northern climes of Europe and Asia, the Hanging Gardens of Babylon, or the twentieth-century landscape icon: Freeway Park in Seattle.
5 Gary O. Robinette, *Plants, People, and Environmental Quality: A Study of Plants and Their Environmental Functions* (US Department of the Interior, Government Printing Office, Washington, D.C., 1972).
6 *An Introduction and User's Guide to Wetland Restoration, Creation, and Enhancement*, US National Oceanic and Atmospheric Administration (NOAA), Environmental Protection Agency, Army Corps of Engineers, US Fish and Wildlife Service, and Natural Resources Conservation Service. Available at: www.habitat.noaa.gov/pdf/pub_wetlands_restore_guide.pdf.

Further Reading

Readings on green and sustainable landscape design:

Meg Calkins, *The Sustainable Sites Handbook: A Complete Guide to the Principles, Strategies, and Best Practices for Sustainable Landscapes*, John Wiley & Sons, Inc., Hoboken, NJ, 2012.

Daniel Czechowski, Thomas Hauck, and Georg Hausladen, *Revising Green Infrastructure: Concepts Between Nature and Design*, Taylor & Francis, London, 2014.

William Thompson and Kim Sorvig, *Sustainable Landscape Construction: A Guide to Green Building Outdoors*, Island Press, Washington, D.C., 2007.

Heather L. Venhaus, *Designing the Sustainable Site: Integrated Design Strategies for Small Scale Sites and Residential Landscapes*, John Wiley & Sons, Inc., Hoboken, NJ, 2012.

CHAPTER ELEVEN

THE FUTURE OF LANDSCAPE ARCHITECTURE

Introduction

T he opening paragraph of the Preface introduced the idea that the genesis of landscape architecture can be traced to the Early Greek and Roman concepts of Arcadia and the pleasant place, the *locus amoenus*: idealized places of refuge and beauty having regenerative powers for the visitor. The future of the profession is the focus of this final chapter. The future of the profession will maintain close ties to the past ideals of gardens and humanity's place in the larger garden, the Earth. The future of the Earth is largely dependent on the knowledge, ingenuity, and creativity of humans to better manage their actions affecting the larger environment and human survival. Landscape architects will be important contributors, ensuring the Arcadian ideals of a healthy world of beauty where regenerative powers are achieved.

This chapter is meant to be encouraging for students who have chosen a career in landscape architecture, by providing a window on the opportunities that will open as they advance in their professional careers. The student can anticipate a bright future of professional opportunities with landscape architecture's focus on the design, planning, and stewardship of the natural and built environment as well as the development and redevelopment of urban centers such as Los Angeles, Shanghai, and London. This potential extends to taking a leadership role in emerging civic engagement initiatives that shift conventional land and resource development toward approaches that conserve and restore natural systems, offset development impacts on the environment, mitigate hazards and provide the essential benefits that humans and other organisms depend on for healthy lives and even their very survival.

Giving Back

There are many terms like borrow pit, square meal, and others that we find useful and are understood by others when we use them but are curious in that their heritage and origins may not be known. *Borrow pit* is one of those curiosities of our language that if you stop and think about it, it may not make sense. Why is the word choice *borrow* when to replace (borrow) the rock or soil material taken from one site to deposit for some specific purpose at another site was never actually intended? It was never intended to return borrowed woodland, wetlands, and farm landscapes used for urban development and other human development enterprises. We find ourselves in the twenty-first century having to consider returning portions of these borrowed landscapes as part of larger strategies to make our cities safer (from storm-caused floods, pollution, and other undesirable impacts), reducing the impacts of global warming, and instead improving water quality and increasing biodiversity. The objective of these *giving back* strategies is to enhance the resilience and health of environments we have altered and even erased from the Earth. Rebuilding wetlands, re-establishing woodlands, converting high water-consuming urban landscapes into less demanding ones by establishing drought-tolerant landscapes are examples of the growing areas of demand for the expertise of landscape architects. The process of rebuilding or giving back normally involves a great deal of catch-up as the economically driven consumption and utilization of the environment and its resources seem to leave dysfunctional landscapes at a faster pace than does the awareness of our political and governing mechanisms to mediate against the losses and resulting deleterious impacts.

Repurpose

Repurposing is an initiative that considers the reuse of built places, structures, and facilities that no longer serve new populations and economic initiatives that have replaced an earlier demographic or economy. In many cases repurposing will require retrofitting older facilities that no longer serve the needs of new users with new designs to accommodate the new uses or programming changes. Retrofitting with new designs may also be necessary to address changing environmental conditions such as rising sea levels or increased threats from flooding conditions in a region. Building retrofitting could include elevating structures or modifying the grounds to increase their water-holding capacity in the form of detention ponds or redirecting storm water to safer locations (such as wetlands, if they exist). Examples of facilities that may need to be retrofitted due to changing demographics include parks, commercial and industrial areas, and street landscapes. Adaptive reuse is the converting of structures or spaces for new uses of derelict and even abandoned buildings, such as commercial malls and whole districts, such as warehouses and industrial sites. Warehouse districts, because of their desirable close proximity to urban centers, are being converted into highly desirable and valued living and commercial space. Railroad rights-of-way no longer in use are being converted to walking trails and bicycle routes. Industrial zones have been converted to other purposes such as the industrial area of North London that was converted first as the venue for the London 2012 Olympics. Subsequently the same Olympic site was repurposed for outdoor recreation, new housing, and commercial uses.

Water Conservation

Water is a limited resource that is essential to humans and all forms of life. Demand for water continues to rise at the same time as the availability of and access to clean water and water quality are diminishing. Traditional approaches to managing storm water have been to get rid of it as quickly as possible by directing surface water from roofs, paved areas, and landscaped grounds to be disposed of via costly storm-water infrastructure systems. The Sustainable Sites Initiative, developed by the American Society of Landscape Architects, promotes the design of landscapes that reduce water use, improve filtration, and promote healthy rivers, lakes, and oceans. The emerging water management approaches that are being designed and implemented essentially mimic natural systems.

> Rather than getting rid of storm water as quickly as possible via gutters and sewers, smarter strategies exist to create systems that mimic nature's capacity to efficiently manage water. A sustainable approach to storm water management involves finding ways to capture storm water on site and use it for recharging groundwater, irrigation purposes, or in ornamental water features.[1]

Landscape architects have the necessary knowledge and experience to lead or to contribute their expertise in the design of more sustainable approaches to water management and land development. They have been applying low impact water management and design principles on new development projects as well as retrofitting older streets and neighborhoods. Other areas where landscape architects are being involved are in designing new developments or converting older designed landscapes, selecting plant species with low water needs, including endemic species, instead of using non-native species, including lawn grasses that require significant supplemental water for irrigation and maintenance.

Conserve and Rebuild Soil

Soil is an important and limited resource that, like water, is essential to human and other forms of life. Intensive use of agricultural soils and poor stewardship of soils associated with resource extraction activities (such as forest harvesting and mineral extraction) will over time result in the degradation, contamination, or the outright loss of soils. Eventually areas where the soils have been degraded or lost will require a rebuilding strategy. While landscape architects may not necessarily be trained in soil management, like agriculture agronomists, they will still have a role as part of a team of experts in the soil-rebuilding process. Their involvement will be particularly needed where extensive tracks of land are targeted for renewal into native habitats as part of a larger conservation management policy. For instance, depleted agricultural lands may be converted to native grassland cover, low-lying areas rebuilt into wetlands, and upland slopes reverted to forest cover. The rebuilt landscape may be incorporated into parklands or areas of national conservation interest.

Landscape architects who accept as their professional responsibility the concept of stewardship of the environment will consider design and planning strategies that do not exploit or abuse the soil or associated natural resources. As human populations grow and the pressures to develop the land, water, and other resources become more acute, designers who think globally—that is, consider maintaining to the extent possible the Earth's natural resources—will produce designs that are sustainable, causing less disruption and abuse of limited natural resources.

Specialization

Landscape architects may find themselves at an advantage in developing areas of specialization as projects become more complex. The anticipated increase in project complexity will require designers to have greater expertise and experience in developing strategies that mitigate between human needs and the capabilities of the environment. It is anticipated that specialization within the profession will become more prevalent, just as engineers have developed specialties in geotechnical, structural, civil, and environmental engineering. Right now landscape architects claim to be able to do everything but as all these "everythings" become more technical and scientifically based, landscape architects must prepare academically and through targeted experience in order to be considered credible in their claims. Take, for example, green roofs and walls. The city of Shanghai, China, now requires that new buildings must have 30 percent of their roof area landscaped. As other cities adopt similar requirements for green roofs as well as low impact water management, reducing the heat island effect and other quality of life and environment improvements, specialization will be the logical response for the profession to embrace. Areas in which landscape architects have developed and will continue developing specialized expertise will include, for example, the design of sports fields/facilities, more walkable and livable communities, a sustainable approach to golf course design, water management, including LID and BMP, wetlands restoration and management, and historical and cultural conservation of heritage properties.

Global Practice

The profession will continue the trend of being a part of the global practice of providing design services, particularly in developing and emerging regions. Global practice will have the additional characteristic of involving teams of consultants with a multi-national composition. This will require greater knowledge and appreciation of other cultures in order to work effectively in teams and in diverse language and cultural situations. Cultural studies as part of a professional curriculum would help landscape architects in this regard. Giving them the tools in cross-cultural communication through cultural literacy would prepare them to assume a more effective role in the global environment of design and planning. China, for instance, has planted unsustainable landscapes along its extensive road building and new town development throughout the country. As water becomes scarce, it will not be practicable to continue maintaining these landscapes as they are today. The lush exotic plantings in the roadway medians and parkways will need to be replaced with more drought-tolerant plants. Consider California and other parts of the American Southwest that have experienced water shortages plus a warmer climate. The climatic conditions have dramatically deviated from years of adequate rainfall and cooler temperatures. With the reduction of rainfall and rising temperatures, landscape architects must approach plant selection and planting methods from the perspective of making decisions under xeriscape (low water demand) conditions. Older plantings may need to be replaced with drought-tolerant plants and might need devising planting schemes that incorporate ground cover materials that reduce transpiration so as to conserve water and reduce irrigation requirements.

Multi-Disciplinary Team Approach to Design

It is common today for landscape architects to work on projects with professionals from other disciplines. The ramifications of a world experiencing ever greater threats from global warming, fresh water scarcity, increased demands on already over-cultivated lands, and the loss of productive landscapes from resource extraction and urbanization will require a multi-disciplinary approach to planning and design. Utilizing multiple disciplines will enhance the effectiveness of work approached as a team effort. More creative solutions can be expected when individuals with different sets of eyes and expertise join forces. Thinking outside of the box will become the norm when diverse disciplines seek design strategies, challenging each other in the process. Individuals with effective communication and people skills will be sought in the team-building process. Communication skills include verbal, writing, and graphic skills. Graphic skills include digital and analog capability. Being well organized and having good reasoning ability are important and desirable attributes for members of a team supported by a depth of knowledge and experience.

Technology

Where technology will take the profession is a wide-open proposition. Perhaps science fiction writers have already spun stories with a central cast of space-age landscape architects and their fellow disciplines designing with hardware and software that seamlessly guide the construction of a project as the required documentation is produced. This notion is nearly within our grasp today. The office of the future or the future working environment will become more and more dispersed as people will no longer need to be physically located in a traditional office. Landscape architects will work in an environment or range of environments that are convenient and more readily accessible, negating the necessity of daily commutes or trans- or inter-continental travel.

The technology of wearable computers and remote access to home appliance and utility systems can easily be adapted to self-maintaining environments, including landscapes. Irrigation systems are already operating that are self-regulated. Sensors in the ground "tell" the computer that controls the electrical valves to turn on the water when the soil moisture falls below a specified range. Sensors also trigger another set of related controls when additional fertilizer and other elements need to be applied through the same irrigation system. Genetic engineering will certainly be a part of future landscapes, allowing the designer to identify physical and growing qualities desired so that plant geneticists can produce specialized, grown-to-order plant species.

Any attempt at looking into the crystal ball of what to anticipate as far as future technology advances is probably futile. Technological advances already have been so rapid and dramatic and will continue to bring applications that are best left up to the science fiction writers who entertain us and tantalize our imagination at this time. The key descriptor of how we might anticipate working in the future is the word remote: working remotely, interacting and exchanging working files with clients and consultant team members remotely, and relying more on sensors to remotely provide data to improve our design and planning decision-making. With the rapid advances of technology we will have greater capacity and ability to work globally, thus extending our professional reach to more diverse markets.

And, finally, looking back at the traditional areas of practice in which landscape architects have excelled, such as garden and planting design, these required great skill and knowledge associated with selecting plants in creating memorable landscapes. A similar knowledge and skill set will become even more relevant to the future of the profession. Landscape architects who are knowledgeable about plants and who have the skill in making well-informed plant species selections will extend their competence well beyond creating gardens for pleasure in the future. The plant knowledge of landscape architects will be applied to extensive, more complex design strategies in areas such as:

1. green, non-structural approaches for cleaning surface storm water in the creation of rain gardens and low impact water runoff detention systems;
2. rebuilding wetlands and other damaged or reduced ecosystems;
3. rebuilding polluted soils in brownfields or reclamation sites.

Those in the profession who are experienced and prepared will be involved and contribute as communities and nations seek to rebuild losses of habitat, water resources, and landscapes damaged by the excesses of narrowly focused land use and the resource development decisions of the past. Landscape architects will be engaged in rebuilding and reimaging more healthy and sustainable futures by applying non-structural design solutions. This is quite an exciting prospect for those thinking about becoming or preparing to be landscape architects. Thinking about landscape architecture may not be a field for you but someday soon those who join the profession will be changing the world for the betterment of the lives of others.

Note

1 www.sustainablesites.org/benefits/water.

Further Reading

Readings on the future of landscape architecture:

Frederick R. Adler and Colby J. Tanner, *Urban Ecosystems: Ecological Principles for the Built Environment*, Cambridge University Press, Cambridge, 2013.

Marina Alberti, *Advances in Urban Ecology: Integrating Humans and Ecological Processes in Urban Ecosystems*, Springer Science + Business Media, New York, 2008.

Jared Green, *Designed for the Future: 80 Practical Ideas for a Sustainable World*, Princeton Architectural Press, New York, 2015.

Tigran Haas, *Sustainable Urbanism and Beyond: Rethinking Cities for the Future*, Rizzoli International Publications, New York, 2012.

S.T.A. Picket, M.L. Cadenasso, and B. McGrath (eds.), *Resilience in Ecology and Urban Design: Linking Theory and Practice for Sustainable Cities*, Springer, New York, 2013.

INDEX